THE MONCTONIANS

Scamps, Scholars

and

Politicians

Hon. H. R. Emmerson
— Photo courtesy N.B. Archives

Volume II

THE MONCTONIANS

Scamps, Scholars

and

Politicians

by

John Edward Belliveau

Illustrated

LANCELOT PRESS
Hantsport, Nova Scotia

ISBN 0-88999-171-5

All rights reserved. No part of this book may be reproduced in any form without written permission of the publishers except brief quotations embodied in critical articles or reviews.

Published 1982

   Second printing August 1984

LANCELOT PRESS LIMITED, Hantsport, N. S.
Office and plant situated on Highway No. 1, 1/2 mile east of Hantsport

Dedicated

to

Dennis Cochrane

the youngest mayor

in

Moncton's history

PEOPLE ON THE FRONT COVER

Among the most notable Monctonians of the Twentieth Century are those pictured on the book's cover. They are: Top left, Walter U. Appleton, railroad vice-president; top right, Rev. Dr. Clément Cormier, university founder; centre, Maude Burbank, musician; lower left, Hon. H.R. Emmerson, politician, and, lower right, Prof. Northrop Frye, world-renowned literary critic.

CONTENTS

A Word of Introduction 9
Politics and Patronage............................. 17
Moncton was Cooking with Gas 28
The Days of Sport and Murder 33
No Language Divisions in the Cemetery 41
A Well Contended Mixture 57
Derby Hats and Pegtop Pants 69
Biscuits and Barter 76
Family Dynasty in Wood 81
Heroes and Railroaders............................ 91
The Great Promoter.............................. 108
Growth, Gallaghers and Parlees.................... 119
Prohibition, Eaton's and Society 129
The Local "Characters"........................... 137
Family Race Horses and Fancy Cars 147
Broadcasters and Burbanks 153
Up in the Air with Jenny 163
Hard Times and Cadillacs......................... 174
Grammar, Papers and Politics 189
Rise of Wealth and Power 199
May, Murder and Abduction 209
The Incredible Monctonian 224
A Man and his University......................... 232
A Mayor in Violent Times 249
New Mayor Bites the Dust 263
No Fiddlers on the Roof.......................... 273
The Tammany Twins 283
The Old (But New) Neighbors 287
A City Come of Age 301

A WORD OF INTRODUCTION

An earlier volume, *The Monctonians,* recalled the city's beginnings and early development. It dealt with the people who made it a town and a city. This second and final volume begins with the opening of the 20th Century, and it is about those who developed the kind of community it had become toward its close.

When Moncton was a smaller place, before 1930, the more colorful local "characters" were easily spotted. So were the leaders in society, in business, industry and politics. In the larger community, a more mobile society, providing many new elements and changing texture more frequently, the picture becomes more complex. More than that, since the middle of the present century there has been a tendency everywhere toward a kind of middle-class prosperity and middle-class morality which makes it more difficult for individuals to stand out. Still, there are always those who do and this book attempts to portray some of them.

This work deals at some length with what has become known as "The Language Question." To some who find it difficult to accept the increase in proportion of a people here since European settlement began in Canada, it is "The French Question." The issue arising from the accommodation of two cultures indigenous to the city's immediate surroundings has been a pervasive factor of Moncton life during the present century. It has changed the city in a fundamental way. Therefore, it has seemed essential to chronicle its origin and development and this book is the first in either English or French to discuss the issue in depth and to detail its history.

Unlike the first volume of this work, a good deal of this one is from the author's personal recollection as well as from standard research and the remembrances of older citizens. These have contributed directly through interviews and by answering endless inquiries, and they have always been helpful. So many have responded generously that it is hard to list their names. However, in one place or another throughout the pages, their names have been mentioned. At least a dozen residents between the ages of 85 and 100 who had retained their full mental faculties have enlightened the writer about the early years of the present century. Some went beyond the ordinary to provide valuable background and understanding.

While both volumes of *The Monctonians* concern themselves with the people of Moncton, the years between 1950 and 1980 brought a new dimension to the community. It had become Greater Moncton with two substantial and growing satellite towns, Dieppe and Riverview. Because of their modern state and their historically close association with the city, something of their origins and development became appropriate to this second volume. The author is particularly grateful for the generous and detailed assistance given by Mayors Caseley of Riverview and Cormier of Dieppe and their town administrators, R. James Wood of Riverview and Mme. Rolande Gallant of Dieppe. Moncton's city clerk, Michael B. Sullivan, and the city engineer, W. M. Steeves, have also given valuable technical assistance.

The book is dedicated to Dennis Cochrane, the youngest mayor in Moncton's history, because of his progressive attitude toward his hometown and mine. Also for his cooperation and support of this history.

My wife, Gertrude, has been a constantly helpful critic, spotting inconsistencies and over-emphases which were then eradicated. My sons, grandchildren and other close relatives have been tolerant of repetitive references to my work and to tales of other times before their experience. Indeed, they have been encouraging and supportive throughout.

Some of those who have assisted in a particular way with this book are mentioned in the introduction to the first volume. However, a few who have been notably helpful and given of their time to provide information for Volume 2 must be thanked. They are Rev. Clément Cormier, C.S.C., H. Reuben Cohen, Q.C.; Ewart B. Gaskin, Frank Walsh, my sister, Mrs. R. A. Dysart; my two sons, Bill and Peter, of *Atlantic Insight,* and the staffs at the Moncton Public Library, the Moncton Museum, the provincial archives in Fredericton and the Nova Scotia archives in Halifax. Volume One includes most of the bibliography used for the entire work.

John Edward Belliveau
September, 1982

Chapter One

A CITY MEETS THE NEW CENTURY

When the twentieth century came to Moncton, it came without fanfare. A community of 9,026 confident residents whose trust in prosperity lay with a thriving railroad, it boasted a still-busy river port but the rich smell of natural gas was in the air. The ebullient, sometimes pugnacious, Frederick William Sumner was mayor and he was a Tory. Not just a man who voted Conservative but a Tory in the social, economic and imperialist sense as well. As the new century began, he and Moncton were both on the edge of a challenge to the kind of power, progress, influence and wealth which had brought them to the present juncture.

Whatever the local powers were in 1900 and the years immediately thereafter, the dominant figure coming onto the Moncton scene was not a Monctonian at all but a resident of Dorchester. He had, however, the wisdom to marry into one of Moncton's oldest and richest families, the Records, and he represented the Grit side of politics which would dominate the growing city for a full quarter century.

In the end, it would be Moncton that would see this powerful new man's downfall and the site of his last resting place.

He was Henry Robert Emmerson, 47 years of age in that year 1900 and a member of the provincial legislature for 12 years. He was premier of New Brunswick for three years but his greater glory was yet to come. In the early decades of the twentieth century, a federal cabinet minister was much more prestigious and far more powerful in some portfolios than the premier of a small province. Moreover, Emmerson, who had been elected M.P. for Westmorland in 1900, would in four more years become federal minister of railways and canals. Not only was that in itself a major cabinet post but, in Moncton and Westmorland, *the* vital one.

The Hon. Henry's years of that glory would be short, yet important as they were for Moncton they would end in scandal just three years after the cabinet appointment. He was named in 1904 and removed in 1907. However, Emmerson's political life did not end there because, whatever his enemies thought, his supporters continued to send him to parliament to represent the constituency in Ottawa until he died in 1914. What destroyed his cabinet career was a ruse set up by his enemy, Moncton's chief of police, the righteous George Rideout, an ardent temperance avenger. Nor did that happen until Hon. H. R. Emmerson, M.P., had saved the city as the railroad headquarters for all Atlantic Canada. Indeed, the city's sway would yet extend in railroad control all the way to Winnipeg.

Something else was happening in Moncton as it moved into the new century, something which would change its character within the next fifty years. This was a fundamental social change which challenged the previously settled power of the old established families. Moncton had been, and continued yet awhile, to be an English-imperialist and largely Protestant community. It had sent a contigent of forty young men, English, Scots and Irish, off to fight for the British in the Boer War. For an Acadian to enlist would have been a sort of political travesty, for the Boers, those voortrekker Dutch-descended South African settlers being fought by the British empire builders, were almost an identical kind of minority in an imperial state to the French-Acadians in Canada.

Now, after the turn of the century in Moncton, the first important signs of transition in the social, political, religious and economic structure of the town made a city only in 1890, had come with the first upward thrust of the French fact. The

14

Acadians, who had been the settlement's first inhabitants after the Micmac Indians, had begun their return in shipbuilding times. They embellished their numbers when the railroad came and again when the textile and iron industries were at their height in the late 1880's.

Soon, the names of Simon Melanson, the merchant-nationalist; Henri P. LeBlanc, the then-considered radical orator and pamphleteer, and Valentin Landry, the newspaper publisher, would be often on the lips of Monctonians. And the words from the Acadian lips and from their pens would be in French as well as English. This was something very new and different for Moncton.

In an earlier volume of this social history of the city at the bend of the Petitcodiac river there was little reference to the people of Acadian French extraction. That was because in 19th century Moncton they were so few. Still relatively impoverished and powerless as post-expulsion returnees, the Acadians then could exert very little influence on the community. And, in fact, even though their numbers were greater than the Irish, the church parish to which they were attached was led, from its creation as a regular parish, by pastors of Irish extraction who were insistent on their very Irishness, and the pulpit language was English.

Within the county of Westmorland, the French-speaking were not without strength numerically and this was reflected in their political allegiances. When Albert (later Sir Albert) Smith was the Liberal M.P., a majority of Acadians voted Liberal, but provincially they had supported Conservatives heavily when Pierre Landry of Dorchester (later Sir Pierre) and Olivier M. Melanson of Shediac were the candidates. Emmerson coming on the scene had won with the help of John T. Hawke, publisher and editor of *The Moncton Transcript,* the undying loyalty of the French-speaking element in all of Westmorland. Their allegiance to his party has remained until this day.

Moncton itself in Emmerson's day and for seventy years afterward was inclined toward Conservatism but as his influence on the Intercolonial Railway and its jobs increased with his entrance into federal politics, the pendulum began to swing. When Westmorland had chosen its first federal Member of Parliament in the year of Confederation, 1867, Moncton was an unimportant part of the constituency and its voting preference had minimal effect on the riding.

After the crash of the shipbuilding industry, the population had fallen to about 600 residents until the railroad headquarters came to The Bend (then recently renamed Moncton) and it began its rise as the population centre of the county. Both Shediac and Dorchester were much bigger than Moncton when Albert Smith became a federal cabinet minister. However, by the time Henry Emmerson succeeded to that eminence, it had achieved more than 9,000 citizens compared with the 6,430 in Shediac and 6,068 in Dorchester. The majority in Shediac civil parish were also of Acadian French extraction though the population of the town proper was more evenly balanced with English-speaking residents.

Chapter Two

POLITICS AND PATRONAGE

For all of the counties of East coast New Brunswick, Moncton as the railroad centre had become the distribution and commercial nucleus and so it grew rapidly in the first years of this century. It began with the ICR shops and offices and housed many residents who worked in the running trades; it still had a cotton factory, a major foundry, a machine shop, a flour mill, three woodworking factories, a barrel plant, a woollen mill on the outskirts (Humphrey's) and a brickyard at Lewisville owned and operated by the Cummins family which made 1,000,000 bricks a year.

Politics in Moncton then occupied its people to a degree difficult to appreciate now, and it was extremely partisan. The newspapers were almost rabidly biased, the morning *Daily Times* Conservative, the evening *Transcript* Liberal. There wasn't much happening for local news and papers were filled with events in other parts of the country and the world, with Ottawa and governmental affairs dominant. To fill the papers, local political issues were built into prime news. At that stage in national history, provincial government and provincial affairs were not nearly so important in the New Brunswick public mind as federal affairs. In a way, this was strange since in 1900 the province was only thirty-three years away from having been a British colony with its own representative, colonial and quite independent government.

The ministers of railways and canals ran the railroads, and if they did not manage them directly they controlled the jobs and made the appointments. In Moncton, Henry Emmerson through the eyes of his representative, Publisher Hawke and the Westmorland Liberal patronage committee, saw that not a sparrow went into the Intercolonial as an office boy without Liberal approval. And as the Liberals were in power twenty of the thirty years between 1900 and 1930 and Conservative Robert Borden's government mostly a wartime coalition when partisan patronage would be somewhat in abeyance, it is not difficult to discern the reasons for Liberal dominance on the Moncton employment scene.

And yet in those years the city, as opposed to the county, retained a strong Conservative core. The local establishment might be weighted toward the Conservative Party outside the railway but Hawke and Clifford W. Robinson held the reins politically. Robinson, whose father had founded *The Transcript* and who himself had been premier of New Brunswick for a year before the Liberal government was defeated in 1908, later became a Canadian senator. Besides, since the county vote so much over-balanced

J.T. Hawke

the city's, for the first twenty-five years of the century, Westmorland sent Liberals to Ottawa. (Actually, Hon. A. B. Copp of Sackville labelled himself Independent between 1917 and 1921 as a hangover from coalition days, but he afterward sat as a Liberal secretary of state in a Liberal government).

Between 1900 and 1958, only Dr. O.B. Price, the Moncton dentist, served as a Conservative from the riding and that was between 1925 and 1930 when partonage control of the railways had passed out of local M.P.'s hands with the amalgamation of lines into the Canadian National. Then, too, by 1929 when the last major shift of railway amalgamation completed the transfer of power from Moncton to Montreal, the C.N.R. had ceased to be under direct political influence. And, of course, Moncton's headquarters function had become only regional and under the control of a central executive in Montreal.

So, in the three decades of continuous growth and generally steady prosperity before 1930, Moncton was still very much a railway town, increasingly a distribution centre with still some manufacturing, yet in its social makeup notable changes had come about. It had been the end of the nineteenth century when the first Jewish residents arrived in Moncton to sow the seed of change which would take Moncton from its narrow base of English-speaking, British-oriented, traditional citizenry. There had always been a few Acadian French but now, from 1900 onward, their increase would revise the city's character.

By 1901 when the overall population had yet to reach 10,000, there were already 2,000 of Acadian-French extraction. In the succeeding eight decades their numbers would rise until they formed some 35 percent of the city's total. Even then, having gained the distinction of creating the city's first institution of higher education and of — in a sense — owning the city hall itself, they had yet to produce a mayor. Tiny as it was, the Jewish minority did generate one chief magistrate.

Individually, the city had its own cast of personalities. George Peters and his six daughters who acted as telephone operators, controlled the 228 telephones of 1900. Hattie

Tweedie, the school trustee when there were 1,717 pupils in the same year, ran her book store on Main street. For fifty years she would remain a trustee, and a most active one, all the while advising teachers and principals of their book and stationery requirements, always available at Hattie's place.

Miss Tweedie served the board from 1899 to 1948 and as to her business, she never waited for customers to come to her. She went to them. Her trustee functions she took seriously and would appear frequently in the schools to see for herself what was going on. Though she was much of the Protestant Establishment, Hattie Tweedie's favorite visiting spot was the school at Mary's Home where the Catholic Sisters of Charity were in charge. The nuns treated her with sweet gentleness and, as the principal's eithth-grade room gave off through double doors into the convent, she would be ushered through the doors and onto those hard birch floors polished to a mirror-shine, and served tea and the Canadian equivalent of crumpets. No school board ever neglected Mary's Home school while Miss Hattie Tweedie was on the board.

The Moncton Speedway was opened in 1903 to provide the community with what became for some years its favorite entertainment, harness horse-racing. The grandstand held 1,200 at first and was then expanded to handle 2,000. By 1912 when Old Home Week took over the little city, it could draw crowds up to 5,000 to the races, most of them standing and cheering their favorites from enclosures below the stands and along the rails.

Lounsbury's mercantile business was being set up in the city's downtown then, along with Sherman Blakeny's Cape Breton Coal and Ice Co. whose partners were Frank and Edward Hall. It was the start of a business expansion which the Blakenys would carry into the present time, meanwhile turning out a family president who would become mayor in the person of C. Hanford Blakeny, later a provincial minister of education. A more recent president was C.H. Blakeny's son-in-law, L.G. DesBrisay, who also succeeded to the title of "Honorable" as provincial minister of finance. Today, the business is operated by DesBrisay's son, Richard B.

And at this period, 1901, Peter McSweeney, whose family was prominent in the first volume of this history, opened his fine new three-storey department store. And two years later R.R. Colpitts began the stationery and office supplies business which greatly expanded today carries on still but R.R. Colpitts and his son, Lorne, are gone and the business is controlled by William Burden. *His* grandfather, Isaac Burden, to a whole generation of schoolboys was well known as the city's truant officer and Isaac's son, Cecil, for a time followed in his footsteps.

Before 1911, Moncton's streets were unpaved although concrete sidewalks were common. Bobsleds were numerous on the frozen, snow-covered streets in winter when transportation about the city was softer and swifter than in summer. When Capt. J.E. Masters was mayor in 1917 he pushed a paving program. Masters was a pioneer insurance man who had deserted the sea to engage in that business and in importing, for a time. He was a leader in campaigns to have Moncton's name spelled with a "k" since it was named for Col. Robert Monckton, and he even succeeded to this extent: For 46 days in the year 1930, the city was officially "Monckton" before reverting to the erroneous but popular and accepted spelling.

So in 1917 the paving smoothed out Main street for the motor-cars which were then beginning to clutter the few passable streets. The first paved loop included King street from the new Moncton Hospital, established in 1903, to Main street, then along Main to High, up to St. George and eastward to Highfield, where it went south to Main.

To one who lived on St. George, which was residential and just beginning to attract a few places of business, the hot tarring on the street is a clear memory. For little boys to try it out was a temptation not to be resisted; asphalt then did not harden quickly as it does today. The result was to find sandals, then popular summer footware for those under six, stuck in the black goo. The wearer was forced to step out, tug the sandals from the muck and run home carrying the ruined shoes dripping tar.

Captain Masters was backed in his efforts to make the streets suitable for automobile traffic by F.P. Gutelius, the general-manager of the Canadian Government Railways which had taken over the I.C.R. He gave engineering support for a subway to be built on Main street at Archibald where there had been a level railway crossing. Four tracks had crossed the city's chief street and, though there were gates and signals, the place was a menace and a nuisance even to the heavy horse-drawn traffic.

Excavation for the cut was done by steam-shovel and this proved to be a novel attraction for the gawking citizens. The paving itself was put down by Warren Paving Co. which laid six inches of solid concrete base on Main street and four inches on side streets to be paved. On top of this again went the bitulithic.

Wooden blocks set in asphalt remained for many years on the subway hill to provide traction for horses drawing loads up the incline and to keep them from slipping on the way down.

The sugar refinery, whose tall smokestack remained overlooking Main street and Hall's Creek for decades afterward, was burned first in 1896 and again in 1906. Financially, it had already succumbed to the takeover disease but a cooperage plant continued to make barrel staves and barrels for the takeover company, Acadia Sugar in Halifax. The Peters Lock company had become Fergusson Atlantic Underwear; the Record Foundry was still a big industry making stoves and furnaces and shipping them all over the place. Humphrey's mill was turning out great quantities of bannockburn pants, blankets and other sturdy woollen goods and J.A. Marven had bought out P.N. Hamm's little store and bakeshop and began making biscuits, later acquiring the big cotton mill off King street for an industry that would employ Monctonians until 1978.

Above all, there reigned in these years before 1915, David Pottinger, the king of the railroad, who held his own court and dealt with the politicians so shrewdly that, as shown in the first volume of this history, he was considered the sharpest politician of them all. The great fire which destroyed the railroad shops in 1906 has also been dealt with previously.

Its effect on the city threatened to be devastating but in the end proved only a chance for expansion and improvement. The hero, as was said in the earlier book, was none other than Henry Emmerson himself to whom we must return later for the story which so shockingly ended his career.

In the meantime, there was the arrival in 1906 of a Methodist preacher, the Rev. H.E. Thomas, who opened a crusade against liquor without local or regional precedent. He was so effective in a place which had developed a bawdy reputation for alcoholic consumption in earlier times, that H. Bruce Jefferson, the newspaper man with the elephantine memory, once wrote that Moncton was about the only place in the Maritimes where a sustained effort was actually made to enforce the despised Canada Temperance Act, known widely as The Scott Act.

"Back in the 1870's," Jefferson recalled, "every other building on Main street was a refreshment or entertainment joint. On Duke street, there were eight buildings which housed seven bars and the police station." Then, for eleven or twelve years after Thomas came to town, the trade was driven underground. An aggressive chief of police, George Rideout whose son became a Liberal Member of Parliament (as did his daughter-in-law) and his grandson a busy alderman, was the man who kept things in check. In Jefferson's words, "he pursued the liquor traffickers to the gates of Dorchester" (jail) and encouraged his sidekick Daddy Atkins, the scourge of school kids, to arrest whom he could. So famous did Atkins become that a local amateur show sang this jingle:

> "Daddy Atkins, he seems to think
> The citizens of Moncton can't get a drink —
> But someone else is getting it, getting it,
> Right where they sold a drop to me."

And when Rideout and his liquor-chasing buddy found a keg, they made a public display of it and poured it down the drain beside the boardwalk street. If life was hard for the tipplers, there were always the drugstores for those who could find prescriptions, and the list of ailing gentlemen and a few

Chief George Rideout, seen with his force dumping beer barrel while carrying out Temperance Act in 1907. Rideout is in centre with flat-top cap.

Courtesy Westmorland Historical Society

ladies for whom such restoratives were deemed necessary never seemed to shorten.

Chief Rideout was physically tough, a big man who sported a black handlebar moustache and disdained the stiff helmets of the London Bobby style worn by other members of the force. He went into his battles only with a soft peaked officer's cap, and with bare knuckles. For reasons which have never come to light, Rideout had a particular vendetta against the Hon. Henry Robert Emmerson, M.P., former premier and now minister of railways and canals. It may have been simply that Emmerson was known to be a drinking man and fond of women and the righteous Rideout found this reprehensible. Still, as the late Col. D.B. Weldon, H. Bruce Jefferson and Elmer Ferguson have hinted to the writer at one time or another (all were Moncton newspaper reporters about that time) there was something more behind the feud.

In any case, it was Emmerson's custom to travel from Ottawa frequently by train to his home constituency, and when he came on departmental business he would use the private business car provided for the ministers. It was also his habit to stay overnight in Moncton and during the course of the evening slip into certain known houses where spirituous liquors were available. Rideout and a character named Bruce McDougall who ran a local scandal paper called *Free Speech,* and who also had a grudge against the minister, kept a watch for him when he came to town. More than once Rideout had Emmerson escorted to the police station for his misdemeanors and once, if not more, kept him all night in the local lockup.

On a particular occasion in 1907, just a year after Emmerson had become Moncton's all-time hero and savior for having the railway shops built after the disastrous fire of 1906[1] the word came to them that the minister was spending the night in his private railway car on a siding near the railway station. Furthermore, it was reported, a married woman had been seen to enter the car and was believed spending time alone with him. Whereupon, Rideout dispatched a constable to enter the car and apprehend the minister for entertaining improperly another man's wife. Emmerson, at the time, was a widower.

The doughty constable did what he was told; the woman was indeed in the car with Emmerson and he was taken into custody. On what charge, if any was actually laid, it has never been possible to determine. Whatever the legal basis, the story was out and Bruce McDougall made the most of it. The woman was the wife of a railwayman whose husband was believed to know of her extramural dalliances and she was found "within" the railway car at two o'clock in the morning.

On an earlier occasion, the minister had been in difficulties after being seen emerging from a Montreal hotel in a merry mood with two women of doubtful repute on his arms. He was understood to have been clearly in a bibulous state and the prime minister who had appointed him, Sir Wilfrid Laurier, is said to have issued a warning about the public behaviour of a federal minister of the crown.

Indeed, the most notable parliamentary event in 1907 began with the declaration of a Conservative M.P. that he would not be stopped from discussing a Liberal MP's connection with "wine, women and graft." The line of inquiry thus opened up, ended with the resignation of Hon. H.R. Emmerson. He went down with all flags flying, however, as he told the House of Commons: "I have never been, mark my words, Mr. Speaker, and I make them with the full knowledge of the solemnity of the occasion and the dignity of my position — I have never been in a hotel in Montreal with a woman of ill-repute."

Whatever he had been doing in the hotel, he had broken the temperance pledge Laurier had forced on him, on penalty of resignation, the year before.

Still, it had been McDougall's report of the Moncton affair which made the whole matter one of national scandal. The record shows only that Emmerson "was compelled to resign his portfolio as the result of charges brought against his private character."

The voters of Moncton and Westmorland were more forgiving; they knew what he had done for the area. They knew, too, that Emmerson had been under a heavy strain after the death of his wife, Emily. She was the daughter of E.B. Record, Moncton's biggest industrialist (Emmerson is buried beside her in Elmwood cemetery). So the voters who remembered that his previous position and power had assured Moncton of its permanence as a railroad headquarters, continued to send him to Parliament until he died. Then, from 1935 to 1945, the same voters sent his son, Henry Read Emmerson, M.P. to the same House of Commons as their member.

Emmerson was called to the provincial bar in 1878, made a Queen's Counsel in 1899, practised law in Dorchester and sat in the provincial legislature two years, in the legislative council for two years and again in the legislature for eight more years, being minister of public works, attorney general and prime minister, as the title then was, of New Brunswick for three years. He was first elected to the House of Commons in 1900. In 1899, he was president of the Baptist convention of the Maritime Provinces and in 1900 president of the Baptist Congress of Canada. In almost any circumstance other than the one in Moncton, the place for which he had done so much, his human frailty might have been overlooked. Nor was Bruce McDougall himself the ideal man to bring such frailty to public attention.

After shocking and titillating Monctonians for a while, McDougall was run out of town, in a manner of speaking, and set himself up as editor of a Sydney, N.S., scandal sheet called "The Vindicator." It didn't vindicate him but soon was reported defunct. And so was McDougall. In the early months of 1911 he died after a fall down stairs in the Windsor Hotel in Sydney to a concrete floor. On April 10, his brothers asked for a public inquiry into his death, saying he had been murdered or, in any event, died as the result of foul play. The coroner's jury had called the death accidental but, in Moncton, where his brothers said he was a resident, the question on everybody's lips was: "Did he fall or was he pushed?" What was known was that three nights before his death he had been assaulted on his way to the railway station to take a train for Moncton and had been left unconscious in the street.

1. This story is told in some detail in volume 1 of the Monctonians.

Chapter Three

MONCTON WAS COOKING WITH GAS

It was during this period, starting with 1908 actually, that Moncton came to know a man who came bearing degrees from many universities in Britain and Europe. He was of Scottish descent but born far from the Clydeside in South Africa and his name was J.A.L. Henderson, a doctor of geology and mineralogy, and in Moncton they always called him "Doctor" Henderson. He was the man who found natural gas in Albert county which could make Moncton rich and famous, as everybody soon thought. And, in fact, for something like thirty years such a prospect was reasonable and, as will be seen, seventy years after Dr. Henderson's first explorations, natural gas was still being supplied to Moncton consumers while others contemplated the arrival in New Brunswick of a gas pipeline from the Canadian West.

It was back in 1858 and 1859, at the time of the historic finding of what was known as "Colonel Drake's well" in Pennsylvania, that traces of oil were found in New Brunswick. A Dr. Tweedel of Pittsburg and a Mr. Merrill, a prospector, were exploring the region and made the discoveries but it was many years later before any commercial development was undertaken. However, the Stoney Creek district of Albert County was found to have varied minerals and a company was formed in Edinburgh, Scotland, known as Maritime Oilfields as the result of Henderson's discoveries. Later, the group became known as The New Brunswick Gas and Oilfields Ltd., and their fields yielded millions of dollars worth of gas and oil products.

Three years after Henderson's first 1909 discoveries, another Scot, Alexander Crichton from the Firth of Forth, arrived in Moncton. Alex Crichton who had spent years in India and South Africa, was a physical epitome of the British imperial civil servant. He would have looked at home in any London gentlemen's club with his stoutish Robert Morley figure and his bristling Col. Blimp moustache. But Crichton was no Colonel Blimp. He came to assist Dr. Henderson and for many years thereafter he was a familiar figure in the city where for some thirty years he never so much as took a fortnight's holiday. He supervised all the detail work of the organization in the fields and in the offices. His own geological and mineral finds were notable.

Alex Crichton   J.W.Y. Smith

Marcel Bourque, who had retired in Moncton during the 1930's, used to recall the excitement at Stoney Creek when the first well blew in, and "blew" is the correct expression. First, the drill was lost in the bowels of the earth and workmen spent four days trying to extract it. Finally, it was decided to blow it out with nitro-glycerine. The drillers found the drill right enough, but the explosion wrecked the derrick and destroyed everything else employed in the operations. Still, no one was injured and the drillers kept going until they brought in a producing oil well. Gas came from above the oil sands and was piped into Moncton. At one time, it reached a daily volume of 1,300,000 cubic feet. Most of that was in the 1930's and a great portion was actually kept in reserve.

The city came to be one of the few in North America heated almost exclusively by natural gas. At one time when the city had 23,000 residents it would have been hard to find a home without natural gas for both heating and cooking. Before electric lighting took over, the most popular means of lighting in Moncton was by gas. A promotional brochure in 1916 advertised "cheaper gas than any city in the Maritimes"-- when there were 1,914 consumers as against 1,500 users of electric power. The electricity was for lighting only.

In all, some 120 wells were sunk and millions spent in exploration which extended to almost every part of Albert County. Great hopes had been held for major oil production, and there still are those who believe valuable oil can be extracted from the fields. However, and much to the surprise of many of today's generation, about 500 homes in Moncton remain consumers of natural gas from the Albert source in 1982.

From 1915 when the second British company took over the fields and utility company, Moncton boosted itself like a present-day Albertan community offering unlimited cheap natural gas to industries that would come and establish. The city produced a slick brochure entitled "Moncton — City of Opportunity" with a sub-heading that said: "The centre of the greatest natural gas producing field in the Dominion of Canada." Alberta's discoveries were far in the future. Eventually, the Moncton Electricity and Gas Co., Ltd., took

J.M. MacDonald's Overland car service station and dealership about 1915. Overland was forerunner of Willys cars and Jeeps.

over and became the sole distributor for the Gas and Oilfields Company.

When the gas begun to peter out, no new gas lines were put down in the city where, in what is now the older part of Moncton, the original loop runs. This is on King street, along Main to Cornhill street, part of St. George street and along Dominion street to Mountain road and west to Emmerson. Streets such as Church and Botsford running off this loop are also still given service but there is no gas available north of Mountain road. A private shareholding company, Moncton Utility Gas Ltd., continues to serve about 500 domestic consumers and forty commercial. Normally, the use now is for cooking and water heating only, with very few still heating with gas. A branch of the Irving Oil Co. has a lease on the Stoney Creek field but the supply is limited though steady. One recent director of the company believes that if the transmission pipes were cleaned and new drilling done, there could be a much larger flow of natural gas available but others believe the project much too expensive to undertake for the known potential.

The Moncton Citizen's Band as seen in 1915, one of several which gave concerts in the park. Back row: John Malenfant, Will McStay, William Douglas, Will Gaudet, Walter Cosman, James Morrissey, Burel Douglas, John McMillan, Walter Melanson, Alyre LeBlanc and one unidentified. Third row: Norman Beaton, Gordon Douglas, unidentified, another unidentified, Jack Dunlap, Bill McMullin, Roy Dann, unidentified, Ovila Williams, Fred Ryan, Edward Girouard, Robert Malenfant, Roy McQuinn; Second Row: William Pujolas, Adolph Gaudet, Ned O'Brien, Percy Ayer, Fred Cosman, Walter Bowness (the director), another O'Brien, John MacDonald, A. Gaudet, unidentified, Stuart Bowness, Ned Williamson, another Gaudet, Y.C. Cosman, Ferdinand Malenfant who later led Assumption Band; Front row: Leo Leger, C. Bowness, Alyre Leger, Frank Ryan.

Chapter Four

THE DAYS OF SPORT AND MURDER

In the years of this century before the first World War, when there was no radio, and two generations before television provided general home entertainment, Monctonians diverted themselves in a variety of ways. They staged amateur concerts and plays, groups went to the Opera House in city hall to see performances of Gilbert and Sullivan operettas, to hear sometimes really notable vocal and instrumental performers. They gathered to hear bands playing in the parks. In winter there was high calibre hockey. And people skated in the old Victoria rink which, when it burned in the disastrous fire of May 6, 1913, took with it the handsome white wooden First Baptist church, a barn, the church parsonage and hall.[1] In summer, they watched baseball and horse races and track meets. A few played golf, fewer played tennis.

Though they were used actively in all the years between 1890 and 1933 except for the war years, the grounds of the Moncton Amateur Athletic Association familiar to two generations as "the M.A.A." were busiest in the first decade of 1900. It was a place down on the marsh, at the foot of Westmorland street surrounded by a high board fence, having a cinder track, baseball diamond, football field, tennis courts and a lacrosse field and a cricket pitch. Bicycle racing went on there at times and on one occasion in the 1920's a world-class speed skating meet was held there and the world champions Charles Gorman of Saint John and Harry Smyth of Moncton, were among the competitors.

MONCTON VICTORIAS 1913

Players — J. Walker, H. Scott, J. Cross, E. Carpenter, W. McGregor, A. Kyle, Jack Carroll and J. Landers
Others include Mayor William Gross, Alderman Frank Robinson, Bob MacKie, P. A. Belliveau, and William McMullin

Both amateur and professional baseball attracted large audiences and, at the beginning and end of the sports seasons, there was a constant battle to keep the river from flooding the park. Cricket had been emphasized in the beginning but never took hold in Moncton, as it did not much anywhere in Canada except with a minority in Toronto, Halifax and Victoria. Most English who were in Moncton had come generations before, when there was no time for leisurely cricket, and those who would come later arrived after World War One.

Two Moncton hockey teams gained national fame, the three-time Allan Cup winners of the 1930's, the Hawks, and the Victorias who played for the Stanley Cup in 1911. The Victorias played from 1906 to 1912 and their players included some of the most exciting ever to skate in the Maritimes. Names like Chester Gregory, the Brown brothers, Frank and Jack, who for decades afterward were noted as referees all over the region; George "Shorty" Trites, who was almost as noted a baseball player; Kennedy, Norman, Crockett, the rover; Cushing, Wortman, Baird, McGrath, Wortman, Smith, Murphy, Doherty, and particularly Louis Berlinquette who went on to the big time but stunned Monctonians by his shot which, at times, went right through the boards. The Victorias, as Maritime champs in 1911 and 1912 played the Quebec Aces in the eastern playoff for the Stanley Cup. They lost in two games, 8-3 and 9-0.

Other historians have handled these sporting recollections in greater detail but the running feats of Moncton's Jimmy Humphrey, whom Elmer Ferguson encouraged to compete beyond regional borders, must be mentioned. In 1902 he ran the first 100 yards under ten seconds ever recorded in the Maritimes. An all-round athlete, he had done the first ten-second 100-yard dash officially on Labor Day, 1895, in Truro. The 1902 run in Moncton was at nine and four-fifths seconds but it was later found the track was slightly short of the 100 yards. He became a professional and won many races, climaxing his career in Saint John against Elbridge Eastman in a nine and four-fifths timed dash. However, a controversy arose over this and another nine and four-fifths run in Halifax was over-ruled on a technicality.

Humphrey was chief clerk at the Moncton railway ticket office, a clean-living, straightforward man who was put off by the shenanigans of the race promoters and betting business. So he retired from the game. In 1923 he was transferred to Montreal and retired in 1940 after fifty years of service to the railways. He died when he was 71, never having smoked or drunk alcoholic beverages, never having had top training for his running or professional coaching but still proving that he was the fastest man afoot ever to run in these parts.

Sports were so important that sports writers themselves became celebrated and, in Moncton, the young man from Prince Edward Island whose name was Elmer Ferguson became the local big star. In later years, as sports editor of the old *Montreal Herald,* columnist with the now defunct *Montreal Star* and as a National Hockey League official and radio "Hot Stove Leaguer," he went on to national fame.

Doug Weldon, a local boy who with Ferguson was mentioned briefly in the first volume of this history, was particularly interested in horse racing. He went up the financial ladder when he left Moncton for London, Ontario, became a millionaire and chancellor of the University of Western Ontario. When he was still active as board chairman of a major investment house and I was writing for the old *Star Weekly* of Toronto, we chanced to meet for the first time at a fishing lodge on the Restigouche river. Weldon's immediate question was whether Phil Belliveau was my father. Assured that he had been, we became bosom friends because the one thing Weldon never forgot was that my father, one of the city's early car owners, would drive him to the out-of-town race meets. "I was a young fellow, and of course no newspaper reporter then could imagine owning a car. The *Transcript* didn't pay travel expenses, so this was the only way I could cover the outside races."

Ferguson has been remembered by other historians but one story which no one else has told was his own version of covering the hanging of Tom Collins who murdered Mary-Anne McAulay at New Ireland. "Fergie" wrote to me about it at a time when a magazine article on the notorious case was in preparation. While the events themselves took place in Albert County it was from Moncton that the news was reported. In a time when exciting news was rare, either at home or abroad, the killing of the parish priest's sister and housekeeper held Monctonians in thrall.

On an August day in 1906 Father Edward McAuley, pastor of St. Agathe's Catholic parish in New Ireland, was away on his mission rounds to the Fredericton Road and to Elgin on the other side of the Shepody Hills. While he was gone, his sister was bludgeoned with an axe in the church rectory. She was found by her brother on his return in the evening and the handyman, young Tom Collins, was missing. The day before the slaying the young Englishman, who had been befriended by McAuley when he got off a boat from the Old Country at Albert, had been seen drinking heavily and was in a bad mood on the morrow. Traced to the railroad station at Elgin and then to St. George, Collins was arrested before he crossed the border into the United States and in his possession was Mary-Anne McAuley's prized pendant gold watch.

This was the only direct evidence, although later a mass of circumstantial evidence developed. There were three trials and, in the end, Collins confessed to the murder. He was hanged in the little jail at Hopewell Cape which today is part of the Albert County Museum.

Ferguson, although he was known mainly as a sports writer, had in the custom of the times done general reporting as well. John T. Hawke, the publisher and editor of *The Transcript*, himself dispatched Ferguson to cover the trials. Ferguson's own description given in that recollection of 1970 when he was an old man and retired from newspaper work was this:

"Collins had three trials. He was defended by the late Jimmie Sherren of Moncton, was sentenced to hang after the first trial, but there was an error found in the judge's charge to the jury. He was tried again and found guilty, but again a legal hitch was discovered and he was tried a third time. By this time, the good citizens of Albert county were aware that these trials were costing money.

Maddison of the Times

R.W. Hewson, K.C., Judge and Historian

"Collins was found guilty with no legal flaws and hanged on a hastily-built gallows at the rear of the small jail at Hopewell Cape on a rainy, cold morning and buried just behind the little jail. He had gained tremendously in weight, for the good people of the district had forgotten, perhaps forgiven, his crime and plied him with excellent food during the long months he spent in the little jail.

"Sheriff Lynds was a grand old gentleman, in charge of the administration of justice in Albert County and he was horrified that he might have to do the hanging. So he sent for Tom Radcliffe, the high sheriff of Canada as Tom styled himself, and he was a sort of official hangman. Radcliffe came to Albert County from his Toronto home a few days before the hanging, supervised the scaffold erection and drank a good deal of whiskey to settle his nerves. No one would speak to him, except myself, so we became quite chummy. He grew nervous as he ran out of whiskey.

"The night before the hanging he and I played cards in the little parlor of the small hotel and upon retiring, or at least preparing to do so, I warned Tom to be sure to waken me in time as I wanted to be on the job for my first assignment of the kind. Tom said he might forget, suggested I bunk in with him, which I did. We walked in the dawn, through the rain, to the little jail. Collins pleaded for another half-hour, so he could die in daylight, and Tom grudgingly assented.

"The Reverend B.E. Thomas had come over from Dorchester to offer the last religious comforts to Collins and he asked me to shake hands with the killer. This I refused to do, which probably was a cruel attitude, but he had murdered a nice old lady in cold blood to steal a ten-dollar watch and the hell with him was my thought and this I expressed to the slightly horrified minister of the gospel. He was so horrified that he wrote a lengthy letter to John T. Hawke, editor of *The Transcript* and one of the best friends I ever had in my boyhood as a newsboy. Dear Mr. Hawke told me it wasn't quite a polite thing to let a man go to his death without a comforting word, but he wasn't too emphatic about it.

"I wrote my story, in pencil, on the boat across the river and on the train to Moncton, to have it ready to set into type on my arrival. It was a lurid tale, as I recall it, the first hanging I had ever attended, but not the last. These things left me, and now in my later years I wonder why, entirely unaffected. I met Radcliffe in the afternoon at the American Hotel in Moncton, we had a couple of drinks together, small beers for me, as I was then an athlete, a sprinter, in training of a sort and didn't do much drinking."

There is a strange, almost mysterious, sequel to this first and only hanging in Albert County. Collins died at the end of a rope on a January day in 1907 and the community began to die at almost the same time. Less than a month after the execution, Father McAuley himself was dead of heartbreak and sorrow, exhausted by the stress of the trial. It was not alone the death of his beloved sister which sent him to his grave but the terrible burden of innuendo which had surrounded him, to the extent even of pointing the finger of guilt at himself before the murderer confessed.

And New Ireland itself began to disappear almost at once. Today, a seeker has to look very hard — and with guidance — to find the foundation stones of the large church beside Priest's Lake. The graveyard is there, fenced and preserved by descendants of founding settlers, among them Jerome Morris, the Moncton merchant who promoted the work. There lie the murdered housekeeper and, beside her, her tortured brother the priest. That is all of what was once thriving New Ireland.

Chapter Five

NO LANGUAGE DIVISIONS IN THE CEMETERY

In the late 1970's, English-speaking parents of the middle class in Moncton were agitating for French immersion school classes because they wanted their children to get ahead. At the start of the present century, a small French-speaking elite was pressing for the teaching of French but the Acadian working class in the city wanted their young to learn English so they could get ahead. Thus history turns.

During the three-score and more years between the first open advocacy of French language teaching in Moncton and the 1980's when such instruction was available from kindergarten through university, there had come about what may have been the most striking and basic social change in the community's long history. While English was still the dominant language by far in 1975, Mason Wade could write in the *Journal of Canadian Studies* that "Moncton has become the unofficial capital of the Acadians."

The decades between 1905 and 1980 had not always been quiet; controversy flared from time to time. Indeed, at times so noisily that Moncton became the focus of national attention of the English-French issue when bilingualism became a federal political factor. This latter period has been well reported. Less well known as part of Moncton's local history is the origin of the French linguistic and social movement which began in the city around 1905 and had, eventually, a most important influence on the province as a whole.

The forgotten and previously unwritten story is that the first and perhaps bitterest of all the local language controversies arose not between Protestants and Catholics but between Irish Catholics and French Catholics. Perhaps they were the more bitter because domestic quarrels make the most painful wounds and leave the deepest scars.

The quite coincidental arrival in 1905 of two men who were to be at the core of the language issue, the one a French-Acadian nationalist, the other an Irish-Canadian patriot, marked the beginning of a major change in Moncton history. The two were Valentin A. Landry, a publisher, and Rev. Edward Savage, a priest. They had come to the city just at the time when a young group of elitist French-Acadian nationalists were forming themselves into an amateur dramatics and public speaking society aimed at making Acadian citizens proud and aware of their language and traditions.

In retrospect, it was this tiny group of educated Acadians who could — like it or not — be said to have launched the movement which gave their people the institutions and the character which makes them today a potent factor in New Brunswick society. Their leader and most radical member was Henri P. LeBlanc, a man easy to dislike if you were on the other side and in fact an abrasive man often hard to like even if you were on his side. His associates included Bliss A. Bourgeois, a moderate and cultured man who later became a senior official with the railways, a man known for the stiff cylindrical high collar he wore and the formal looking fly-fronted overcoats and black umbrella he affected.

Another was Simon Melanson, the Main Street grocer, and his colleagues in these cultural enterprises were Dr. Fred A. Richard, the physician and surgeon; J.J. Bourgeois, who became one of the city's largest shoe merchants; Dr. L.N. Bourque, Moncton's first Acadian alderman and a prominent school board trustee; Clément Cormier, Sr., the vociferous Henri P. and Valentin Landry, the newspaper publisher. LeBlanc was the orator and pamphleteer of the group. Simon Melanson's children and grandchildren were themselves to be prominent in Moncton.

Henri P. LeBlanc in regalia of a papal knight. He spoke for parish division.

One of J.J. Bourgeois' sons, Joseph, became a provincial cabinet minister. Clément Cormier's only son became the president and founder of the Université de Moncton.

Valentin A. Landry was the man who founded the French-language weekly *l'Evangeline* at Digby, N.S., in 1887, later took it to Weymouth and then to Moncton where it became the principal organ of the French language in the Atlantic region which it remains to this day. However, when Landry came to town with his printing press in 1905 the chief French newspaper was *Le Moniteur Acadien* published by the Robidoux family in Shediac for half a century. Nor did *l'Evangeline* remain the *only* French paper in Moncton as will be seen.

In his 1975 doctoral thesis published at Dalhousie University, Martin S. Spigleman said of Valentin Landry: "He was like his Quebec colleagues; where others were defensive he was offensive. He was a fighting type and antagonized even those on his own side. Many Acadians were Conservative and at first Landry published a Conservative newspaper but, later, it became so Conservative that a rival had to be created on the Liberal side."

Rev. Edward Savage, a native of Melrose, New Brunswick, an Irish nationalist all his life, was appointed pastor of St. Bernard's in 1905, the year Landry came to town. He had been educated at St. Joseph's and le Grand Seminaire in Quebec, was ordained by the French-Canadian Cardinal Taschereau and spoke French well. He was the antithesis of a French-baiter and he came to Moncton seeking harmony among his mixed French-Irish parishioners. All of the parish pastors before him had been Irish and, as he himself wrote in his memoirs, "a majority of the congregation was of the French race." In fact, at one time the proportion of parishioners of French-Acadian origin (though not necessarily all French-speaking) was almost three to one.

What happened was that Father Savage soon found young Acadian leaders demanding a separate parish. More than that, they were using St. Bernard's parish hall to develop their cause. The new pastor wanted to put down the

First French-language social centre in Moncton housed two societies on top floor. Two windows at left have the following script decipherable in original photo: "Centre Catholique Beauséjour, Soc. la Jeunesses." (Beausejour Catholic Youth Centre) and "Ordre des Forestiers Catholique, Court Leo XIII, Nu. 1422." (Catholic Order of Foresters, Court Leo XIII, No. 1422). Toombs & Son were oldest wholesale grocery and provision house in city, corner Main and Duke.

movement, fearing divisive disruptions which he deplored, but Henri P. LeBlanc at one meeting spoke up and objected. A battle arose which ended in the creation of a new church parish, but that was not until 1914 and in the meantime much else would intervene.

As early as 1901 when the Acadian population in Moncton had risen to 2,000, a Beausejour social club was organized and had rooms on the third floor of the Robertson building at the corner of Main and Duke streets. By 1905 the LaTour branch of la Société l'Assomption was formed. These were really the first manifestations of a French-language presence in the city which had as its ideal the preservation and development of the French language which had fallen into disuse or become bastardized.

Landry and his newspaper cooperated with the local chapter of the society which, as a major insurance company would in future years become la Societé Mutuelle l'Assomption (Assomption Mutual). At this time, however, it was a small insurance and fraternal organization. The newspaper tended to become nationalist in the struggle between Irish and French clergy and it attacked the Knights of Columbus as a Catholic fraternity which the Irish controlled.

As things grew hotter, moderate Acadians turned against Landry, the Canadian apostolic delegate who was the Pope's diplomatic representative, objected as did the Irish, and Valentin Landry sold his newspaper to a specially constituted company and departed. He left J. O. Gallant as editor but he too soon found himself in difficulties over the parish separation issue. We shall return to this but, meantime, no discussion of the "French Question" can be understood without some knowledge of the historic forces behind it.

The Irish-French clerical and linguistic dispute had arisen out of a long-festering condition which may be summarized. After the Expulsion of the Acadians from Nova Scotia in 1755, the original and French-speaking inhabitants were restored to their civil rights but as they settled in isolated parts of Nova Scotia and what was to become New Brunswick, they were without any clergy. Governor John Wentworth of Nova Scotia was well disposed toward the Acadians and in 1796 sent to London their petition for a French priest.

The fabled Abbé Jean-Mandé Sigogne who knew English as well as French, reached Baie Ste. Marie in 1799 to serve the Acadians of Nova Scotia. Other French-speaking priests were unavailable and those later found to come to the French-speaking colonials in the Maritimes were Scots in Nova Scotia and Irish in New Brunswick. Neither supported the French language. For nearly a century after their deportation in 1755, the Acadians had no ordained Catholic clergy but kept the faith through local patriarchs like Joseph Gueguen of Cocagne who witnessed marriages, performed baptisms, led prayers and kept parish records. Irish priests began to arrive during the heavy immigration of Ireland's famine refugees while a few missionaries came from Quebec. It was the Quebec clergy which founded the institutions of education in the Maritimes but these were supported and supervised by Irish bishops. It was partly for this reason that Quebec-French influence and attitudes had never become those of the Acadian French.

An illustration of the long absence of French-speaking clergy can be found in the fact that the first Acadian native ordained after the Expulsion became a priest only in 1870. (A single exception had been Abbé Mathurin Bourg, an Acadian refugee in France ordained in 1772 and serving as a missionary in Acadia). The man elevated to the priesthood in 1870 was Rev. F. X. Cormier, a graduate of St. Joseph's College in Memramcook who had studied at Ste. Anne de la Pocatière in Quebec. He died on August 4, 1907, and his nephew and namesake, Rev. F. X. Cormier, became a curate at St. Bernard's.[1]

Beginnings of the so-called Acadian Renaissance lay in the national conferences (which the novelist Antonine Maillet has called "historic phenomena") held at Memramcook in 1881, at Miscouche, P.E.I., in 1884 and at Church Point, N. S. in 1890. They had set the tone for cultural, linguistic, educational, nationalist and perhaps even religious revival. They adopted an Acadian flag, the tricolor with star, took the Latin-titled hymn "Avé Maris Stella" (Hail, Star of the Sea) as their anthem and declared August 15 as their national holiday.

These events were the work of an elite but they brought about a sense of restored pride in a people who had been isolated for a hundred years after their dispersal and regrouping along the coasts. It inspired education in their mother tongue and in English. It began the raising of an Acadian-French clergy and increased a professional and business element of French language orientation.

Nevertheless, in civil matters the French-speaking population was under English rule and in church matters under Irish. In such a low state was the education of the Acadians as late as 1871 that, as Dr. Alexandre Savoie has shown in his study, while Westmorland County had 30 Acadian teachers in one-room schools or their own lodgings, 26 of them lacked teaching licenses. There was no such wild dream as a high school for French-speaking children and in that year only 21 per cent of French origin attended any school at all.

Many of those who learned to read in adult life did so by reading *Le Moniteur Acadien,* the weekly newspaper published in Shediac. T. W. Wood, the school inspector for Westmorland, had reported in 1867 that schools for Acadians were "in a pitiable state and will remain so unless the standard of teaching is improved." However, between then and 1907 things had improved moderately and in Moncton the school board yielded to a request from the French-speaking leaders. It was recognized that children having no English and coming from homes where the spoken language was French could not learn much nor long remain in schools where they understood nothing of what was being taught.

So in that year a petition signed by a large number of Acadians was presented to the Moncton school trustees asking that teaching in the primary grades where the mother tongue was French be in that language. The board passed a resolution to the effect that French could be taught exclusively for the first four grades.

Moncton wasn't prepared to continue any such concession. So on December 9, 1909, *The Daily Times* ran a headline reading "Former Resolution Rescinded and French to be Taught to French Pupils in Grade One and English to Grade 8." The story disclosed that at the monthly meeting of the board, it had been noted that the 1907 resolution applied only to the Wesley street school and that whereas there had at that time been unanimous agreement among French-speaking petitioners, that was not so now. No substantiation of this was given and the newspapers did not report discussion at the board meeting.

Mover and seconder of the rescinding motion were Mrs. C. T. Purdy, wife of the doctor (whose 100-year-old home at 24 Church street burned to the ground in November, 1980) and H. Seeley Bell, whose home, once a Moncton showplace at Church and St. George, remains but is much altered. A new resolution was moved by Bell and seconded by Purdy to the effect that, while Grade One could be taught French exclusively to pupils of French origin, after that and up to and including grade eight the teaching of French pupils "shall be in English as well as the French language which was the practice before the 1907 resolution." While there seems to be some ambiguity in this, no further explanation of the resolution was offered. Board members present were: Chairman John T. Hawke, Mr. McCully, Hattie Tweedie, Mrs. Purdy, J. Flanagan, H. S. Bell, H. H. Ayer, J. H. Harris, James Doyle and Dr. L. N. Bourque.

The full board voted yes, except for Dr. Bourque who left the meeting earlier. While the resolution applied to all public schools in Moncton, the teaching of French and in French was done only at the Wesley street school. Some years later, French was also taught in four classes at Mary's Home school where French-language pupils who lived in the north and west parts of the city attended. In practice, as Rev. Clément Cormier, a Wesley street pupil who enrolled there in 1918 recalled, French was available if and when there were French-speaking teachers. By the time the classes started at Mary's Home there were French-speaking Sisters of Charity and they taught the various grades. French was taught but, as textbooks were all in English except for French literature and grammar, the language of instruction as elsewhere in New Brunswick was in English. And this did little to improve the reading or speaking of French or, indeed, to encourage those of exclusively French tongue to remain at school.

The old Wesley Street school about 1920, showing portion of St. Bernard's church at its rear. First French was taught here.

Between that first resolution and its rescinding, other agitation was rising among the French-language activities. This concerned a movement to establish a separate church parish for the French-speaking, a breakaway from St. Bernard's, and the pressure for an Acadian bishop. The diocese of Saint John had ecclesiastical jurisdiction in the province everywhere except the northeast where the diocese of Chatham prevailed. It, too, had an Irish bishop.

That was the situation when, on January 19, 1908, a delegation of twelve Moncton Acadians waited upon Father Savage and read him a letter they were sending to Rt. Rev. Thomas Casey, the bishop of Saint John. The name of Simon Melanson stood first on the list of signatories. As the pastor recalled in his memoirs *Thirty Years in Moncton,* the tenor of the document was for the early division of the parish into two distinct parishes, "according as the people spoke the English or French language." In his reply, Bishop Casey told the twelve: "The fact that I have given three priests instead of one within a period of six years will show how clearly I am attentive to your spiritual needs. That St. Bernard's will one day be dismembered seems now to go without saying."

When Father Savage accepted the pastorate in 1905 he had asked the bishop to let him have two assistants, both French-speaking because he had known of the need. Later, he wrote that "unceasing agitation" had come to a head in 1907" and a committee had waited upon him concerning "an absolute separation" even though services were available in French. Within a few years, he as pastor had built the church of St. Louis de France in Lewisville for people living in that section of the parish. Those people "by their own exertions and without help from St. Bernard's financed the undertaking."

While this was going forward, the pastor was erecting Mary's Home as a home for the aged which was to be a memorial to his predecessor who had begun the project by acquiring extensive lands from the McSweeney family. When it was completed, the interior had to be altered for use as a school.

It had cost $40,000, but the stone used had been left over from the building of St. Bernard's. No direct subscription had been asked but a door-to-door collection was taken. Father Savage recorded later that he was "met with all sorts of grumbling opposition, particularly from a class of people not understanding how powerless I am in regard to the kind of secular instruction given in the public schools. They seem to hold me responsible for the fact French is not more largely taught. Now, as the proportion of French houses invaded by me is very great, the proportions of the moneys collected from the French people must be correspondingly large."

It was during this same period that Valentin Landry and his newspaper were having trouble with the Canadian Catholic hierarchy. The *Daily Times* of Moncton ran an item quoting the Saint John *Globe* as saying that *l'Evangeline* had for years "been criticizing the Catholic church authorities, assailing the Irish race, and denouncing the Knights of Columbus. Why the latter organization should be especially selected is not clear," *The Times* went on. "It is not an Irish society. There are in it descendants of English, Scotch, French, German and other races as well as Irish."

Threatened with possible excommunication for his divisive and inflammatory writings, Landry desisted. Not only because of ecclesiastical disapproval but because a large part of the Acadian community opposed his methods.

For a time, under Landry, *l'Evangeline* tended to be neutral in politics after its earlier Conservative tone and for a time its orientation was Liberal. It became Conservative again when J. O. Gallant took over and, as well, it soon ran into financial difficulties. Gallant and a committee went to Ottawa in 1914 to see Ferdinand Robidoux, the Conservative M.P. for Kent, and Hon. J. D. Hazen, the Saint John cabinet minister responsible for New Brunswick patronage. The committee sought funding for the paper and the national Conservative Party agreed to raise $3,000, which it proceeded to do. It purchased shares of the newspaper and made it into a Conservative organ. Clément Cormier, Sr., who had been manager of the weekly objected, whereupon A. B. Copp, the Liberal M.P. for Westmorland, Clifford W. Robinson of Moncton, Ivan C. Rand, the Moncton lawyer, and Peter Veniot who would become leader of the New Brunswick

Liberal Party, decided there should be a French-language newspaper that was definitely Liberal. They supported this idea with cash and established *l'Acadien* as a weekly and made Cormier editor and publisher. It remained in business until 1921 when Cormier was stricken with tuberculosis and entered a sanitarium.

Had Clément Cormier remained in health, his newspaper might have steered French-Irish and French-English relations in Moncton on a smoother course than they ran in the ensuing decades. He was a moderate, reasonable and intelligent man whose same qualities would mark his son, Rev. Dr. Clément Cormier, C.S.C., who in his time became the most genuinely effective Acadian of them all and whose remarkable career is told elsewhere in this book. As it was, the senior Cormier never went back to journalism but died in 1928 at the early age of 45.

To return to the Irish-French difficulties, it should be remembered that the division of church parishes was common with all Moncton denominations. It happened with the original Baptists, with the Anglicans, the Wesleyans (Methodists) and Presbyterians as well as with the Roman Catholics. The one and fundamental difference was that the Catholic separation was brought about not by theological, liturgical or ritualistic disputes but by language and nationalism. And because in the end it changed radically the character of the city and created its most lasting contentions, it is worth considering in some detail. As Richard Gwyn has quoted Pierre Trudeau in his biography, *The Northern Magus,* — "Of all political issues, language everywhere is far and away the most explosive." And, as Trudeau himself wrote in an official declaration of language policy: "Language is related to man's life in society as breathing is related to life itself."

Moncton, New Brunswick, was one of the first places in Canada where the difficult problems of a bilingual community were raised in a religious context and acted out in a public way. This apart, and considering only the repercussions on Moncton itself, this issue (never previously discussed in any history of the city) can be seen as of first importance. More

Very Rev. H.D. Cormier, first pastor of French-language parish. Courtesy, Centre of Acadian Studies

Rt. Rev. Edouard LeBlanc, first Acadian bishop of Saint John.

than that, it is clear now that bilingualism in New Brunswick and the establishment of the Acadian social structure as a force in provincial affairs can be traced directly to the small group in Moncton. "Troublemakers" they may have been called by their contemporaries — and trouble they did make — but they were pioneers as well.

As the Moncton dispute on church division along language lines proceeded, French-Acadian agitation for appointment of an Acadian bishop succeeded. Rev. Edouard A. LeBlanc, of Weymouth, N.S., an unremarkable bilingual Acadian-French country priest, was named Bishop of Saint John in 1912. At that time, what is now the Moncton archdiocese was within the Saint John diocese. This appointment resulted almost immediately in the creation of a French-language church parish in Moncton. When asked for his views, Father Savage replied that division of families on "racial or national lines" was impossible. "I will never be a party to the segregation of the French people, or indeed of any people, as a distinct body in the community.....It was always my hope to see two churches in Moncton — harmonious, sympathetic, undivided in faith or sentiment — where naturally English-speaking people would go to an English-speaking church and French-speaking people to a French-speaking church, in every case keeping the family intact and quite independent of what race of lineage their ancestors might be, following the language habitually spoken in the family."

On February 10, 1914, the parish was formally divided and Rev. Henry D. Cormier became pastor for the French-language parish of l'Assomption.

After the split, many Acadians remained with the English-speakers at St. Bernard's and not a few of them in fact spoke little or no French despite their origins. Others were bilingual Acadians married to English-speaking spouses and often these themselves might bear an Acadian name but be half-Irish and wholly English in orientation. For others who were Acadians and had French as a mother tongue yet preferred to remain in the old parish, it took some courage to do so. Nevertheless, a good many did. One who did and recalled it in 1980, nearly seventy years later, was Ovila Williams, the printer. (In New Brunswick, the name Williams, like Finn and Casey, is often now an Acadian name, with Gilbert Finn rector of l'Université de Moncton as this is written). Williams recalled those days of language conflict within the parish with great sadness.

One of the little ironies wrought by time was that Simon Melanson, the number one signer of the original separation request, found himself in old age asking to be accepted into the congregation at St. Bernard's. He had remained living on a little street off King, a long way from the new parish of l'Assomption and without means of transportation. He asked Father Savage if he and his wife, Ozite (Richard) Melanson, could attend Mass in that church, and they did so for the remainder of their lives. Like almost every member of the original detaching group, Melanson was fully bilingual. It is a further irony that his granddaughter, Lorraine, (the daughter of Dr. A.J. Cormier and his wife Alvina Melanson Cormier) should be married to a man bearing the most English and aristocratic of old Moncton names and become Lorraine Chandler.

To all of this history of language and church division, which was the forerunner of events which would mark much of Moncton's Twentieth century experience, there is a footnote. The pamphlet "Thirty Years in Moncton" put out by Monsignor Edward Savage and recording his side of the long dispute was never published generally. When the Moncton archdiocese was created and Archbishop L.J.A. Melanson named in 1936, he considered the mimeographed, magazine-sized document likely to cause disharmony. It disappeared but, here and there, a few copies were made on an old and weary stencil machine. It was the author's good fortune to have unearthed one of these. The correspondence it contained was fascinating and this reproduction of some of it is the first in any language.

Drily, the old pastor commented at the end: "None of the arguments ever touched St. Bernard's cemetery. Presumably it was felt that in the cemetery they all spoke the same language."

---

1. The curate, F.X. Cormier, was sent into clerical "exile" during the separation troubles in St. Bernard's parish. The Irish bishop sent him to the remote parish of Kingsclear, an Indian reserve on the upper St. John river where no French was spoken. He had sided with the French-speaking dissidents in Moncton.

Chapter Six

A WELL CONTENTED MIXTURE

For a majority of Monctonians, squabbles between the Irish and French seemed to be only congregational difficulties. Basic as they might prove to be in a changing city, the general public heard them only as echoes. As for the then small Acadian group, individuals might attain standing in the general community but working-class folk were more or less hived off in the east end.

A few of the middle-class were beginning to move uptown and by 1916 there were for the first time two bilingual aldermen elected to city council, J. J. Bourgeois and P. A. Belliveau. The famous "conscription election" of 1917 found a provincial focus in Moncton. When a Liberal trend was indicated, "a seething mass of people crowded Main street for nearly two blocks," and the Conservatives lost their formerly large Acadian support. It would be another 60 years before they could regain it to any substantial degree.

Eight years later when the Ku Klux Klan was active in the 1925 election and Peter Veniot, an Acadian Catholic was leading the Liberal Party, Monctonians provided an unusual result. The Klan's slogan was "A Vote for Veniot is a Vote for the Pope of Rome" but E.A. Reilly, an Irish-Catholic Conservative, was elected as the member for Moncton. Apparently, the local citizens considered an Acadian more papist than an Irishman of the same faith. And, at that, Veniot

Hon. E.A. REILLY, M.L.A.   WINSTON A. STEEVES

wasn't very much of a French-speaker. Raised in Pictou, N.S., he spoke no French until he came to Moncton as a Transcript printer in his young manhood.

As in all Canadian communities with mixed Protestant and Catholic populations which in Moncton were approaching numerical equality by 1920, there was the usual disputation and schoolboy taunts about the ultimate destination of rival denominations. Moncton's school population grew so rapidly after World War One that the total number of schools actually was doubled between 1920 and 1930. But there seemed to be reasonable agreement as to the separation of religions in the schools and in 1923 "The Academy" on Church street became the first all-French language school in the city. Whereas in previous decades French-speaking people might cease talking when passing their English-speaking neighbors in the streets, now the second language had come to be taken for granted.

Something of the new character of the city might be seen in the area which was our immediate family neighborhood. Just over the fence lived the Rev. Bowley Green who had come from the United States to be pastor of the First Baptist Church, in 1917. He wore a batwing collar, pince-nez glasses on a ribbon, often carried a walking stick. Above all, he had a snappish toy bulldog which became a natural target for neighboring children. Sometimes they joined us on the sloping roof of father's garage overlooking Green's garden. When the reverend gentleman, a distinguished churchman who later accepted a call to a church in London, Ont., came out to attend the dog, the boys and girls — Protestants and Catholics, Irish, English and French — were caught throwing stones in its direction. Shaking his stick, the Rev. Mr. Green, threatened the miscreants by saying he would tell their fathers. But he never did, and on the street all of them greeted him respectfully.

The area bounded by Highfield, Park, Cameron and St. George streets had by 1915 become a substantial and fairly new uptown residential section. It had a good mixture of population and, if it was typical of the Moncton which existed between 1910 and 1930 then Moncton was in those years a generally harmonious town. During the quick expansionary period of the 1920's this section may have been more representative of the city's mixed composition than any other district, being as it were at the residential centre of the overall community. Thus it may be useful to examine its nature in people terms.

Right beside the Rev. Bowley Green's house was a family of Irish-Catholics whose head was Dennis Sweeney, a man who could raise the roof at Holy Name Society meetings when things didn't suit him. (One of his daughters married a man of Lebanese extraction named Bouzaine; a grandson, James Walsh, survived the horror of Japanese imprisonment in Hong Kong during World War Two). On the other side of Mr. Green was a MacLeod family of Scottish background. Across the street were the Robert K. Buzzells, Mrs. Buzzell having been a Hannigan and the daughter of one of Moncton's early Irish families. Around the corner on Dufferin was T.J.

The Victorias hockey champions (Maritimes) of 1921 when they played in the Independent Hockey League and all players were local men. Lineups then included a rover, point and cover-point with one spare defenceman, one spare forward and one spare. Left to right standing at rear: V. Doncaster, J. Flannery, H. Smith (trainer), Frank Brown, manager; F. Carroll, J. Carroll. Seated left to right: B.O. McLeod, A. Wheaton, William Rogers, H. Carroll. Reclining in front are, left, Jack Ingram, and G. Carroll. The Carrolls were brothers and members of the Carroll Brothers family team later. Picture provided by Mrs. Adrienne (Brown) Lent of Vernon, B.C.

Allen, the railway solicitor and former school principal from Port Elgin. On the east side of Highfield on Dufferin was the W.U. Appleton family before Mr. Appleton became the C.N. vice-president and moved to the general manager's house on Main street, and they were Presbyterians with roots in Nova Scotia. Across from them was the family of Amos O'Blenis, the school superintendent, of Baptist persuasion and originally from Salisbury. At the corner of St. George and Highfield was Adolph Comeau, the Acadian fish merchant from Nova Scotia's Clare Shore district. Cater-cornered from his shop was the Highfield Baptist Church where Rev. A.K. Herman was pastor after Rev. W.B. Wiggins. Facing the church on Highfield was Dr. O.B. Price, the Conservative M.P. and dentist who was thought unfriendly to Catholics. Beside him, on St. George, were the Acadian-Catholic Legers and the family of Herbert Brewster, a Protestant C.N.R. clerk.

Half a block from Rev. Mr. Green's house, on St. George, were the Irish-Catholic Montgomerys and the elderly Mr. and Mrs. Hayes. Then, the Baptist Randalls who ran the butcher-shop and grocery. The head of the family was Benjamin Randall and he had nine sons, Ben, John, Percy, William, Fred, Russel, Kent, George and Willard. Ben Jr. became a sheriff and at least three of his brothers were city and railway policemen afterward. Near them lived Marg Osborne, the later famous Canadian country music singer with Don Messer and Charley Chamberlain. In the same double house resided a Lemieux family from Quebec whose boxer son "Biff" was a favorite around New Brunswick boxing rings in the 1920's.

The Randalls kept a big and wonderful farm-style hay barn where they stabled both work horses and harness racing horses. There were always cats and dogs around, and birds. Whatever the birds were, perhaps racing pigeons, neighborhood boys thought they were magpies and were forever shooting at them with arrows and BB guns. Moncton then still had a good share of horse-barns in backyards and a couple of active livery stables.

To continue with the makeup of this part of the city and indicate its representative texture, Sterling "Whitey" Hains, the jazz and classical pianist and composer, lived with his parents at the corner of St. George and Weldon, and almost next door was Miss Georgie Hains whose home-cooking shop was a marvel. She was, oddly, "a far-removed relative" of the musician. Now retired in Tottenham, Ontario, and still composing, "Whitey" Hains was among early radio performers in Moncton and later in Toronto where he was promotion manager for Capitol Records.

Beside us on St. George was the Methodist mayor, Frank Robinson, the senator's brother whose wife was an early woman-driver. It is not male chauvinism to recall that she was a bit of a menace and both the Robinson fence and the Belliveau fence frequently needed mending because of her erratic handling. Her husband was a car dealer and, for a time, so was his neighbor. The backyards adjoined, both entered by a mutual drive and often there were used cars parked temporarily on the way to the garage lots. Metal mayhem was always a possibility with Mrs. Robinson. Because car driving was a popular sport then, she would frequently invite friends to go driving — cars were rare, and few in Moncton had them before 1920. Much as they wanted to go driving women froze at the idea of being chauffered by the good Mrs. Robinson.

Behind the Robinsons, (later replaced by the eminent merchant tailor, James D. LeBlanc, a learned fellow who had picked up a smattering of Micmac phrases,) were first the maiden-lady and elderly Irish-Catholic McSweeney sisters, Aggie and Jo. When they went, Presbyterian Alex Crichton moved into the house — or was he there *before* they bought? Next to them were the Methodist Bedfords. There were also the Catholic Tom O'Neills (O'Neill and LeBlanc men's wear), the Baptist J.C. Keatings (manager of *The Daily Times*) and next door the C.C. Haywards (he was Lounsbury's top man and a Baptist,) and beside them the Catholic McCarthys — there were eminent Protestant McCarthys in Moncton, too.

The older Baptist Steeveses who are mentioned in the first volume of this book were represented in the present century at the corner of St. George and Highfield by David Steeves and his wife who ran a cracker-barrel type of grocery store. Nearby, on Weldon, was the Leslie Lynds family. Mr.

Mayor Frank Robinson's Ford dealership as it was in 1915. Model T. "in any color so long as it's black" seen above, tops up and tops down. Robinson's wife drove a McLaughlin-Buick, precariously.

First David Steeves block on St. George near Weldon. Shoe store in same building was run by J.B. Sangster whose father built Methodist church and mansion now site of Public Library.

Lynds was the railway station agent who had come from Saint John and his son, Fred. A. Lynds, would become Moncton's first native-son radio and television broadcaster. South of them on Weldon lived the Frank Storeys and the head of that household would be mayor of Moncton six times.

Just to round out that corner of Weldon and St. George and up to Park, there were the Connollys and the Fillmores, the Moores, the Caseys, the Girvans and the Barsses — three Irish and three "English" (or Scots; one was never sure of some names and families.) The Jefferson family of railroaders, journalists and school teachers, lived at Park and Weldon.

In an earlier volume considerable attention was paid to the original Stiefs-become-Steeves for they are important to the history of Moncton. Through generations they have lived quiet lives unspectacularly. They never seem to be involved in scarums and alarms or scandals and sensations. Solid citizens. After Winslow and Isaac, who were met in the previous volume, the first notable Steeves seems to have been Dr. E.O. a medical man who first shows up in the news as "a prominent Orangeman concerned with a special service in the Free Baptist church" on St. George st., Sunday, July 12, 1885, when mention was made of H. McAfee as the first Orange leader in Moncton.

The career of Dr. E.O. Steeves developed in political as well as medical directions. He became an alderman two years after Moncton was raised to city status and again several times later, including 1899. Then he became mayor in 1906. Dr. Steeves and his wife lived in one of the most handsome houses in Moncton, a white Georgian type on the north side of King street at the corner of Steadman. Half a century ago, his wife was known as the rich widow who could be seen chauffeured about in a fine limousine as she went about her prosperous affairs.

Dr. Steeves was one of those brave citizens who joined the first Moncton Salvage Corps, a jaunty body of gentlemen who in 1913 organized themselves into what became more of a social club than an arm of the fire department. It was a most representative group, with a charter member of the Knights of Columbus, balancing a charter Orange lodger, and a whole list of other business and professional men in its ranks. The real purpose of the corps was to race out after the fire wagons and attempt to protect whatever goods might be menaced, removing them from the path of the flames or throwing tarpaulins over them to protect the goods from water. Since the salvationists had to hasten independently day or night to the blazing structures, owning an automobile was a requisite of membership.

Once a year a banquet was held when the merry gentlemen celebrated their previous year's achievements in bibulous style. This went on at least into the 1930's when David Greig, an editor of *The Times*, paid his annual visit and at the same time volunteered to "cover" the proceedings for his paper. But all that got into his paper was the menu, so hazy were the proceedings.

This is to digress and coming back to Mayor Steeves, to recall that he was in the drug store business as well as into doctoring. He sold the pharmacy to W.R. Rodd in 1919 and the Rodd family operated a store in the Main street subway block and later in the Brunswick hotel block. Miss Marjorie Rodd took over the business from her father. She was a World War II veteran who served in the Royal Canadian Army Medical Corps as the only professional woman pharmacist in the corps.

One J.F. Steeves had gone into the wholesale grocery business in 1909. Of him, little else is recorded but many still living remember David, the grocer. He started with little stores in Steeves Mountain and Boundary Creek and came to Moncton with a bounce in 1895 to establish a shop between Lutz and Robinson streets on St. George, which later became the E.A. Fryers & Co. meat business, where anybody who was anybody in the first half of the present century went for the best cuts in town.

Proust, the great French novelist, has told in "Les temps perdu" (The Days That are Gone) how his mind was stimulated, his memory brought to life when he passed a bakeshop in a little village and smelled the wafting delight of a cinnamon cake. To mention Dave Steeves' store as it was six decades ago is to bring back all the delights of childhood in a time when his winter delivery sled known as "an express sleigh" raced along the snow-covered street, the belled horse driven swiftly in the shadowy December twilight. Standing at the front, reins in hands was big and bluff "Jumbo" Elliott whose proper name I never knew. He wasn't the brightest man in town, but he was good to small boys who ran after him, scrambled over the sleigh's low backboard, bells merrily ringing, Jumbo whistling shrilly as he went about his home deliveries.

Long after I had left Moncton and returned professionally to the province to do political work, I would come upon the most prominent of all the modern Moncton Steeveses, Winston and his brother Stephen. No others of the name matched them in the extent of their business enterprise, and while this recollective history had not been planned to include today's active Monctonians, some must be mentioned to permit continuity.

Stephen and Winston got into the construction business in 1945, a bold venture at the time. Later, the company name was changed to Modern Enterprises Ltd., which is an umbrella for several other companies. Active as they were in their own businesses, the brothers became almost as eminent — perhaps more so — in their work for world Baptist causes. And it was Winston Steeves who, with the late George English, could be called primarily responsible for the Moncton Industrial Development project of which more is said later in this book.

Winston Steeves was president of the Board of Trade at the time, as George English was retiring to become general manager of the board. Property which had been owned by the Steeves organization in Edinburgh Drive was made available to M.I.D. (Sold at less than $1,000.-an-acre, it was considered worth $15,000-an-acre in 1981) for the first part of the new industrial park project. Winston became a president of M.I.D. and remained on the board of directors for many years.

The Steeves brothers established an automobile dealership in 1951 and have been involved ever since, continuing to hold the "International" franchise in conjunction with Harold Steeves under the name of

Brentwood Motors. At one time, Stephen Steeves was a Liberal Party candidate in a provincial election in Albert County but suffered defeat in a constituency that was and remains traditionally Conservative. Both Steeves brothers were afterward active in provincial Liberal affairs.

It is doubtful in Moncton's long history that two men have extended their religious activities as far afield as the Steeves brothers. Stephen has been president of the Baptist Men, of the Baptist World Alliance, and Winston, was at one time president of the Gideons of Canada, part of a world-wide association of Christian businessmen who voluntarily distribute Bibles and other scriptural material. More than that, with Gideon International in the International Extension Ministry, he has been responsible for 14 South-east Asia countries.

At one point, Dave Steeves built a business block on the south side of St. George, between Weldon and Highfield, in anticipation of swift business development in this part of the city. Across the way, the Canadian Bank of Commerce had daringly erected a small brick building which was to serve as its uptown branch. It didn't last long. (It was the first Moncton bank branch to leave Main Street.) Soon Dr. G.O. Taylor was occupying it as an office and residence. Steeves' new building, however, was ambitious and it housed a moving picture theatre called The Kent, which didn't last long. Two blocks west, the Colonial theatre was opened in what later became Noble's garage between Cameron and High. Its life was almost as short as the Kent's. It was also in this Steeves building that Lane's Bakery, and the Lane family fortune, got its start.

Francis Lane, having graduated from St. Francis Xavier University, came to Moncton from a farm in Malden (Melrose) to follow the path of the many Irishmen from Melrose who made their careers in Moncton. There had been Frank Sweeney, Q.C., the provincial attorney-general, Hon. E.A. Reilly, the first chairman of the N.B. Hydro Power Commission; Monsignor Savage and the Mahoney family whose wealth derived from the lumbering trade. There was also Francis P. Murphy, the lawyer and alderman whose son,

J. Edward, became one of Moncton's youngest-ever mayors, another son, Henry, a Member of Parliament and judge, still another, Fred a noted local surgeon, and Patrick Murphy, M.D. It is doubtful if any other family in Moncton produced so many professionals in one generation, but several successful Lane brothers came to live in the city from Melrose.

Francis Lane had been preceded by his lawyer-brother, William F. Lane, who was to be Moncton's magistrate for many years and preside at the most famous of local criminal hearings, the Bannister murder case. Other brothers were Leo, Joseph and Corrigan and all now are dead while all the Murphys were still in practice in 1982. Corrigan Lane eventually became associated with Francis in his business enterprises.

From the tiny bake-shop on St. George street, Francis Lane moved to a slightly larger one on Archibald and then branched out into a full-scale bread-making industry. In the beginning, neighborhood boys eager to earn a few cents on a Saturday morning would be taken on as bread wrappers, machines for such work being a future luxury. There had been a Maple Leaf Bakery immediately opposite on St. George street which closed when its manager and his lady-cashier were found dead of carbon-monoxide poisoning in their parked car on the Salisbury Road.

In World War Two years, after continuous growth from such humble beginnings, Lane's Bakeries became a major bread supplier for military installations. Its expansion continued after the war until Lane's was the largest bread-maker in the Atlantic Provinces. Francis Lane sold his interests in 1965 to a national corporation and retired. Having become wealthy in previous years, Lane quietly became a major benefactor to education and charitable causes. He married Mary LeBlanc of Moncton, fathered three daughters and built Lane Hall for women at S.F.X. at a cost of $2,000,000.

In recognition of his services to education, the university bestowed upon him a doctorate of civil laws in 1969. The man who had been first president of the Maritime Bakeries association, died at the age of 77 in 1980.

Chapter Seven

DERBY HATS AND PEGTOP PANTS

Having skipped around a decade or two, it is time to return for a moment to that 1910 period. You can tell the prominent citizens of the day by reading a list of charter members of The Moncton Club, founded in 1909. There had been a previous Moncton Club, that from whose Main Street window Judge Botsford plunged heavily to his ending at a good age, but it had disappeared. Now the organizers were the Sumners, the Harrises, Cavour Chapman (who, unaccountably for a native of Dorchester, New Brunswick, was named for the great Italian leader of the Risorgimento, Count Cavour) E.C. Cole, the merchant and *Times* co-owner, and others such as A.E. Williams, the railway treasurer; Matt Lodge, the civil engineer and C.N. director, hydro-power schemer and oilfields financier; James Geary who ran the McSweeney Brothers' business; James Edward, the Grand Trunk railway agent; Lester Higgins, the shoe manufacturer soon to own more Moncton downtown property than anyone else; Fulton McDougall, the banker; Allie E. McSweeney, the department-store heir; James McD. Cooke, the druggist, whose wife, Lou, later drove a sporty McLaughlin-Buick "roadster with a rumble seat" and played championship golf.

There were also Dr. F.J. White. the quondam mayor and surgeon; Fred C. Jones, the realtor and money-lender who would give Moncton a lake; Charles Fowler Burns, the accountant whose son Herbert would become president and chairman of the Bank of Nova Scotia after his start in Moncton; R.A. Borden, the lawyer and cousin of Prime Minister Sir Robert Borden; J. Fred Edgett, the frequent mayor, school board chairman and wholesale grocer; J.W.Y. Smith, the millionaire whose fortune Edgett kept making bigger by his running of the Smith-financed business whose money had come through the parsimonious Lady Smith of Dorchester who got it first from the Youngs of Halifax, her parents, and her husband, Sir Albert.

Then there was E. Albert Reilly, the lawyer-politician who was first manager of Central Trust and afterward chairman of the N.B. Hydro Commission, a provincial cabinet minister. Another of the organizers was Dr. W.A. Ferguson, the physician and surgeon who had come to Moncton from Rexton and was long prominent, especially for his fast-racing Pierce-Arrow and Cadillac cars of the period; another was Judge W.W. Wells, and there was Clifford W. Robinson, the one-time (later) premier and afterward senator.

J.H. HARRIS, Postmaster in 1920's and last prominent member of family noted in Moncton for four generations.

Moncton was enjoying one of its most expansive periods when, in 1912, the city council and board of trade decided to sponsor an Old Home Week from June 24 to June 30. The automobile had come to stay and the International Auto Co. proprietors of the Victoria Garage, were exclusive agents for the "Mighty Michigan Automobiles." And mighty they were. In the 1920's one of them was parked in our yard as a trade-in on a Jewett and it was the most ungainly looking contraption to be imagined. Recollection says it had a chain drive, though that may have attached to another model, and it stood beside a Rickenbacker which was somewhat sportier.

George O. Spencer, the druggist, was offering for Old Home Week a "beautiful high class real Japanese fan" with every fifty-cent purchase of Rexall remedies and toilet articles. The fans *were* real Japanese, made of delicate bamboo straw strips gaily decorated, and they adorned many a lady's dressing table for years afterward. B.E. Smith offered Gerhard Heintzman pianos, and no proper Moncton home could be without one so that little girls could practise their scales. Their older sisters, home from finishing schools for the holidays, sang to its accompaniment all about "A little boy and a little girl, in an ecstasy of bliss" tying apples on a lilac tree. And "Roses of Picardy."

J.M. Ross, who took pictures and sold photographic supplies along with men's cotton undershirts and such like, (in fact he advertised "Everything a Man Wears Except Boots") provided the news of the world in pictures. In his window at 749 Main street, opposite City Hall, he displayed pictures of news events — "a new one every day". It wasn't television, but it beat Life magazine and its pictures by twenty years.

MacLeod Jr., just eastward on Main between Botsford and Church, called itself "The Home of the Neckwear Beautiful. Dress to impress others and EXPRESS YOURSELF IN PERSONALITY—". The town was full of dandies then, peg-top pants, bowler hats called "derbies" in Moncton, "trilbys" in London, and "old time lids" in New York's St. Patricks Day parade.

Chief attractions for Old Home week were provided, except for the trotting races and parades, by Eastern

One of Moncton's early photographic studios, Crandall's, had this glassed skylight before electric lighting was available. Below is first Spencer drug store. Founder George O. Spencer probably man at far right.

Amusement Ltd., Torrie and Winter managers. Alexander Torrie was the son of the rich soap manufacturer who fought the great land battle with Oliver Jones after Torrie had built his mansion on Bonaccord street — and they named the street just that — *bon accord* (friendly agreement) when the dispute was settled. Torrie then built the lovely house a block away, now the attractively restored Canadian House. Fred Winter was the son of old John Winter who gave the Moncton Club a hard time when he tried to raise the rent on their premises even though they had a long-term lease. Their respective lawyers, James Friel and Austin Allen, battled it out, after he had fixed the roof leaks, and they came to terms several years later.

Don MacBeath was the epitome of the "local boy makes good at home". He had begun his career driving a delivery wagon for the class trade grocer, J.T. Ryan, then sold groceries as a commerical traveller. In 1919 he bought out George O. Stratton at 881 Main and was in business for himself. So well did he know the trade that by 1926 he was building himself a new business block which included a modern groceteria, but it was not called that then. He catered to the upper class trade. The block was later taken over by the Woolco store at the corner of Foundry.

One of Don MacBeath's sons, Ronald E., after World War II, rose in the Canadian Legion to become its national commander. His father's real estate operations included the foresight to develop the area now known as McBeath avenue, which includes among its occupants the Moncton General Hospital. D.A. MacBeath had taken his big store to Mountain Road after buying the Lance Wilbur farm, a landmark on the road to the hills. It then seemed to be far out, and has since become one of the most active retail districts in the city. It was, in fact, D.A. MacBeath's gift in 1949 of ten acres of farmland which made the new hospital facilities possible. The uptown grocery store was run by D.A.'s sons, Ronald and Alexander. D.A. MacBeath went into the real estate business and his son, Ronald, took it over after his death.

In those Old Home Week times, Ern Givan was Maritime agent for the 36-6 cylinder Pierce-Arrow car, the touring model with the soft top, isin-glass side curtains in case

F.M. TENNANT, founder of wholesale fruit trade.

DONALD A. MACBEATH, grocery pioneer and hospital philanthropist.

H.H. MELANSON, first Acadian railway vice president

E.C. COLE, merchant co-owner of Times.

of rain, and a fold-down windscreen. Givan didn't depend on sales of that alone to make a living. He also sold "Orange Julep, the best drink that ever trickled down a thirsty throat. Try it." Next door, just to clean things up, Givan's invited citizens to "See Your Laundry Work at Givan's Steam Laundry." They were, as they said, first to adopt natural gas in Moncton. "Always up to date, at 90 King St., Moncton, Phone 64."

One of the mysteries of that memorable Old Home Week was the crowning of a carnival queen. Curious as to who she might have been, perhaps still living, I went through the daily newspapers to discover the lucky girl. Not one word was there to suggest her identity, or even that the event came off. The only big headlines that week were for the Duke and Duchess of Connaught (She was the royal Princess Alice) then the governor-general and his wife. They came to town for a day and were royally welcomed.

That same day, *The Transcript* recorded that "a visiting Englishman and two Monctonians were injured" when their car went over a bridge embankment at Stoney Creek. "Chauffeur LeBlanc lost control of the brakes" and Septimus Warwick, a London architect, was hurt. So was James Edward, the Grand Trunk agent at Moncton. Quick on the accident scene was Dr. C.T. Purdy "who fortunately happened by."

Chapter Eight

BISCUITS AND BARTER

Between 1900 and 1920 a sort of industrial phenomenon was taking place in Moncton history and it came to be typical of a syndrome which would affect all the Maritimes. Before 1867 and Confederation, the Maritimes had been highly prosperous and developed major local industries. Confederation brought protective tariffs and discouraged the free trade and commerce of the high seas which had made the Maritimes flourish when they were colonies of Britain. Now, industries were protected under the new national system but the Canadian market could not absorb the growth of such industries and the competition within the new nation began. Better organized newer companies with good financing in Quebec and Ontario flooded the market with lower-priced goods and Maritime industries suffered. Several such manufacturing companies had existed in Moncton and are mentioned in an earlier volume. But one industry which begin in Moncton as a tiny biscuit bakery in 1903 bucked all the earlier trends.

When Joseph Avard Marven bought out P.N. Hamm's little bakeshop on Main Street no one foresaw what would happen. Joe Marven, born at Shemogue (then called Bristol) between Shediac and Port Elgin in 1868, had been a commercial traveller representing W. Frank Hathaway and Co., of Saint John. They sold biscuits along with such other staples as Estabrook groceries and Tiger tea, but Marven wanted a business of his own.

As he got his new enterprise moving, Marven went on the road selling his own products and his friends in the trade had a few well-worn comments. "Hello, Joe. How's the hardware business?" they'd guffaw. Or call out: "Well, Joe, I hear that Marven's Biscuits wear like iron." There was another wisecrack farmers would make as Marven came around: "Those sodas you make are great for shingling barns." Just the same, Joe Marven was busy producing a quality product, a first-class product, and it all went so well that he soon hired William A. Walker as a salesman. As the business thrived, Walker became sales manager and others were taken on.

Within a few years, Marven had to find much larger quarters and in 1916 he bought part of the unoccupied former cotton factory off King Street. Marven's White Lily Biscuits became famous in the region and then beyond, proving the business to be a phenomenon of that era when other Maritime industries had been pushed out or fallen by the wayside.

In time, that would happen eventually to Marven's as well but not for a long time yet. By 1920 the little biscuit shop had burgeoned into a million-dollar-a-year business and Fred M. Brown had been made plant superintendent. S.L. Holder was made secretary-treasurer, and the company had warehouses in Montreal and Toronto as well as retail outlets all over the place.

Marven's imported dried fruits from Australia, cherries from France, spices from the Far East, flour from Ontario and Manitoba, arrowroot from the British West Indies. The Maritime Provinces supplied butter, eggs, jam fruit, oatmeal and so on, providing secondary industries of themselves.

Then the "Confederation syndrome" struck, but with a difference. The first results proved only temporary. Foreign capital had begun to exert a controlling force in the Canadian industry as a whole. This was in 1925 at the height of prosperity for the biscuit business.

To counter this, Canadian financial interests worked to form a large and all-Canadian company by amalgamating some of the most important plants in Canada. Marven's joined these to create Canada Biscuit Company with executive offices

FRED. M. BROWN   JOSEPH A MARVEN

in Montreal. The biggest of the joiners was McCormick's and eventually McCormick's took over the whole amalgam. While in 1925, Marven's retained its famous "White Lily" brand, it added "Oven-Kist" to represent the new company.

The organization continued to prosper for some time with F.A. McCormick as president. Joseph A. Marven sold his interest in 1928, then in 1935 W.A. Walker and Clarence E. Fraser bought the local branch of Canada Biscuit Co. Ltd. for the remarkable price of $25,000. Once again the business flourished, additions and improvements were made, E.O. Steeves was made plant superintendent, W.A. "Biscuit Billy" MacDonald became Maritime sales manager. MacDonald was later to be even better known as tourist development chief for the city and area, a sports promoter and one of Moncton's best-known citizens before his death.

This new company had branches in Halifax and Saint John. It added new lines; things were going just fine and warehouses were opened in both Montreal and Toronto. Local competition then took form in 1931, when F.M. Brown and S.L. Holder, who had been Marven originals, combined to establish a new biscuit company known as Brown-Holder Biscuit Co. In time, it too bucked the national trend, and became the largest independent manufacturer of biscuits in the Maritimes. The owners advertised extensively, built a plant on Botsford Street extension and erected warehouses. The business continued until the death of F.M. Brown in 1951 when his son, Harold, became the managing head.

As for Marven's, with many ups and downs over the years, it remained alive until 1978. Unable to retain a sufficient market against a new kind of competition, the industry which had some years before been taken over by Westons, could no longer pay its way. Its going was traumatic for Moncton, not only because of the sad loss of employment at a time when other losses were being felt, but because it had become a local tradition. As a non-railway industry, it had outlasted most others, had become part of the city's fabric.

What was unique about the biscuit industry in Moncton was demonstrated when Brown and Holder formed their own company. In 1931, when the Depression was just beginning to show its worst effects, the prospects of success would have seemed almost insurmountable. However, the biscuit industry had one ingredient (literally) which made it competitive with centralized rivals and allowed it to prosper, and that was lard. Lard made biscuit-making and selling a local and regional operation with which distant and centrally-located factories could not compete until much later in the century.

Cookies made with lard turn rancid in a few weeks. Therefore, they had to be turned over fast and to do that successfully the market had to be close by. Shortening came along and made longer life possible but shortening was expensive and even the major Canadian makers could not use it. In time, an ingredient was found which made the cookies last longer without rancidity.

When Brown-Holder Biscuits got going, Fred M. Brown the president and for thirteen years a Moncton alderman, found the going so tough the salesmen often took goods in barter from country grocers. At some of the most difficult stages, employees accepted vegetables and meat as part of their wages. One wholesale grocer in Minto, New Brunswick, who was also in the coal business, supplied coal for the biscuit plant in exchange for cookies.

Gradually, the business developed and volume was maintained at a high level even in the harshest 1930's because plants in central Canada closed down during two winter months. During this period, Brown-Holder employees worked two shifts a day to supply the shortage in central provinces. In the next decade, wartime demand caused partly by sugar rationing made biscuit sweets particularly attractive. In 1949, when Newfoundland became a part of Canada, the Moncton biscuit industry took on new life and Marven's and Brown-Holders both prospered. There was even some exportation to the United States because biscuits went there duty-free for five or six years.

However, the arrival of supermarkets hurt the Moncton biscuit makers. Centralized buying and the ability to use the new lard without rancidity brought bigger orders from central Canadian factories. However, Brown-Holders continued to flourish. Fred M. Brown had died in 1953 and his son, Harold, took over as president and general-manager. For a long time the business averaged $500,000. yearly in sales (Marven's in its biggest year had gone to $3,000,000.) and employed as many as 150 people. In 1973, Brown who had been connected with the enterprise 42 years, sold out to David Clifford who had been with the Dare Industries in Kitchener, Ontario, but after running it for a year the industry collapsed. Like the machinery at Marven's, it was smashed and sold for scrap. It was the end of an era in Moncton.

Chapter Nine

FAMILY DYNASTY IN WOOD

In Moncton, the woodworking industry goes back at least to 1844 when Stephen Binney arrived from Halifax to make barrel staves. And, peculiarly, like Binney[1] all of its major entrepreneurs have been notably civic-minded people. Perhaps it has something to do with making things out of New Brunswick's greatest natural resource, wood, but from Binney down to the third generation of Lockharts in the 1980's the Moncton woodworkers have been solid citizens who made more impact on the community than most.

While Binney had once been mayor of Halifax, the next big woodworker at The Bend, after it became Moncton, was a Prince Edward Islander who had actually taken part in the preparations for the Charlottetown conference in 1864 which led to Canadian confederation. He was Paul Lea and his part in the welcoming of delegates from the Canadas, Nova Scotia and New Brunswick to Charlottetown was to help decorate the parliament building.

A young fellow with a yen for adventure, three years after that he went to California when getting to California from Prince Edward Island was some feat. There was no transcontinental railway connection and the Panama Canal would not be opened for another 47 years. Yet, on April 1, 1867, he made the 50-mile crossing on the Isthmus of Panama. Whether by horseback on the ancient roadway through the jungle or by rail which long preceded the canal isn't known, but he sailed from the Pacific side up the Gold Coast. He returned to Charlottetown three years later and started a woodworking business.

A dozen years later, he saw Moncton as the place for expansion while Prince Edward Island was losing some of its earlier zip and in 1883 he established a woodworking plant on Westmorland street. It was close to the wharves and close to Main street, and he gradually expanded the operation until it employed some 60 hands regularly and provided finished woodwork as well as lumber for most of the city's rapid growth in the growing railroad years. Not only in Moncton but for institutions well outside its borders.

When Paul Lea built his final home he didn't use wood, however, but was one of the few Monctonians to erect a stone house (others included F.W. Sumner's and the rectory of St. Bernard's parish). However, Paul Lea chose an odd place for his, smack up against the railroad embankment and almost beneath the ugly traffic impediment known as the overhead bridge on Mountain Road. His house still stands there on the south side of the street, substantial and austerely narrow, thin as himself but tall.

As late as the 1930's its orchard produced good apples where schoolboys could approach from the tracks and snitch as many as their pockets would carry. Tall, dignified and handsomely bearded, old Mr. Lea never seemed to protest. Perhaps his hearing had been impaired by the thousands of trains which had rumbled past over the years. At one time there were as many as ten trains a day coming and going to Shediac alone, to say nothing of that being the main line to Halifax. In the days of steam and coal firing for engines, smoke must have been a constant companion to the Lea household but it may have been deflected since the house was never begrimed with coal dust.

Lea sold out his industry to Bent W. Lockhart in 1922, and retired, and thus began a whole new woodworking family dynasty in Moncton. Lea had been a good citizen, community-minded and at least once an alderman, but B. W. Lockhart and his son, Leonard, proved to be two of the most active civic-

PAUL LEA BENT W. LOCKHART

minded men in their generations. As this is written, his son Leonard, Jr., carries on in various public-spirited capacities. The Lockharts produced in Bent W. and his eldest son a pair of remarkably energetic citizens who expanded their industry into one of the biggest of its kind in the coastal provinces.

The Lockhart family, originating in Scotland and reaching Nova Scotia in 1760 by way of sojourns in Northern Ireland and Connecticut, had settled at Leicester in Cumberland County, N. S., near Parrsboro. B. W. Lockhart was a son of Henry B. Lockhart who was long identified with lumbering in Cumberland. When he died at the age of 85 he was the oldest citizen of Leicester in both age and length of residence.

"B. W." came to Notre Dame on the Cocagne River in 1900 to join his brother, Charles E. Lockhart, (whose daughter Jane married J. Edward Murphy, Q.C., of Moncton), at first looking after a store and then supervising milling operations.

He had gone to business college in Saint John and soon was manager of both milling and store operations. When the firm was sold to W. D. Gunter of Fredericton in 1913, "B. W." stayed on until 1917 and then came to Moncton to launch his own business. By 1922, he had bought out Paul Lea who had handled both domestic and imported lumber for both wholesale and retail trade and manufactured doors, sashes, desks, office and bank fittings and interior finish of all kinds.

Bent W. Lockhart had married Annabelle Teed in Notre Dame in 1907 and their first son, Leonard, was born in 1908. Two other children were Mary, who became a teacher in Halifax, and Henry (Ben) who became a medical specialist in California. While the business expanded, they were raised in a modest home on Highfield street, a few yards from the then new Edith Cavell school. B. W. Lockhart soon had business connections in every community in Eastern Canada and developed a volume of foreign trade.

By 1927, the plant was using 3,000,000 board feet of lumber and had a payroll of $75,000. a year. Besides this, of course, there was the employment generated in cutting and hauling wood and in winter, Main and Westmorland streets were often crowded with bob-sleds bringing in logs. Where snow had been removed from the street railway, the screech of iron-bound runners crossing the steel rails as the sleds came down Church and onto Main was an ear-piercing shock, like drawing chalk across a slate.

A stocky man who in a lumberman's mackinaw would have looked perfectly at home handling a peavey in a log-jam, B. W. Lockhart couldn't contain his energy through his business activity alone, grow as it did. He was as well a leader in the United Church, in the Board of Trade, and in the Westmorland County Conservative Association. He was a director of the Y.M.C.A. and president of the National "Y" council; he was founder of the Red Cross Blood Donors Clinic and a director of the New Brunswick Lumber Dealers Association.

Even this wasn't enough to use up all his energy so, like Teddy Roosevelt, he found still other outlets in hunting and fishing and so ardent was he in this that it was at his Square

Paul Lea Co. lumber mill on Westmorland street as it looked in 1915.

P.N. LeBlanc woodworking plant in 1915. It was south of Main street near present Hotel Beauséjour parking lot.

The fire department's pump and ladder truck in a dashing display in 1915. Only fireman who has been identified is Dave Chandler, standing at right. May be first non-horsedrawn fire wagon in town. Note splendid bell and searchlight. Also, the crank at front. No self-starters then.

How Archibald street looked from the corner of Main before subway was built. Picture was taken on a snowless January day in 1915   (Courtesy Westmorland County Hist. Soc.)

Lake camp in Albert County that he was stricken and died in 1935 at the age of 66. At one time, B. W. Lockhart had owned the Shediac Inn and it was the only one of his business operations which proved unsuccessful. However, while he ran it, the historic inn was host in 1933 to the flyers who had made history by bringing General Italo Balbo's fleet of flying boats across the Atlantic for the first mass crossing by air.

Leonard Lockhart had been associated with his father from 1928, having in the meantime married Helen Humphrey of an old Moncton family in 1930. After the death of his father, he became president of the company in 1935 and the name became Lockhart Woodworkers' Limited. If his father had expanded, Leonard expanded even more until he himself was chairman of the board of Lockharts Limited, his son Leonard Jr., president of Lock-Wood Ltd.; his son Marks, president of Lockhart's Limited and his son, James, manager of both Lockhart stores in Saint John.

Like his father, Leonard Senior, an intensely family-minded citizen, Leonard Jr. has a family home facing his father's on Portledge avenue and the family has a compound of summer places at Shediac Cape. Like his father, Leonard Senior became a dedicated fisherman. Like his father again, he is a member of the United Church of Canada, his Nova Scotia ancestors having been ardent Methodists. His most notable public service was to have headed the Moncton Hospital's board of trustees for 17 years, and to have guided the institution through its greatest development and expansion. He was at one time chairman of the Moncton Urban Redevelopment Commission and a member of the Greater Moncton Chamber of Commerce. For 36 years, at the time of writing, he had been a director of the N.B. Telephone Co., a member of the executive committee of the board for many years and chairman for four years.

A Lockhart hobby, farming, became for him a unique business carried on at North River near Hillsborough, Albert County. This involved the operation of a farrow-to-finish hog farm and the annual marketing of some 2,000 hogs. The farm had the distinction of being the first in Atlantic Canada to improve the quality of stock by artificial sow-breeding. There, it was not unusual to see the senior Lockhart in rural work clothes supervising a fence-building or a lake-digging while handling a shovel now and then himself.

Either there or at the Square Lake fishing camp there was always some sort of project moving ahead under his direction, and when he felt the need of change he flew to his home in Bermuda. But Len Lockhart was never long or far away from Moncton and his sons following his footsteps had the same attachment. With their inherited business acumen and civic-mindedness, the Lockhart family seemed destined to be headed for fourth generation business leaders in Moncton.

Another wood products manufacturer in Moncton whose activities supported the theory that people in that business have been particularly public spirited citizens was Harris Joyce. He came to the city in 1926 from Albert County and founded a lumber company which under the later ownership of M. C. Taylor in the late 1970's moved into the city's most historic industrial building, but went out of business in 1982. By taking over the Marven's Biscuit factory which had been idle after the final collapse of that industry, it operated from the place which was once the Moncton Cotton Manufacturing Co., founded in 1881.[2]

Joyce was at first manager of the Moncton Manufacturing Co., which was owned principally by Garfield White of Sussex, but soon became principal owner himself and renamed it the Moncton Lumber Co. in 1933, with office and yards at Main Street east of King. The plant beside a wharf was neighbour to the Maritime Paint and Chemical Co. and of Robin Hood Flour when they flourished in that part of the city. (Eric Kierans who later became a famous Quebec and federal cabinet minister and candidate for national Liberal leadership, worked with Robin Hood in Moncton in the 1930's, before returning to university and becoming a professor of economics.)

As his business flourished, Harris Joyce ran for aldermanic office and was first elected in 1948. He was an alderman-at-large in 1950 and by 1953 had become mayor. A competent chief magistrate who paid careful attention to the city's business in a period of expansion, Joyce was twice re-elected. Always interested in Y.M.C.A. work, he was president of the Moncton board and took part at national levels.

Moncton had a tremendous burst of commercial activity during World War II, not only as a military centre, air and supply base, but because of the railroad. The National Transcontinental Railway had been reactivated and the C.N.R. ran from Quebec to the Atlantic coast via Moncton. The C.P.R. to Saint John from Montreal could not be used in wartime as its lines went through the United States.

It was, however, the joining of Newfoundland to Canada in 1949, according to a theory enunciated by Harris Joyce in 1954, which opened up a whole new push for Moncton's already big distribution industry. Moncton, he then predicted, instead of being a distribution centre for the Maritime provinces and a provisioning base for Labrador, took on that function for four Atlantic provinces.

Joyce promoted this and Moncton proceeded to demonstrate once again the city's history as a natural geographic trading centre with the people dynamism to take advantage of the fact.

In the Joyce mayoral years, Moncton was desperately in need of a major new hotel, and he began working on the idea which, eventually after his death in 1961, arrived in the form of the C.N.'s Hotel Beauséjour. In the meantime, he had tried to have city council develop a multiple-level parking scheme to get cars off the street but that never came until the Brunswick Hotel put up such a facility for itself in 1980.

It was during Joyce's terms, when the quiet-spoken but dedicated mayor moved on plans for slum clearance and rehousing. This, too, came much later but he had started it.

During his terms, university life had come to Moncton with the new women's college, Notre Dame d'Acadie, and the first moves of the University of Moncton from its old St. Joseph's base in Memramcook. Under Joyce, the woodworking manufacturer, the Moncton music festival had become one of the best in the nation. The city area had then a population of some 60,000 and property values jumped to $65,000,000.

Civic improvements were seriously needed and Joyce pressed for them. It had seemed that as he had been successful in all his previous activities, Moncton would quickly move to achieve these. But there was always the Moncton hesitation — go slowly, hold down the tax rate. Like the incredible obstruction known as the overhead bridge beside Paul Lea's stone house, some of the improvements which Harris Joyce saw as essential in 1952 are still awaiting civic attention.

1. Stephen Binney's extraordinary political and business career is outlined in Volume I of *The Monctonians*.

2. The cotton mill, whose operations are considered in an earlier part of *The Monctonians*, once employed hundreds of workers, had 250 looms and 12,000 spindles and turned out 12,000 yards daily of twilled goods, sheetings, wraps and other cotton products.

Chapter Ten

HEROES AND RAILROADERS

When Britain's foreign minister Edward Grey watched the London lamplighters outside his office window on August 3, 1914, he said: "The lights are going out all over Europe." In Moncton, the gas lights were lighted as usual that evening but the next day World War One was declared.

The world was about to change irrevocably. The nostalgic years, the gay and happy years, the era of confidence and certainty, had really ended with the sinking of the Titanic on April 14, 1912. While the loss of 1,500 lives — among them the world's richest and most famous — shook the world, it took time for the impact to sink in. The biggest, strongest, fastest and safest "unsinkable" vessel afloat, they said. But it sank anyway. Then came war with Germany and an era had surely passed.

On the day war was declared, August 4, 1914, Moncton's 19th Field Battery was ready and Major S. Boyd Anderson wired Sam Hughes, the minister of militia, that the unit was prepared for immediate mobilization. Formal orders came three days later. In his *A History of Moncton Town and City 1855-1965,* Lloyd A. Machum has documented the record of this period and ensuing war years. It would be redundant and presumptuous here to do more than mention some its prominent figures.

For one who as a five-year-old boy heard the horns and watched the street parades of November 11, 1918, there is only the recollection of the grand procession up Highfield Street turning at the corner onto St. George. There was a decorated tank or a simulated tank and other military equipment. Then there were the names one heard so often. Capt. Arthur Barton, who was the Battery's second-in-command, and Lt. Frank H. Tingley and Dr. L.S. Doyle, the veterinarian for the militia. To him were reported all horses offered when word went out that 169 were needed for the battery.

Frank Tingley was wounded many times in France and, after a most distinguished battle career, was killed in action. It was symbolic of the Moncton then developing a mixed English-French orientation that the first two Moncton casualties in the war were Tingley and his signaller, Gunner Arthur Comeau. Wounded by the same shell, Comeau died overseas but Lieut. Tingley was invalided home to a great civic welcome in 1915. That same year the Moncton Irishman, Launce O'Leary, received his commission in the field. Tingley returned to England in 1916 and was decorated with the Military Cross at Buckingham Palace.

Meantime, the citizens at home waited for news, watched and did all the wartime things that people do who are fighting. A Home Guard was raised in 1915 and a citizens' recruiting committee formed, and also a Victory Bond committee.

"Major" Anderson became "Colonel" Anderson and the Moncton Club records show that even in the midst of the worst battles — or just after — he would take the time to write letters of appreciation of those who had sent parcels for the "boys over there." One letter told of parcels arriving just as the men of his brigade had returned from the terrible Somme battle. "I do not think that any of them were forgotten, and the gifts came at a most opportune time."

The 19th Battery which became the 8th Battery during the war, was in all the battles of the Canadian Army; Ypres, the bloody Somme, Vimy Ridge and Hill 70. Frank Tingley on his second tour had been wounded again and returned home to recruit a draft. The third time he went back to the front he was badly wounded on September 5, 1918, and he died a month before the Armistice was signed. He was one of Moncton's true heroes.

The number from Moncton and the Parish of Moncton who were killed or died of wounds totalled 199 men. Their names were the old family names of Le Coude, The Bend, Moncton — of Sunny Brae, Lewisville, Leger Corner, Georgetown, Newton Heights, Humphrey's, St. Anselme and the Irishtown Road. Names like Alward and Bingham, Bourque and Brown, Calkin and Cassidy, Coffey and Coles, Comeau and Cormier, Cuthbertson and Cripps, Davis and Densmore, Donnelly and Driscoll, Duplessis and Emmerson, Fowler and Gallagher, Girouard and Goodall, Hagerty and Horsman, Jones and Landry, Leaman and LeBlanc, Lutes and Manning, McKinnon and McHugh, O'Brien and Patterson, Pellerin and Peters, Price and Randall, Ripley and Richard, Roy and Robinson, Starratt and Steadman, Stiles and Sullivan, Talbot and Thibodeau, Tingley and Trites, Wilbur and Wheaton, Wilson and Wortman. And all their dead comrades whose names are on the roll of honor.

Some Moncton businesses suffered during the war years, others prospered because those at home were at work and wages were good. A few got rich. The Maritime Hat and Cap Company made 10,000 military caps and the Record Foundry was sustained for a while longer by making shells for the war. Part of the foundry was used for administrative offices and a barracks for the 145th Infantry Brigade drilling and training in Moncton. The Record Foundry had been started by Charles B. Record back in 1857; by 1880, his son, E.A. Record, took over assisted by R.F. Boyer but they had trouble and the plant which had employed hundreds and once been the biggest Moncton industry apart from the railroad was sold at auction for its creditors. A.E. Peters and a joint stock company bought and then revived the industry, employing 150 and manufacturing thirty types of stoves, 17 models of plows. In 1889 it had a payroll of $50,000. Then a few years later the stove business went to Sackville and the general Moncton foundry decline had set in. The Record plant had occupied 12 acres and stood where Eaton's later took over.

Picture taken soon after Main street subway was opened. On left may be seen Opera House and "flatiron" building and at right old Windsor (Wilbur) Hotel.

Gorbell's drygoods store was one of the first west of Cameron street on St. George. It was typical of a British variety shop.

As it did elsewhere in Canada, the 1917 federal and provincial election known as "the Conscription Election" had its influence in Moncton. The overtones of racism and imperialism which had been raised in Ontario and Quebec, fanned by the inept and awkward Sam Hughes, were rampant in New Brunswick. Moncton stayed aside from most of the bitterness that had been stirred up between Ontario English and Quebec French Canadians but some was found to exist.

As Spigelman says in his study of Quebec-Acadian relations, the Acadians had been loyal to the monarchy and the empire but "the issue in Quebec and Ontario had been made into a racial and religious issue and politically the Acadians supported their French-speaking fellow Canadians." They had understandably become alarmed at sentiments expressed and, as Spigelman has written, "English Canadians rarely distinguished between Acadians and French-Canadians" and quoted Major J.A. Leger as saying to Hon. J.B.M. Baxter: "The Acadian race is now sharing the opprobrium everywhere being showered upon the French Canadians."

As *Le Moniteur Acadien* pointed out, at the start of the war, Acadians had enlisted spontaneously to go to the aid of the British "because they understood, better than other people perhaps — having themselves been victims of persecution and injustice."

The French-speaking leaders in Moncton supported Conscription, and these included Sir Pierre Landry, Senator Pascal Poirier, Bliss Bourgeois and editors of both *l'Evangeline* and *l'Acadien*.

Troop movements, goods transportation for ships waiting at Halifax and the heavy general freight carriage kept the city extraordinarily busy during the war years. With almost no out-of-town travel by automobile and long before commercial air travel, the railroad handled everything that moved except that which went by horse and wagon for short distances over dusty country roads. So it was a prosperous time for local citizens. Not only was there the trade on the tracks but the making of the railroad equipment, repairs and maintenance and the demand for manufactured goods from the woollen mills and other materials manufactured in

Moncton city hall in 1916 as it looked new after old one burned, with country market extending down Market street, now gone (as is this particular city hall). Men on steps believed to be Mayor L.W. McAnn, Ald. P.A. Belliveau (in raccoon coat) and two unidentified aldermen, perhaps P.D. Ayer and H.H. Warman. Below is the C.N.R. office building as it appeared at the same time, having been built earlier for Intercolonial.

Moncton such as uniform caps and shell-making kept Moncton very busy.

At the start of the 1914 war, the government railroads held in Moncton 437 acres of land while the National Transcontinental, still privately owned, had 55 acres. By 1916 employment in all was close to 3,000 people in shops, running trades, offices, station and yards of the railways. Annual wages totalled $2,000,000. All of which made the railways of first importance in the city.

Though the people still called the main railway system the I.C.R. (and for years afterward) the name had actually been changed to Canadian Government Railway (C.G.R.) in 1913. This signalled the beginning of major developments which altered this railway community. The N.T.R. had reached Moncton from Winnipeg in 1912 and Moncton became its headquarters in 1915. Eventually, all would be amalgamated into the Canadian National.

In those years and for a good many afterward, the Moncton day began at seven o'clock when the waking whistle of the "New Shops" sounded. (The old shops had burned in 1906). Then, precisely at 8.40 a.m. the shop workers' train from Pointe du Chene, Shediac, Scoudouc and Painsec (where it picked up commuters from Dorchester, Memramcook and as far away as Springhill) rumbled over the Church and Lutz street crossings. Sixty years later the gate-guarded city crossings remain an aberration and obstacle to traffic.

Before Eaton's came, everything seemed to rotate about the railway and when a newspaper column signed by the mysterious "J.B. King" appeared it became extremely popular. So much so that people would stand outside The Transcript building at Westmorland and Main in the afternoons waiting to be first to read the latest railroad gossip. Some thought the column was written by John T. Hawke, the publisher, with the connivance of various politicians and railroad insiders. No one ever found out, not even senior reporters on the newspaper itself.

There wasn't a hotbox between Montreal and Sydney that J.B. King didn't know about and not a breath of gossip about a railroader from Riviere du Loup to Mulgrave that didn't reach the pseudonymous King's journalistic ears. He published it all. Under Gutelius, the I.C.R. became the C.G.R., and all manner of railroad decisions on amalgamations were being taken in Ottawa. The column predicted with amazing accuracy the results of all the decisions. "King" could tell when it came time for an executive of the railway to clean out his desk, pack his bags and look for new employment, and the actual happenings bore him out.

In the years between 1911 and 1921 when *The Transcript* and the Liberals were in opposition for the first time in a generation, its editor and his un-named columnist could exploit to the full the general dissatisfaction with the recent managerial changes. More came between 1913 and 1920 than at any time in local history. Almost daily, King's predictions of impending changes aroused consternation in official and political ranks.

J.B. King kept murmuring about "foreign management" when Gutelius and Ottawa-Montreal control had come, and once when the reporter Bruce Jefferson asked him for a certain piece of railway information, Gutelius replied: "Why don't you just ask J.B. King? He knows more about this road than I do." The general superintendent of the C.G.R. at the time, J.B. MacNeillie, used to say that he grabbed *The Transcript* the minute it came off the press because "I can find out a lot more about what's going on than I ever will from official reports."

One situation King carried to such an extreme that when Hon. Frank Cochrane, then minister of railways, arrived at the Moncton station, a fistfight was in progress. Dr. O.B. Price, the Conservative candidate who would become M.P. for Westmorland in 1925 and stay for ten years, was fighting with "Dynamite" Richardson the current railway superintendent. The hot-headed Price, dukes at the ready, then bearded Cochrane in his private business car and he, like Richardson, was invited to step outside for a general settlement of grievances "in a democratic fashion." Cochrane didn't accept. Next day, *The Transcript* reported the famous bout of fisticuffs as "a naval battle off the port of Moncton" and used nautical rather than railroading terms to describe it. Hawke wasn't a descendant of the great British Admiral Edward Hawke (hero of the Battle of Quiberon Bay) for nothing.

When Frank Sayer was publicity representative of the Canadian National in the 1930's, the J.B. King column had been gone for more than a decade. Still, he was well remembered by railroad officials and when this Transcript reporter turned up, Sayer would often hail him as "J.B." (Sayer had been secretary to the royal commission on railway amalgamation and came to Moncton as Gutelius' secretary in 1913, later becoming regional director of public relations until his retirement, a mine of railroad information.) Dr. O.B. Price was still around in the Thirties.

"None of the railway or political performers could outdo Doc. Price in his younger days of blowing the Tory bugle," Bruce Jefferson once recalled. "He was a terrific fighter and one of the Transcript reporters once told me that when he had incurred his wrath it was necessary to keep out of his way for months. Another time, when a drunk showed the bad judgment of sticking his head in a Tory Party doorway to yell 'Hooray for Laurier' one election night when Doc's friends lost the decision, the dentist-politician heaved him down three flights of stairs, one flight at a time."

There was another time when the pugnacious "Doc" Price got into an open brawl. Elias Wetmore operated an all-day and all-night "dog car" (a restaurant made to look like a street-car and theoretically mobile). There in the car, Charley "Shediac" McDonald, the tailor, was attacked by Price in the heat of a political quarrel. It was so serious that both Price and McDonald — in Bruce Jefferson's words — "had to be dry-docked for repairs."

When, at first, the N.T.R. reached Winnipeg and the Canadian Northern came within the C.G.R. system, things looked very bright for Moncton but later amalgamations and a fully national system reduced it to a regional headquarters only, with a general manager in charge. The C.G.R. and the Canadian Northern had come under a government-appointed board of directors in 1918. The Canadian National Railways system was formed in 1922 and combined all the lines mentioned except the privately-owned C.P.R., the Grand

This view of the C.N.R. passenger station and general manager's house was taken in 1920's. View is from east showing corner of office building and greenhouse behind residence.

Locomotive erecting plant of railway at C.N.R. shops as work progressed in 1915.

Trunk and the Grand Trunk Pacific. But in 1923 the latter two were merged with the C.N.R., leaving the great C.P.R. as an independent, privately-owned entity. And so, control moved to Montreal. In this sense, Moncton was put on the back burner while the opening of the West caught the nation's attention.

Still, it was Atlantic regional headquarters from Riviere du Loup to Sydney, and until Eaton's came to town with their mail-order centre, the railroad executives were the industrial elite of the city. In the hearts of Monctonians the nostalgia remained — and so did most of the local employment. But Eaton's with an eventual thousand employees ran a strong second.

Many years later, when the spacious old railway station opposite the Brunswick Hotel was demolished, a wail of anguish arose from the citizens and that was understandable. Its grounds had held crowds watching troops come and go in three wars, had welcomed kings and queens, governors and prime ministers. Its platforms had known countless welcomes and farewells, and for generations the station or "depot", had been the place to go to watch the comings and goings of society. Moncton's anguish was genuine for that callous demolition marked the end of an era — to be replaced by a bland parking lot. A shopping plaza arose where the vice president's house, flower garden and hot-house had for so long been attractively set out. Loss of the Victorian-age station was a psychological blow and a symbolic one. A glassy new high rise office building went up but no glassy, featureless highrise could compensate for that human place, the railway station, where people came and went, met and knew one another and found a gathering place in their community.

If David Pottinger had personified the railroad in Moncton in his lifetime, his successor, Walter U. Appleton, was to occupy the same role in a new century. Appleton was the son and grandson of railroaders on both his mother's and father's side, his grandfather McHaffie having been master-mechanic for the old I.C.R. Walter Appleton's parents had come to the new railroad town from the Annapolis Valley and Walter, born on Foundry Street in 1878, became the general manager and then vice-president of the C.N.R. in 1924. He remained as such until his retirement in 1943. By then, he had been 53 years with the railroad.

Walter Appleton's mother had been widowed early. As the eldest child, though only twelve years old, Walter went to work as an office boy for Pottinger in 1890. He worked ten-hour days and it was seven years before he could earn as much as seven-and-a-half cents an hour. Since he could not qualify for apprenticeship until he was 16, he had studied when he could and was taken into the mechanical department four years after his initial employment.

Walter U. Appleton had gone upward step by quick step once he had become chief clerk of the mechanical department. In that post, he was served by another early-starting office boy, Jeff (S.J.) Lockhart who went to work as W.U.'s 13-year-old runner in 1907. He was still with him in 1943. At retirement, Lockhart had been assistant to no less than four other vice-presidents. Fortunately for Appleton as he began to rise in the days of political railway patronage, he was a Liberal, because the Liberals were usually in office. Like Pottinger, he learned to play that political game and still do a first class job of running a railroad.

Walter Appleton had first caught the eye of S.J. Hungerford when Hungerford was head of the mechanical department of the Canadian Northern. Later Hungerford was president of the C.N.R. and as he progressed so did his younger protegé. No matter how Appleton rose, he would remember his youth and the difficult times of those years. Those who had known him then always had access to his office even when he was general-manager and vice-president.

Typical of this, perhaps, was Mary McGowan who married W. O. McAllister, a highly inventive machinist. When Walter Appleton was an apprentice in the shops he boarded with Mrs. Connolly on Albert Street at the corner of Euston. The McGowans lived across the street and Mrs. McAllister in later years would remember the young apprentices washing up and calling out to the girls from Connolly's pump shed. She also remembered Walter as he remembered her and when she had four grown sons to be employed, she would simply walk

Walter U. Appleton, Moncton native who became railway general manager and vice-president. He was 53 years in railroading.

over to the V.P.'s office, ask for Mr. Appleton, and another son would be put to work. As it happened, they were all excellent workers, and some even inventive and imaginative like their father.

When the I.C.R. became the C.G.R., Appleton was made general superintendent in the region and then general manager for the Atlantic Region. Later, he was the first native Monctonian to become a railroad vice president, and when he retired he had been in that post for nineteen years. Only old Dave Pottinger had been there longer.

Jeff Lockhart, who remembered all of this, would recall in 1980, when he was in his 90th year, how in Appleton's days as general superintendent, he would frequently receive important telephone calls at night and relay them to the Appleton home. Walter was often out, sociable, a good club man and frequently at meetings, so Jeff Lockhart talked to Mrs. Appleton. She would say: "Well, Jeff, what do *you* think should be done?" Lockhart would suggest the appropriate solution. "If you think that's the right thing to do, go ahead," Mrs. Appleton would say, adding: "I know Walter would agree with whatever you say." And he always did.

The fact was that, through the years, Lockhart became Appleton's alter ego. As such, for generations and through countless changes of management and executive, Lockhart himself became a power. Having begun with the railway at the age of 13 and having been through all the changes, Jeff Lockhart knew everything there was to know about the railway and its personnel. He knew the names of men who drove the trains, knew all the shopmen because he saw the pay lists and the pension lists; he knew all the office people. More than that, he knew *all* the executives from the Montreal presidents on down to the chief clerks. With general-manager after general-manager as assistant, he became so valuable they wouldn't promote him and he was never highly paid. Indeed, until very close to his retirement he was never properly rewarded via the very pay envelopes he himself knew so much about.

Jeff Lockhart became a local legend in his own time, and an encyclopaedia of railway lore, not to mention Moncton lore. His mother, the former Jessie Scott, had come to Moncton from Jardineville in Kent County in 1879 when she was ten years old. Since she lived to be 103 and died only in 1972, and as Jeff had lived with her most of his life, he had come to know more of Moncton history at first hand than most. He was born in the city in 1891 and went to work at a time when everybody knew everybody else in Moncton. What he didn't remember, his mother did.

There are some things about which he is insistent. The historians and record-keepers have held that Salter's big shipbuilding wharf was at the foot of what is now Mechanic street. Lockhart says it was not; it was at the foot of Foundry street. "That's why Records and Weirs went there to establish foundries; they did Salter's work," he once told the author.

Jeff's father, Melvin, a native of Cook's Brook which is now known only as a railway crossing at Lakeville, bought a house at the corner of Foundry and Albert-Waterloo. This was built by Allan Rand, an uncle of Moncton's most famous jurist, Ivan C. Rand, and overlooked the marsh and river. When Jeff was a boy there were five wharves to be seen — the public wharf at King Street, Sumner's wharf, Master's wharf, Winter's wharf and Dunlap's. Together, they stretched along the waterfront. The Winter family, in the amusement business in its second Moncton generation, brought imports from the West Indies and owned the big Columbia Farm. Its house was at the present corner of Mountain Road and Weldon facing what is now Winter Street and occupied by the Westmount Apartments building. Lockhart says the big trees about it are the same as were there when the land was farmed.

He also remembers that lower Robinson, Lutz and Westmorland streets exist where they are because of the shipyards. These streets were within the then city boundaries, he maintains, while Salter's yard was outside of the city, actually beyond the "John Jones line." This marked the town limit and ran about 60 feet east of Foundry Street. Salter himself lived in town.

The so-called Jones Line ran from the river to Archibald Street, Lockhart says, before the town was extended westward. Earlier, the first town western limit had been at Botsford Street, then Church Street and afterward High Street. High Street was in place long before Highfield or the streets in between which were developed by Oliver Jones. From earliest highway days, the present High Street had been the connector route between Main Street (once called the King's Highway and which continued westward along the river to Salisbury) and Mountain Road which went to the Mountains. Historians and geographers don't seem to agree as to whether the stage coach route went from Irishtown Road across the ridge north of Moncton to the mountains and on to Sussex, or by way of Main Street and Salisbury. However, Lockhart insists that the Post Road from Dorchester to Sussex Corner and, eventually, Saint John, came into Moncton by way of the present Dieppe (Leger Corner) to Lewisville around the marsh, south on King Street to Telegraph, then westward along the mucky river road now Main Street, to Salisbury. He says, though, that you could also take the High Street route to Mountain Road and go out that way.

One thing is certain: Travellers from Nova Scotia and Dorchester going to Hillsborough or Hopewell when the ferry was not running from Dorchester Cape or Island, came to the Bend, went on to Salisbury, forded and crossed into Albert County there. This was before the long bridge was built across the Petitcodiac from Moncton to Coverdale (now Riverview).

And, while it puts us well ahead of the story of Moncton's post-World War One railroad days, it may be a good place to mention another of Jeff Lockhart's entrenched memories. "People keep talking of Moncton's first industrial park being up between St. George Boulevard and Baig Boulevard. It wasn't there at all. It was on the site of railway land which had been given for air force use during World War Two from Killam Drive to Vaughan Harvey Drive and Wilbur Street. At the end of the war, this was turned back to the railway — including the streets, sidewalks, sewers and so on — and it became the first industrial park. The C.N. sold the buildings to private buyers and the city benefitted. All of the development, streets, water lines, power lines, sewers were turned over to the City of Moncton by the railroad."

After the amalgamation of the Canadian railways in 1923 when Sir Henry Thornton was made first president, Moncton felt the first and only major shift of employees away from the city. Some 100 clerks were moved to Montreal, being members of the passenger and audit departments and the decentralized accounting department. When the C.G.R., Grand Trunk and Canadian Northern-N.T.R. became the C.N.R., there was a triplication of titles which was confusing, so control went to Montreal's central headquarters. The move brought a good deal of concern to Moncton and fear that many more people and many other services would be removed, but that never came about.

Earlier, in 1915, a few employees of the C.G.R.'s mechanical department went to the Canadian Northern shops at St. Malo, near Quebec, and Point St. Charles, near Montreal. Among these was Frank "Pokey" Mackasey, who was the father of Bryce Mackasey, the future federal cabinet minister and brief, controversial Air Canada chairman.[1] (The latter job at a time when Claude Taylor of Salisbury, N.B., now a Moncton suburb, was president.) The Mackasey family had come originally to Moncton from Halifax and were among the founders of St. Bernard's parish. Frank's brother, Andrew, was a dapper, commercial traveller. (His wife was a Gillespie). So strongly do family traits and nicknames carry along that Andrew's son, Reginald, was also known as "Pokey", a successful businessman now in Toronto.

In an earlier chapter on Moncton's railway affairs (in the first volume of this work) there is a description of the patronage practices of both early and later periods in Moncton. This persisted to some degree until about 1930 but by 1940 had ceased to be a factor.

1. Bryce Mackasey, the consummate politician, lived several places and when he sought election (and won) as M.P. for Lincoln, Ontario, he claimed St. Catharines as his hometown. He had once lived there briefly but he had also lived in Quebec, his birthplace, and in Verdun when he sat for that area in the House of Commons.

Chapter Eleven

THE GREAT PROMOTER

If the 19th Century had been Moncton's years of trading, shipbuilding and railroad development, the first thirty years of the 20th were its promotional years. And if two men typified the characteristics of those decades they were Clifford William Robinson and Mathew Lodge. The former was the Provincial cabinet minister and briefly premier; he was essentially a behind-the-scenes man. Matt Lodge, as everybody in the area knew him, was the front man, the visible promoter, the engine that provided the steam for the continuing operation.

There seemed hardly to be an industrial or financial promotion in Moncton between 1900 and 1930 in which the two were not principals. Sometimes, Frederick W. Sumner, Capt. J.E. Masters and Christopher Harris were involved in the same promotions but, being Conservatives, they were usually operating on a different wave length. The two men were close contemporaries, Lodge, born in 1858, being eight years older than Robinson. Both were Mount Allison graduates and both had started their careers as bookkeepers and accountants in Moncton.

In their maturity, they were gentlemen of the old school, quiet-spoken, conservatively yet stylishly dressed. They were of good physical stature, strong and active in their occupations until they died.

MATHEW LODGE

Married in 1884 to Adelaide McCarthy, a daughter of Moncton's prominent Edward McCarthy, Lodge had lived first on King street and as he prospered moved uptown, buying the Croasdale estate with its fine house on Mountain Road. This occupied the entire block opposite Mary's Home to John street, between Bonaccord and Highfield. Mrs. Sarah Croasdale had been a daughter of the great land-holder Judge Botsford and she and her husband, also a civil engineer, had developed the estate into a sort of farm-town combination property. In winter it had been the best coasting hill in town, near the orchard, and the Lodges never objected to the scores of children who daily had their snow fun there.

Senator Robinson and his wife latterly lived in a large house at the corner of Main and Weldon, now covered by office buildings. Earlier, the Robinson house was the beauty bought by John O'Neill, the merchant, and later Dr. E.W. Ewart. After the Senator and Mrs. Robinson died and a public auction was held to sell some of their possessions, one buyer discovered a treasure.

A professional antique dealer, he had bought unopened a large case found in the basement. The auctioneer had found it difficult to open and thought it might hold tools or other odds and ends. What it did hold was $6,000. worth of sterling silver brought over from England and apparently never used. It cost the auction buyer about $10.

Senator Robinson was born in Moncton in 1866 and never lived anywhere else. Matt Lodge was born in Cumberland County, N.S., in 1858 and begins to come to attention in the city's development and as a curler in the late 1890's. He was a member of the famous Flatiron Gang of young men, almost all of whom became prominent in civil life and met every New Year's until the last member was gone. By 1901, Lodge was secretary-treasurer of the New Brunswick Petroleum Co., later Maritime Oilfields Ltd. Like Robinson, he was an early shareholder in *The Transcript*, but Robinson's father, William, had been the founder and principal owner of the paper sold to John T. Hawke for $800. and notes. Senator Robinson became the largest shareholder after Hawke's death and again after Otty Barbour died in the 1930's before it was sold to J.K. Grainger and his backers.

Robinson, who was a distinguished senator in later life, started his career as a bookkeeper but after a short stint with the Moncton Cotton Company studied law and entered political life. He became mayor of Moncton at the age of 31 and held the record as youngest ever until Dennis Cochrane was elected at the age of 28 in 1979. That parallel is interesting because in 1897 when Robinson was there the city was making a forward-looking turnaround much as happened when Cochrane won a surprising victory. Neither had previous experience.

If it is a useful omen to Cochrane, Robinson went on to become the only Monctonian ever to hold the provincial premiership. (James Alexander Murray, premier for two months in 1917, is said to have been born in Moncton but is not known to have lived there. His home was in Sussex.) Cliff Robinson was sent to the legislature the year he became mayor. Twice re-elected, he was Speaker of the House and minister of lands and forests, and from 1907 to 1908 was premier when Hon. William Pugsley left to take a cabinet portfolio in Ottawa. Described as a "quiet, respectable businessman-lawyer," Robinson remained titular leader of the Liberal party after its defeat in 1908, but asked to be relieved of the job in 1916, apologizing for not giving it enough time. But he remained a power in provincial politics until his death in 1944, though usually well behind the scenes.

Like Lodge, Robinson was a curler and a noted golfer, one of Moncton's first. The two men had been together in many enterprises but, as interesting as any, was the Petitcodiac river tidal power project. Robinson was chairman of the organizing meeting and Capt. J.E. Masters secretary. Directors elected were Lodge, Masters, Robinson, F.R. Sumner, J. Fred Edgett, and A.E. McSweeney.

Robinson was a lawyer and while Lodge seems to have had the skills of a civil engineer, his college background does not indicate that he studied engineering. He was certainly self-taught in mineralogy and energy engineering. Perhaps he had taken courses without a degree because one of his strongest supporters in his energy-producing projects was a Harvard professor.

Mathew Lodge attended the local Southampton school, went to the normal school in Truro, then Mount Allison University. He came to Moncton as an accountant for The Moncton Sugar Refining Co., was then with the Moncton Gas, Light & Water Company where he came to know all the local entrepreneurs and investors. Afterward, he contracted for construction of a branch railway line and then went into mining in various parts of Canada and the United States. In Oklahoma he learned about gas and oil.

Back he came to Moncton to discover and promote gas and oil wells in the Stoney Creek area of Albert County, about which something has been noted earlier in this book. He fought skeptics for years, but he knew he was right and, at last when money and developers came in, he was of course then looked upon as a great fellow by all those who had stood in his way. The experts may have brought in the wells and financed them; it was Matt Lodge who had first seen and believed in their potential, fought for them and in the end was credited with saving Moncton millions of dollars in energy costs and bringing millions in revenues to the city. He, himself, made only moderate gains in this or any of his civic promotions, and when he died his estate was modest by any standard. As the newspapers then said, "He was a moneymaker — for others."

Matt Lodge never had a peer in Moncton as the promoter of enterprises and, before he died when he was 80, he knew the heads of almost every important banking and financial firm in North America and Britain. He had crossed the Atlantic so many times that he lost count, but O.L. Barbour, the publisher and his sometimes business partner, said it was between 75 and 85 crossings. Even the shipbuilder Salter was far outdone in this and certainly no Monctonian of this time, or perhaps of any time, had travelled more frequently than Lodge.

He was returning from Edinburgh where he had been on a business trip connected with the tidal power project when he had a stroke on the liner *Cargaric*. As it reached Father Point, near Rimouski, Mrs. Lodge went aboard and Sir Henry Thornton, president of the C.N.R., provided a special railway car to bring the stricken man to his home. It was there in his house on Mountain Road (then called Union Street) that "he ended a career of wonderful activity." His life, one editorial said, had been "an enrichment to the country and to Moncton."

At the time of his death, Lodge was a director of the railway, a director of New Brunswick Gas & Oilfields, president of a British Columbia mining company, director of an oil company, director of City Land Co., and of course director of the Petitcodiac Tidal Power Project.

In the midst of all his industrial activities, Mathew Lodge was always in the forefront of civic and social development in Moncton. It was he who convinced Thornton, the C.N. president, to let the city have the handsome Archibald house and land on Subway Hill on Main Street as a public library for $1 a year.

This proved to be one of Lodge's most lasting and valuable contributions to the growing city for, hard as it is to credit, Moncton until then had no real public library. The Fort Cumberland chapter of the I.O.D.E. and the city council had fitted out two tiny rooms back in 1911. The grant was tiny. Then the city hall burned and the books and most of Moncton's historical documents went with it. Instead of helping to restore the library, council actually withdrew the grant. Moncton has never been a Parnassus of literary culture, but this was the limit. However, the women found a smaller space and tried again. With a Mrs. Snow and Mrs. Lottie Bishop as successive part-time librarians, they carried on. By 1926, the Knights of Pythias began to agitate for a library and Matt Lodge went to work.

He was so successful that by August 12, 1927, the new public library opened with its own fine building. This was the converted Archibald house on Subway Hill now covered by the Times-Transcript building. Today, anyone who frequented the premises in its first years would recall two dedicated women, Mrs. Berdia Moore and Miss Betty Condon, trained librarians, who worked for so many years for so little. When Miss Condon retired after an adult lifetime of helping Monctonians to read, she did not draw so much as a cent of pension for the intelligent life of the city. The city had never bothered to provide one.

The Mathew Lodge house on Mountain Road. Built for Croasdale family, faced Mary's Home (Now a home for the elderly).

Home of Senator C.W. Robinson and wife on Main street at Weldon, now 1111 Main building. A showplace painted yellow in 1920.

Mathew Lodge's most ambitious single project was to have been the harnessing of the Petitcodiac and Memramcook rivers at their confluence for hydro power. With himself as managing-director and Robinson as president, a new company was formed in 1928. Lodge was the originator, had long talked of the project and now pressed forward but when he died the scheme faded away. Not entirely, however, since the idea persisted as late as 1950 when Walter A.S. Melanson, a retired district highways engineer, made a new study of the tidal potential. Without a Lodge to promote it, nothing more happened.

When he acquired personal property between John street and Mountain Road near the turn of the century, Lodge had shown other foresight. John street was opened around 1910 to create a direct road to the "New" shops of the railway from Bonaccord street. Previously, a roadway had skirted a stream which flowed from the shops vicinity to a grist mill at what is now the corner of Brydges and Bonaccord. The mill is long gone but the miller's house remains. Presumably his name was Brydges but no one now recalls. Along the street named Brydges, however, its bogginess remains beneath the homes and sump pumps find frequent activity.

As for Mathew Lodge, for all the prosperity he achieved for Moncton, he left an estate valued at only $25,000 of which $20,000 was insurance. It went to his wife of 44 years who, with his one son, Mathew Cabot Lodge of Montreal, survived him for some years.

To return to the junction of Mountain Road, John and Bonaccord streets, E.H. Cunningham built a fine brick house on the Bonaccord side in 1917. His son, Lauchlin, who continued to occupy the residence in 1982, remembered that Lodge built a house for his son next door on the corner of John and occupied as this is written by Dr. Clement Cormier and family. It is one of Moncton's more attractive older houses and was sold by the Lodge estate to the late Edward McManus. When he went to Memramcook to take over the family farm and the quarrying business, his brother, Reid McManus, bought the house and there raised his family of six daughters and one son.

Facing that property there is now a tiny city parkette which sits on a hemisphere of land which was once part of the Rufus Bulmer farm. The farm and some adjoining property were purchased by the T. Eaton Co. Ltd. when it came to town as a sub-division site for homes sold to its managerial people who had been transferred from Toronto. All of these houses between William street and Mountain Road and on both sides of Bonaccord remain.

The Reid McManus family was one of those which had been a mainstay of the Moncton Irish community in the days of controversy. The family had come from the Memramcook-Dorchester area where the original John McManus family had conducted a large general supplies and construction industry. Two of John's sons, Edward and Reid, became civil engineers and engaged in construction trade when they came to Moncton. Born in 1874, James Thomas Reid was remarkable for his time in that he was graduated from the Massachusetts Institute of Technology in Boston in 1895.

Reid McManus worked as a draftsman with the Boston Bridge Works, was a steel inspector on the Boston subway and rodman on the crew which surveyed the Crow's Nest Pass Railway in the Canadian Rockies. By 1899 he was in construction work with his father and brothers, and became president of John W. McManus Ltd., in 1902. The firm carried out projects in various parts of the Maritimes, Quebec and Maine and, when Reid McManus brought his family to Moncton in 1910, he immediately became involved in the city's business and political life.

He had married Margaret Mary McDonald, of Sydney, N.S., in 1905 and in Moncton they lived first in the Sheriff Willett house at 105 Church Street, and then moved to the splendid Oliver Jones house on Main Street. McManus became an early director of the Central Trust Company, and was first elected to the Moncton board of school trustees in 1919. In the next year, he was elected to the New Brunswick legislature for Westmorland County and sat until 1925 when that legislature was dissolved. In the election of 1925, he was defeated and retired from elective politics.

Until his death in 1948, however, Reid McManus remained a power on the Liberal scene, so much so that when the former Oliver Jones property was sold by him to the federal government there was a considerable uproar raised by local Conservatives. An ideal site on that part of Main street whose south side had been original railway property, the McManus place was also across the street from the Brunswick Hotel. On this site the federal government built a post office and federal office structure.

Reid McManus, who in 1937 was decorated by Pope Pius XI with the medal Pro Ecclesia et Pontifice, was particularly popular with Moncton newspaper reporters during his long tenure on the school board. *Times* reporters had a deadline to make for the morning edition; *Transcript* reporters were working evenings (overtime without overtime pay) and both wanted to get away early. At every meeting, when it seemed enough business had been transacted, the two would catch Mr. McManus' eye. He would then nod almost imperceptibly and, almost immediately, would rise and say: "The business of the meeting being concluded for this time, I move we adjourn." His fellow trustees invariably accepted the motion and the secretary, H.H. ("Hezzie" and later "Harry") Trimble, would stow his papers. Harrison Hezekiah Trimble, a high school teacher previously, became superintendent of Moncton schools and remained for many years an influential and well-loved public servant. A Moncton high school has been named for him.

As this is written, four of the six daughters of Reid McManus and his wife who died in 1925, remain in Moncton. A fifth is in Montreal, a sixth in Shediac. Their one brother, John, died at the end of the 1970's. The McManus women are Misses Mary, Margaret, Catherine, Janet (Mrs. J.A. de Niverville), Frances and Winnifred.

It was something of an historic irony that Mr. McManus' somewhat less diplomatic nephew and namesake Reid McManus of Memramcook, should in his time have become a controversial member of the district school board so often mentioned in the 1970's newspapers. This Reid McManus had attended school in Moncton and, upon graduating from St Joseph's College, worked for a very short time with *The Transcript* in the 1930's. His early writing showed promise as he submitted material to such magazines as the literate New Yorker but he did not pursue that career. Instead, he returned to the Memramcook farm and the large quarrying operation. A scholar, outstanding naturalist, he gained a reputation among ornithologists. At one time he taught school in the Valley and continues to carry on the family tradition on the family estate, the last of his immediate family in the district.

Chapter Twelve

GROWTH, GALLAGHERS AND PARLEES

It was 1919. The Great War had ended the previous November and already many soldiers had been returned home. Now, in the first post-war year, Moncton reported that 853 warriors were still overseas or "in convalescent homes." But there was good news at home where the country's largest retail and mail-order company was buying land on Foundry street for its catalogue business. Downtown merchants were worried, but the word was put about that it would not effect them much because this would be strictly mail-order.

Still, a good deal of Moncton's retail business depended on people coming into the city from nearby towns, villages and farming districts. The major New Brunswick drift away from the farms had not yet begun, though it soon would. What with returned soldiers and others moving into town, the city's population had increased by 2,000 in a single year, and it would continue to grow. The school population stood at 2,559, the city's 17,410, and it is interesting to recall that 113 local children attended "private schools." This was a carryover from the past when many parents found the public schools inadequate or distant for walking.

There was a special "cachet" about it, of course, and the boys and girls met on the streets near these private schools would suffer the taunts of public schoolers. These considered the privateers prissy or over-protected. Among the private schools the "in" ones were those of Miss Willis on Weldon street and Mrs. Wilcox on Mountain Road and they ran close social competition.[1]

One of those sent to Mrs. Wilcox's was T. Babbitt Parlee[2] who one day would become the lawyer-mayor of Moncton and a provincial attorney-general. His tragic death in a small airplane crash when returning from Fredericton on an inclement night in 1957 ended a career which almost certainly would have seen him as premier of the province. In his protected childhood, one would meet him as he trudged along from his Bonaccord street home. An only child, Babbitt was the son of William Parlee and his wife, who had been a Babbitt from Fredericton. Bill Parlee worked in the business office of *The Transcript* where his sister, Babbitt's aunt, Emma Parlee, was martinet and "ran" the whole place during Publisher Hawke's long illness.

Miss Parlee had also run much of it, people said, when Hawke was in good health for she had been "his great and good friend," some said his mistress. Like Hawke, she was an ardent Liberal which makes Babbitt's adoption of the Conservative Party the more surprising.

Harry Lodge, an uncle of Babbitt Parlee's by marriage, was the man who supervised the country market in the basement of city hall and his brother, W.W. Lodge, had married a daughter of John T. Hawke. (Another daughter married J.E. Berry, a travelling salesman and photographer). Both the W.W. Lodges and the Berrys lived in the Hawke house at 65 Wesley street with their families, and the somewhat altered house is still there as this is written. It still has the handsome "H" in the frosted glass of the front door.

Because of conflicts in politics and, undoubtedly in the family attitude toward Miss Parlee, Hawke's widow did not benefit by his will though Emma did. His daughters also inherited from the handsome estate.

So the Hawkes, Parlees and Lodges were all connected and it may have been the political quarrels among them which in the end influenced T. Babbitt away from the Grits. At any rate, before he became involved, he attended Aberdeen High school straight out of Mrs. Wilcox's and was the victim of cruel pranks. Moncton was what some called "a lunch-pail community" in temperament and Babbitt was "different" because he went to a private school and had such connections. On one occasion, the brilliant young student who would one day be a prize debater in university and then one of the legislature's most effective, was so abused in a classroom that his mother took the matter to the school board. This made it a matter of public gossip (Some boys, two now fairly distinguished local residents of retirement age, put needles in their shoe toes and kicked Babbitt) which made things worse.

Yet, as an adult in civic and provincial politics, the same youthful persecutors did not hesitate to seek out Parlee for favors. In a later chapter, the political Parlee will come into our story again.

Meantime, to return to that year 1919 when the big Eaton building was being put up, local bricklayers went on strike. However, it didn't last long and the structure was not seriously delayed. This brief delay, however, recalls another obstacle the giant merchandising corporation ran up against. Dominick DeVona, who may have been the city's first citizen of Italian birth, kept a fruit and variety store on Foundry street abutting the Record property which Eaton's had acquired. They wanted DeVona's land, too, but Dominick didn't want to move or sell. It was his livelihood and he held out for a long time. Finally, he agreed and profited well by his sale. DeVona's sons later went into business in Moncton. A daughter, Alvina, married Nick Athens, the local restaurateur. She had a sister, Daisy, and her brothers were John and Bill.

In the year 1919 Moncton's school-teachers, sensing post-war prosperity and the growing school population, asked the board for a whopping 25 percent salary increase. The matter was put over. No teacher's union then.

The Employment Service of Canada's Moncton office at the same time advertised for "a few second-class carpenters" (Sixty years later that sometimes seemed to be the only kind one could find). There were also openings for "women to do washing and ironing. Good wages for the right parties." A first-class cook for a private family was sought by one employer who would pay $25. a month. "A good maid" was

No. 2 Hose Company, fire department, in 1918 photographed by Jack Ross. Identified are: Robert McKay, second from left, and "O.P." Burns, third from left.

also required and her pay would be $16. a month, which was considered very good since the girl lived in. The availability of young women as housemaids continued for another decade or so and then, in the thirties, for the few who could then afford any help at all, the pay would be as little as three dollars a week. A good many girls were glad enough to get that because a room and board went with it. Many were newly in from the country and there was no unemployment insurance.

As 1920 dawned, the English and Scotch Woollen Co. opened one of a chain of tailor shops, later (if one recalls correctly) taken over by David Dunkelman and his Tip Top Tailors of Canada. Suits and overcoats made-to-measure for men went for $20. They were made of British wool, well tailored. The Peakes from England had opened a store on Mountain road where the Moncton High School afterward covered their ground.

Men's boots were offered for $3.98 and women's for $4.98. When the Peake family moved downtown they established one of Moncton's memorable women's fashion stores which their sons, Cecil (who had been a Western Union telegrapher) and Bill took over. Cecil, a corpulent young man who married Florence Gallagher, the daughter of Thomas, a Moncton hotel man whose father, Patrick Jr., ran The Minto Hotel, became one of the city's best known men-about-town. He was into everything, the hockey teams and summer sports, the golf club at Lakeside which he ran as "the way of life," amateur dramatics, and various club activities. "Cece" Peake before his death would become almost a legend in his own time. A *bon vivant* and wit, he was forever organizing and play-acting, even to doing Father Neptune for the first Shediac lobster festival.

The fashionable Peake-Gallagher wedding before 1923 caused considerable stir in Moncton because the Catholic bride was "married outside the church." Florence was said by her Irish friends to have "turned," a local rarity in the second decade of this century. It was also disturbing news to the Jewish community about the same time when the fur-buyer Harry Rich was married to the Irish-Catholic Mary McHugh. That wedding, the even rarer union of a Catholic and Jew, took place in St. Patrick's cathedral in New York.)

CECIL PEAKE, MAN-ABOUT-TOWN

The new Mrs. Peake by the way, was descended from an Irish family long in Moncton and widely known in the hotel trade. Her brother, Bill, soon made a Moncton first by going to Hollywood and mingling with the stars. He was for years secretary to the noted movie actor, Tyrone Power, and his picture appears in the book of Power's life called *The Last Idol* by Fred L. Guiles (Doubleday). The two were very close friends for the rest of their lives. Gallagher died in 1969. Mrs. J. J. O'Rourke of Winnipeg, a younger sister of Gallagher, recalled another book about Power which was, in her words, "very vicious and filthy, and pushed to the back shelf quickly because Ty's wife sued for $5,000,000."

Patrick Gallagher, the father of Patrick and grandfather of Thomas the hotelmen, had come to Saint John as Irish immigrants during the potato famine. A priest who met the boat found them work washing dishes in an hotel and thus started them in the business. Both thrived and were proprietors of hotels in Moncton and Shediac. Once, when Patrick wanted to add a third storey to the Minto Hotel on Main street, near Robinson, the city refused permission. Gallagher outwitted them by raising the structure and putting the storey underneath.

Another Gallagher story has to do with the twin sisters of Florence (Gallagher) Peake born at 29 Alma street on May 24, 1904. They were two months premature when delivered by Dr. W. A. Ferguson and they caused a lot of excitement. Ferguson was assisted by a druggist who lived next door, probably J. McD. Cooke, and between the two of them rushed about getting equipment to keep the tiny twins alive. Meantime, the townfolk, having heard of it, waited breathlessly to see if they would survive. They survived and quickly came to be known as "Nid and Nod," celebrated because they were so tiny. They were baptized in September at St. Bernard's church, but Nid died of pneumonia the following January. Nod lived to attend St. Mary's convent in Newcastle with her two older sisters, and married the dentist, Dr. J. J. O'Rourke. In 1981, she was still living in Winnipeg. Her sister, Florence Peake, at the time of writing was living in Halifax and in delicate health, having also achieved advanced old age. Miss Ann O'Rourke, a niece of Mrs. O'Rourke, lives in Moncton but all the Gallaghers are gone. William Peake, the man-with-the eyepatch, lives in retirement near Stoney Creek.

When the Gallagher girls were young, they lived at one time in what became the Barker House hotel. It had been bought by their grandfather, Patrick, the first of the hotelkeepers, as a private home for Tom and his family because Thomas Gallagher had been plagued with rheumatism and, after a few years in Arizona, had come home to die.

Hon. Thomas Babbitt Parlee, B.A., B.C.L., Q.C.

Now to come back to Babbitt Parlee's political career, a boy of the Twenties who came to be mayor in the Fifties. His entry was as a Conservative candidate in 1948 for one of Moncton's two seats in the legislature. (It now has three seats). He ran on a ticket with Francis A. Leger, a lawyer whose father, Hon. Antoine J. Leger, had been provincial secretary-treasurer in Conservative governments and later was appointed to the Canadian senate. It seemed like an ideal ticket for Moncton, nevertheless the two were defeated by Liberals Claudius I. L. Leger[1] and Ernest A. Fryers.

As it turned out, the defeat of the Conservatives was Moncton's gain for Parlee contested the mayoralty and won it in 1950. Then, in 1952, he again was a candidate for the legislature and this time with Joe. Bourgeois, a genial cigar-smoking Acadian tobacco-and-newstand proprietor whose father, J.J. Bourgeois, had been a successful businessman and early leader of the French-speaking revival in the city. Parlee led the poll.

The real surprise of that election was in knocking off C.H. Blakeny who had joined the Liberals and become a candidate for that party with Claudius Leger.[3] There were two C.C.F. (fore-runner of the N.D.P.) candidates, Lloyd Ayer and Lawrence Goguen. At last, after seventeen straight years in power, the Liberals provincially went down to the Conservatives and Moncton retained its reputation of being a belwether riding, always going with the government. Almost immediately, Parlee was made president of the executive council and named to the cabinet as minister of municipal affairs in 1954. He and Bourgeois were re-elected in 1956, defeating Leger and Fryers.

Only a year later, Babbitt Parlee's career was ended. He was hurrying to Moncton from Fredericton for a speaking engagement in the evening of January 23, 1957, flying with Howard Smith and Pilot L. C. Russell in a chartered Piper Tripacer aircraft. They had left Fredericton in near minimum flying conditions and never made it. Not until the next spring was the wreckage found, with their bodies, in the woods north of the flight path. Parlee was only 42 years of age and few who knew him ever doubted he would have one day been leader of his party had he lived. In ability and intellect, he was head and shoulders over most of his colleagues. His widow, the former Evelyn Moran, died in Florida in November, 1980. There were no children and the Parlee name, long part of Moncton tradition, disappeared from the community.

1. Mrs. Ora Wilcox (Mildred) was still living in Moncton at an advanced but alert age when this was written in 1982.

2. Parlee Beach near Shediac was re-named in his memory. Previously, it had been Belliveau Beach named for the extensive land-holder, John Belliveau who developed the area as a beach resort.

3. Claudius Leger's defeat may have been fortuitous for he continued to practise law in Moncton and was later appointed to the Supreme Court of the province and soon had a reputation as one of its ablest jurists.

Chapter Thirteen

PROHIBITION, EATON'S and SOCIETY

On January 1, 1920, the new Arena skating and hockey rink opened for the season with natural ice in good condition. Starr skates were much prized and many a family which had delighted in at least one new pair for Christmas turned up either at the Arena or on the marsh behind the pumping station. Three days later, a large part of the Record Foundry burned but it had already been sold to Eaton's — or at least the land had and the foundry would have been demolished anyway. Nevertheless, it tugged at the heartstrings for this had been Moncton's oldest big industry and few families there were which did not have some relative connected with the firm at one time or another since the 1850's.

Then, two days after the fire, the first New Brunswick Poultry Show opened with a fine flourish at the city hall. Mayor Hanford Price, winding up his term before moving aside for Cavour Chapman, who had been elected for the bright new year, welcomed a batch of notables. The deputy minister of agriculture was there, and Hon. C. W. Robinson, also Hon. Frank J. Sweeney, K.C., the attorney-general, practising in Moncton but a native of Melrose, and Ald. S. Forbes was present. The event was big enough to make the first column at the top of page one in *The Transcript*.

It was the start of a big year for Moncton and one which, then unrealized, would more than subtly change the social history of the city. There was a post-war boom and a sense of euphoria which would dissipate as the decade advanced and more and more people left for New England and jobs.

As the first year of the new decade got going, "Elmo The Mighty" was running as a serial at The Dreamland three-score years before television re-discovered the mini-series. Dorothy Gish was at The Empress in "Nugget Nell." Crime was light and the local newspapers made a front page story out of it when three fellows appeared in court charged with "taking articles from local parties." Most of the rest of the page was given over to Chicago gangland killings.

You could get the Boston Sunday Advertiser in town and the demand for the garish weekender was such that it could be had "at all dealers on Friday afternoons." No mail delays then. All the excitement was in the newspapers because radio was just on the verge, with Mr. Marconi's invention stirring the imagination of youthful inventors.

Moncton's finest stone residence built by F.W. Sumner in 1914, occupied later by son, F.R. Sumner, and family, then by Catholic archbishop. Demolished to be replaced by federal building and 1111 Main street building.

Filled with the go-ahead spirit of the new decade's first year, the new city council urged development of the Natural Park away out there on St. George street extension (Snobbishly, a boulevard today). Besides, a civic hothouse was recommended but the Board of Trade objected to a proposed increase in telephone rates. Chief of Police George Rideout, the redoubtable George Rideout, thought there should be a new police station but he said that more attention was being paid to traffic laws. The motor car was coming into its own. Alongside this news were advertisements for Minard's ointment for those who might come up with an abrasive accident; Dodds' liver pills for other ailments and Scott's Emulsion to ward off winter colds.

This was timely because Moncton was about to be hit by the biggest gale since Saxby. The wind on February 19, 1920, swept up the river at 60 miles-an-hour and interrupted train service, lifted some roofs and did other damage. Then, the Abrams and Sons foundry and machine shop was struck by fire and almost wholly destroyed with losses up to $30,000. and only half insured.

Prohibition, which had replaced the old Canada Temperance Act in 1918, was enforced with a vengeance, but there was always relief for the thirsty. The gentlemen's clubs had to dispose of their supplies already on order from the Halifax wholesaler, (whiskey was $7. a gallon wholesale from J. V. Turney & Son). They did this with some dispatch by selling it to Holstead's and Keirstead's drug stores where it could be dispensed on prescription. Prescriptions were not difficult to obtain and the number of ailing residents whose health could be improved by partaking of such spirits as rum, gin and good scotch, increased markedly. Porter and stout were considered more ladylike but the ladies never went into the nicely and comfortably furnished back rooms at the stores. As for the men, they had to wait some time for their prescriptions to be filled and they might as well be seated in comfort. Further, since there was the danger of evaporation if the stuff was carried home for consumption, it was safer to down the horrid medicine right there on the spot.

Thaddee and Azime Leger, brothers, operated hardware store and tinsmithing shop on St. George before and after 1920's. First uptown hardware.

Inside Holstead's pharmacy, 741 Main, in 1915. Door at rear led to backroom popular watering place in Prohibition days. Adjoined Sumner's.

This was one case where the Catholics had it over the Protestants, because none of the Protestant nabobs who hustled to Al. Holstead's — right beside Sumner's big store — on thirsty Sunday mornings could make it until the long 11 o'clock service was over. (Everybody, but everybody, went to church then). A lot of the Catholics got up for nine o'clock Mass and had a big headstart on their Protestant friends at Holstead's.

Quite apart from this sort of spirit, there was in the Moncton of that period a better relationship between the major religious denominations than there soon would be. They had long since learned to live together and work together, people with their own convictions, people who "believed" and people who had a fine sense of Christian charity and fellowship. That would be damaged in the near future with the coming of some elements of Orange militancy from the then Tory-Protestant-imperialist Toronto and the rise of French-Catholic nationalism.

The year 1920 was the year of the Lindsay Crawford riot in Moncton which was described in detail in the first volume of this work. The newspapers of the day had mentioned charges that "imports from Toronto" had stirred up the trouble. The truth was that some of the middle-range employees who had come to Moncton with Eaton's were in the forefront of the attack on the Irish Nationalist (himself a Protestant and former Orangeman) Crawford. It would be dishonest to avoid the historical reality that the Eaton company of that period was itself a very Protestant organization. Founded by North of Ireland dedicated Protestants, it had grown in the Orange Toronto of those years when the biggest annual event was unquestionably the Glorious Twelfth of July celebration and parade.

Some of those who came to Moncton, and it is also only honest to say that this attitude was not that of senior management, brought with them the old hatreds. These had been nourished in a Toronto where the whole police force, with a handful of exceptions, were Ulster-born bobbies and where T. T. Shields on Jarvis street was excoriating Catholics.

133

Tommy Church, the perennial Toronto mayor and then federal politician, kept the place in a politico-religious ferment. As a reporter, this writer once asked the otherwise affable Church how he could tour the Maritimes and never mention his Toronto prejudices and he said, "Well, you know I'm also a politician."

In Toronto where the newly-arrived first Catholic archbishop was once stoned by a mob as he rode from the station in his carriage, the hiring practices of some big firms could go unquestioned because of the then majority atmosphere. That could not be the case in Moncton, and employment at the new Eaton's was not "Protestant only." Yet it was well understood in the 1920's that no Catholic was likely to be promoted to a departmental manager's post, regardless of ability. There was one man, an Irish-Catholic named Keogh, who had come to Moncton with Eaton's from Toronto as a manager. He married a Moncton woman and always attended Mass at seven o'clock Sunday morning so that he would not be obvious. This is not hearsay for the man and his family once spent part of a summer with the writer's family at Shediac Cape, and told them all about it.

These are not pleasant subjects to remember sixty years later when such practices are so greatly altered, but it would not be historically accurate to avoid mention of them.

Nothing like this would mar the delight of Monctonians on that day in February, 1920, when R. Y. Eaton himself came from Toronto to walk through a snowstorm to turn the key that would open the new mail-order building. Some eight thousand visitors went in the first day to inspect the premises. This was a very big thing for Moncton; it would bring employment to thousands, steady work at decent if not generous pay. For some, it provided lifelong and well paid careers.

The directors of T. Eaton Co. Ltd., threw a great banquet to mark the opening, with a long list of distinguished guests. William Pugsley, the lieutenant-governor, was there and Senator Robinson and all of the city's bigwigs gathered at the feast in the Brunswick Hotel. During the banquet a choir sang — and all of the guests joined in — "Moncton By the Sea"

A.H. GRAINGER OF EATON'S

and such Irish favorites as "Mother Machree," "My Wild Irish Rose" and dozens of other selections. The menu was scrumptious and Harry McGee, the chairman and second vice president of T. Eaton Co., Ltd., read a telegram of regret from Sir John Eaton, the president, who could not be present.

    A. H. Grainger, who soon would become second only to Walter U. Appleton, in Moncton's industrial and commercial hierarchy, as the head man for Eaton's in the Maritimes, Newfoundland, Bermuda and the West Indies, proposed the toast to "Our Guests."

    The first mail order package was soon shipped off to Bathurst, and the downtown Moncton merchants who were concerned about the impact on their trade of this national giant were lulled into believing that only mail-order business would be done, and no retail store should be expected.

    Nevertheless, that came in 1927 and many local merchants were hurt. It was the first impact of retail chain stores, a whole generation in advance of those which would fill the shopping malls of Canada after the 1960's. Here in

Moncton, the merchants had for generations extended long term credit. The great majority of customers worked for the railway, for the government in one way or another, and the pay was good and regular. On paydays the custom was to make regular payments on account.

Not a few of the merchants, right into the Twenties, would take potatoes and other vegetables, barrels of apples, hay for their horses, and sometimes even knitted goods from rural folk, in payment of purchases. Money might be slow in coming from those with little cash but it came. The merchants carried them. Credit and lengthy credit terms (Men bought $30. suits in the 1920's at $2.-a-week, joining "suit clubs" to do it) had been part of doing business. Now, Eaton's mail-order business meant cash with order, and country people who had often paid annual store bills when they sold their crops in the fall or when fish harvest yielded a good amount, now managed to scrape together cash for intriguing catalogue merchandise. The smaller merchants were hurt.

Since the cash only policy applied with the retail Eaton's at first — something the present generation may find hard to believe in the age of credit cards — the local merchants often got *only* the credit business. Toward the end of the 1920's those who fitted themselves on credit, formerly good accounts, and then disappeared into the United States to live thereafter, were numerous. Several merchants were bankrupted with tens of thousands of debts outstanding on their books. And, though poor management and family feuding were the big factors in doing in the first big local department store, Peter McSweeney Ltd.[1], the success of Eaton's with its modern and efficient merchandising policies competitively gave the *coup de grace*. One Moncton merchant who went under, and who is still living handsomely well up in his nineties in Moncton, scratched a living for his family for several years after 1930 by collecting fifty cents-a-week apiece from scores of his debtors, after his business went bust.

1. This story is detailed in a previous volume.

Chapter Fourteen

THE LOCAL "CHARACTERS"

In the period between the two great wars when the city was compact enough for local "characters" to be visible and known all over town, Moncton had its quota. There was poor Bessie Gray who ran alongside the open garbage wagon of her mate, Caleb Morrell, railing at him loudly as he made his rounds. There was tragic little Maggie Proctor in widow's weeds forever trudging the streets carrying a bundle in her arms which she had imagined as her lost child.

Later, and of a wholly different mold, was Rosie Wing whose crooked leg resulted from a broken bone never properly set. A Caucasian married to an Oriental restaurant-keeper, Rosie ran a house of ill-repute down by the river side. It was said she sold spirits illegally, provided other services including money-lending to alcoholics. She was reputed to keep large sums of money stashed about her slum dwelling and, finally, she was done in. A young man went to prison convicted of manslaughter. When police picked their way gingerly through her filthy house they found thousands of dollars stuffed into dirty cans and crevices in the foul-smelling den.

Down on Telegraph street was Flewelling "Priest" Wilbur, a slum landlord and political power. He owned the land on which the old post office stood and gained mail-moving contracts, and he was feared, undoubtedly also a money-lender. Once, after a bitterly cold night, he was found alive in a snowbank, fingers frozen.

It was never determined whether Flewelling had simply fallen while inebriated or been pushed by an unhappy borrower. He was a power of sorts and nothing much was reported.

Countering such types was that very happy fellow, Early Steeves. Presumably his name was Earl, and the children thought he was called Early because he drove horse and rig through the early morning streets delivering cream and butter. His farm was on the hill in Lewisville between what is now called Floral avenue and the Shediac Road and he sang his way through town. Well before his one-hoss shay with soft top folded came into sight "Early" could be heard belting out hymns in a stentorian voice. "We'll be washed, we'll be washed; we'll be washed in the blood of the Lamb" would be followed by "Shall we gather at the river?" and "Yield not to temptation; He will carry you through." The wonderful old Protestant hymns were implanted in the hearer's memory by an enchanting evangelical personality whose voice needed no amplification as youngsters ran beside his gig and he called out gaily to passersby: "Are you saved, are you saved?" but never stopping to get an answer, never pressing, never pushing. Just shouting out his faith.

Maybe people were less sensitive in the generation that grew up before 1930 when the sitting-magistrate, who filled in when the regular magistrate was off, was known as "Squealer" McDougall. The lawyer, W.A. McDougall, was deaf and had a peculiarly high-pitched voice which he was inclined to use with effect in arguments from the bench. He was egged on by the shrewd solicitor, James "Jimmy" Sherren, who defended many of those charged with petty and grievous crimes. Their arguments came to be legendary.

While Capt. Mollie Kool was not herself a Monctonian, the city's waterfront made her its own "Tugboat Annie." Mollie's father, Capt. Paul Kool, had built a scow which carried lumber and gravel up the river from Alma. He named it for his elder daughter, "Jean K.," who wasn't interested in

J. FRED EDGETT, frequent mayor and school board chairman in 1920's and 1930's.

W.A. MCDOUGALL, clerk of court and stipendiary magistrate over 35 years.

scows. But Sister Mollie was and soon earned her mate's papers. She sailed on the tides with her father and eventually won her master's papers.

    On a notable occasion in 1938, the redoubtable Mollie had come up on the morning tide with a load of lumber for Thomas H. King. She tied up at the public wharf just along from where Cy's Seafood restaurant sits today and was there when the evening tide brought in a 2000-ton steel Norwegian freighter coming to load pulpwood from Harris Joyce's Moncton Lumber Co. Her skipper wanted to tie up at the wharf where the Jean K. was berthed but Mollie wouldn't move. When she came on deck, the haughty Norwegian skipper said he wouldn't talk to a woman whereupon Mollie advised him to vanish into some dreadful Norwegian hell.

Then he brought his vessel in behind the scow and rattled it until the lines broke and it went adrift. Mollie managed to leap ashore as the Norwegian asked if she wanted him to throw her a line. She said she'd see him in Marine Court first.

A seaman from the freighter then went aboard the scow and beached her just below the present restaurant. But Capt. Mollie Kool wasn't fooling. She engaged Roscoe Allan as her lawyer and won an out-of-court settlement. She was in her early 20's at the time and continued sailing her scow until it was accidentally rammed by the Digby ferry out of Saint John and sank. She had it raised but left the seafaring life to marry a Bucksport sailor from Maine, keeping the Jean K. long enough to have their honeymoon aboard.

Earlier in the same decade, politics of the day brought out the best and worst in Peter Campbell Johnson, son of a Father of Confederation who had come from Chatham and made his home in Moncton. His father, Hon. John Mercer Johnson, was one of New Brunswick's delegates to the Confederation conferences and P.C. attended many political meetings. His special joy was to present himself at Conservative meetings and whenever the name of Prime Minister Richard Bedford Bennett, a fellow New Brunswicker, was invoked to raise a raucous razzberry.

Tall, distinguished in appearance and elderly, Johnson wore well-tailored black suits, a black homburg hat and velvet-collared Chesterfield coat. At Liberal meetings he entertained the folks with a harmonica played through his nose. At these gatherings he came supplied with two kinds of wooden-handled "suckers," one of which was a large lollipop or all-day sucker. When asked to speak, or when presenting himself to speak asked or unasked, he would begin:

"The wealthy have more than they need but Bennett thinks they should have even more, so he gives them this all-day sucker." Out would come the large lollipop with a flourish. "As for the poor, they have nothing, but Bennett gives them something too. No lollipop for them, though; to him, they're just a bunch of suckers and this is what he gives them." With that Johnson would whip out a tiny one-cent sucker and the crowd would roar. "That's telling 'em, P.C." and Peter

Campbell, looking thin and brittle as a lollipop-stick himself, would bow graciously, smile and move off to another meeting.

It seems that the Johnsons were closely related to the millionaire Eddy paper family from Chatham, New Brunswick, where the future Prime Minister Bennett articled in law. Bennett had wooed the future Mrs. Eddy in her maidenly days but never married. When she died, leaving a great fortune, the Johnsons had hoped to inherit. Instead she made R.B. a millionaire Calgary lawyer and he went on to fame.

As will be seen in other chapters, the "French Question" had taken hold in Moncton early in the century. As it blossomed, it produced some notables. You could hardly call the ardent nationalist Henri P. LeBlanc a "character" but he and his friend, Zoel Cormier could always draw attention. As they passed on opposite sides of the street near the Orange Hall on Archibald where both resided, they would shout greetings in French: "Bon-jour, Zoel...Bon-jour, mon ami. Comment ca va?" Being sure to speak very clearly. "Ca va bien, Henri. Et vous?"

It is only the truth to recall that the looks of passing neighbors were often scowly because the French language spoken near the Orange lodge hall was less than fashionable.

From the days when motor-cars were less common and the Gray Dort (built in Chatham, Ont., by the Gray family) made its appearance, Hugh Hamilton of Moncton bought one. A well-to-do bachelor who had retired from the I.C.R. as a senior clerk in 1914 and enjoyed his generous Provident Fund pension for about thirty years, Hamilton made a fortune in World War One Liberty ship investments. Of an old Irish Moncton family, Hamilton had never before driven a car and the Gray Dort dealer gave his a lesson or two. Then Hugh took his first trip alone into the country. He got started all right but he couldn't remember how to stop the danged machine. He headed right out the Shediac Road, went on to Cocagne and up the river to the Irishtown Road, back into Moncton. Then he started the round again, still unable to stop, and just kept making the circuit until the car ran out of gas. At least, that's the story people told.

Atlantic Underwear plant in 1920's once Peters Lock factory, later Wallace warehouse, Church street. Inset is J.L. McDonald, manager of Atlantic Underwear. Artist's drawing 1915.

How wholesale fruit of F.M. Tennant warehouse transported in 1920. Model T. truck and horse-drawn wagon kept busy. Fred. M. Tennant seen in cap, foreground.

Then there was that lively and imaginative fellow J.B. "Jack" Connolly who proved himself a sign of the times when he moved on from ponies to automobiles. One day he went into *The Transcript* newsroom to explain a predicament and a resulting news item quoted him as saying: "Due to my having advertised a car for sale some time ago, the daily and even hourly question asked of me is: "When are you leaving town Mr. Connolly?' Mr. Connolly, it is understood, was acting as agent for another gentleman and laughingly remarked that he didn't drive a car but a 'jitney' and hoped to stay in town for as long as Father Time and Dame Fortune would allow him to do so." A little while after that he left for Halifax, Dame Fortune having failed him at home.

One item from that Moncton period which didn't make the newspapers had to do with a scandal that wracked old Aberdeen High School. Everybody in town knew about it, for the school board had held an investigation which, though kept out of the papers, went swiftly around town. The affair concerned the gift of chocolates to various young ladies in Grades 10 and 11 from various young men. One of the youths involved was the son of a druggist and had learned enough chemistry to discover how to inject what was then considered an aphrodisiac into individual chocolates. These were then restored to their attractive boxes and passed around by the youths to girls of their choice.

What the end results were was never disclosed. Some two or three youths were expelled from the school, but later returned, graduated and were among the very few from Moncton then going on to university. Since the two best remembered are now dead, as are their respected wives, it may at least be said that they came in middle age to be among the city's most respectable citizens.

The cornerstone of the three-storey brick Knights of Pythias Hall had been laid in 1921 and, when the building was completed, it included a splendid ballroom on the top floor. Dances held there were sometimes quite splendid affairs, and the New Year's Eve ball an event of the year. Floor-length ball gowns of taffeta, or whatever, for the young ladies and white tie and tails or tuxedos for their escorts. The ball was still a big

Famous Colleens basketball team of St. Bernard's won Maritime ladies' title 1930. Three standing at rear; left to right: Minerva LeBlanc, Iris Forbes, Marjorie LeBlanc. Seated: left, Evelyn Jeffrey and Phyllis Bourque; below is Agnes McGee.

affair in 1936, even though it was Depression time. A made-to-measure tail-coated suit, complete with white waistcoat was sold by Tip Top Tailors for $33.00. The cloth was of a high quality British wool, the trousers handsomely braided, an outfit that would run to $550 in 1981. Worn rarely, there is just such a suit moth-balled within the house where this is written, much too small for its owner but still in good shape after forty years.

Through the 1920's and occasionally into the 30's, young ladies kept dainty, marked dance programs on which their swains were listed for the waltzes and fox trots. Paul Coté had opened his dancing school on Mountain Road next door to what is now the Moncton Museum. The Flett family of studio photographers, father, son and daughters, lived nearby, having just opened their studio on Main street. The thing to do was to have your picture taken, not "after the ball was over," but just before. Chaperones were no longer required, but woe betide the young man who failed to have a father's daughter home at the designated hour. At New Year's it could be as late as three o'clock in the morning but there had to be a full explanation.

While the practice of "calling days" for socially-minded women in Moncton had fallen away somewhat during World War One when women were too busy with war work, it revived briefly afterward. The ladies of a particular street or district would set aside one afternoon of the week to be "at home," Botsford street on Tuesday, Church on Wednesday, uptown on Thursday. Sometimes, a Society leader would set her own day regardless. The city was smaller and mostly the women walked to one another's homes. There was a strict protocol about staying and leaving calling cards. The visit must last no longer than twenty minutes and no tea was served. The visiting cards were ordered, if you wanted the proper steel-engraved ones, from Flewelling's in Saint John. They were left on a silver tray in the entry hall of the house being visited. If the caller were married, she left two cards, one with her name and one with her husband's. If single or widowed, she left only her own card. Mrs. A.H. Melanson,[1] whose husband owned the fine jewelery store on Main street, remembers those customs well. A tall, stately looking woman, she had reached her 97th birthday in 1981 when she remembered and explained all of this. She had even kept some of the cards left over when the custom died out more than fifty years earlier. It died because "the women were too often out," she said. "They were too busy and they got out of the habit. It was a nice custom."

1. Mrs. Melanson died in 1982.

Chapter Fifteen

FAMILY RACE HORSES AND FANCY CARS

For one born before the 1920's, Moncton was a cozy, lively small town, a good place in which to grow up. Everybody knew everybody, or at least knew *about* them. It was a punch-proud little city close to its rural surroundings, in tune with nature, and prospering. The automobile was still novel and farmers still came to market behind horses in buggies. Horses (and street sweepers who followed them) were still common on the streets as delivery wagons, dump trucks and carriages were common before 1920.

In winter time, those who had cars put them up on blocks in garages, drained the oil and walked. Not a few families kept their own driving horses and rode about in winter in sleighs of varying sorts. Livery stables flourished, snow piled up in the streets though sidewalks were well and quickly plowed. On harness-racing days in summer, thousands from the city and the surrounding countryside came to the Moncton Speedway west of Enterprise street between St. George and John to watch the competing trotters and pacers.

Horses and early automobiles were very much a part of the family life in which the writer was raised. Even as this is written in 1981, older residents stop to reminisce about P.A. Belliveau and his record-breaking trotters. Or to recall the wonderful cars of an era long past. "P.A." was my father and in many ways could be said to illustrate the lifestyle of Moncton's middle class in those years.

It used to be the custom in England, upon the death of a moderately prominent relative, for someone in the family to do a "life." In the circumstances, it would be something less than objective and certainly that might be charged against this book's present chapter. Nevertheless anyone writing of that period in Moncton's history would need to make some reference to Phil Belliveau. In Machum's historical index his name appears frequently, partly because he served on so many public committees.

From his business, civic, political and sporting involvements, a family member could learn much about the community's people and their goings-on. So even if he was a parent, one should mention his career.

"P.A." came to Moncton from the Memramcook Valley where his parents lived on the "English" or Dorchester side of the river. Educated in both languages and being among the graduates of the original business course at St. Joseph's College, he fitted easily into both English and French sides of life in Moncton. Arriving in 1892, he caught on with McSweeney's new departmental store. Four years later, he had become so immersed in Liberal politics as to be on the committee which welcomed Wilfrid Laurier, the future prime minister, to the great Curling Rink rally in 1896.

From then until 1935, when he died of viral infection picked up getting out the vote on a cold and wet election day, he was never far from civic, provincial or federal politics. He had opened his men's and boys' clothing store in 1903 directly opposite city hall. With its opera house upstairs and country market down, that was a mecca for both city·and country folk. So father came to know a wide cross-section of the public through sheer visibility.

He was an alderman and deputy mayor for five years; he ran the racetrack, kept stables of harness horses. He was in real estate, operated a motor-car agency with Frank "Frenchy" Dayton who had come to town from Edmundston. He managed the local Victorias hockey team when it played the Quebec Aces for the Stanley Cup in 1913. He was on World War One recruiting committees, in the Home Guard, on the Victory Loan committee and secretary of the Westmorland

P.A. Belliveau, the horseman, in light road gig, with daughter Catherine in 1908. Panama hat was his fashion hallmark. Bright-eyed woman high collar style is Anna Belliveau, the author's mother, in 1900-era studio portrait.

Moncton Speedway harness-racing track now site of R.C.A.F. supply base, about 1920
Photo courtesy E.W. Larracey

Liberal patronage committee. A gregarious joiner, he was a charter member of the Salvage Corps, a volunteer fire department auxiliary more social that salvationist. He was a charter member of the Ancient Order of Foresters, the Knights of Columbus, la Societé l'Assomption, the Moncton Curling Club, the Moncton Club. You name it, he joined it.

But it was horse-racing blood that ran in the family, inherited from his father André, so well known a horse-trader in the valley that his whole clan was called "The Drivers." P.A.'s youngest brother, Albert, in 1981 and in his 90's, still trained harness horses as a retirement hobby. The first novel Father read was *David Harum*, the great American horse-trading book for boys. Religiously, he read *Trotter and Pacer,* a thin slick-paper weekly published in upstate New York. He went annually to the Old Glory harness sales in Goshen, N.Y., picking up horses for his own stable and to sell to other horsemen.

In those days, harness racing was prominent in the newspapers. Many, if not most, residents were country-bred and horses were part of everybody's inheritance then.

They cheered when P.A.'s trotter *John A. Hal* established the Eastern Canada track record at the Halifax Exhibition in 1917 and lowered it to 2.08 3/4 at Chatham in 1919. Another of his winners was the big black sire *LaCopia* still mentioned by older citizens as the greatest performer of its era. (Bill Daley, a retired insurance executive in Kansas City, wrote in 1980 to ask for current news and recall how *LoCopia* had kicked him in Dick Kinnear's horse-barn at the corner of Bonaccord and Dufferin, back in the early 20's.)

There was one filly from the Old Glory which performed less than gloriously. A matinee racer, she had set up a remarkable record in New England, so P.A. bought her, renamed her *Catherine B* for his older daughter, and looked for great things. But in Canada, *Catherine B.* never won a race; never even came close. There was another trotter called *The Problem*, whose name should have been given to a horse mentioned in *The Transcript* on June 7, 1920. The news item read like this: "The *Fredericton Gleaner* states that P.A. Belliveau has acquired another trotter. The sale was made through an agent, who it was later found, had no option on the horse though he had purported to have one. So Mr. Belliveau may not get the horse, though he has paid for it. The horse was *Billy Jackson* and Mr. Belliveau was buying for spring stables." He never got it.

It wouldn't be the last time "P.A." lost a racehorse. In the late 1920's a "swipes" horse-handler at the track, made off one weekend with a handsome chestnut mare. Leaving his wife and family, the handler was presumed to have got the horse over the American border and neither man nor horse was ever again seen in Moncton.

One of the thrills of boyhood was to be taken on a wintry Sunday afternoon to the harness races on John street between Bonaccord and High. No cars then ran in the winter and the street made a splendid straightaway mile. Riding in the high-runnered racing pung, my brothers and I would be tucked under a buffalo robe while raccoon-coated Father's fur-gloved hands snapped the reins with practised expertise. James Swetnam, the long-retired railway executive, recalled, as this book was in preparation and he 92 years of age, that before that winter races were held on measured St. George street.

At one race meet on the Speedway, the family watched from the 1919 Studebaker, as Father's black stallion "Cochata" bolted and fell, with "P.A." holding the reins. The horse landed heavily on the fence with driver and sulky left on the trackside. Leaping from the sulky, the driver sat on the horse's head and waited until helpers arrived to unhitch the animal.

Not so fortunate was the outcome of an accident involving a family hackney called "Candy Girl." Father had given it to Mother as an anniversary gift and she and her grandmother were taking the children to Shediac Cape. As they passed Cook's Brook, a black bear ambled out of the woods. "Candy Girl" reared and upset the carriage, throwing its passengers into a ditch. Grandmother suffered a broken hip.

Chapter Sixteen

BROADCASTERS AND BURBANKS

It was 1924 and one evening Mrs. Elizabeth Wrynn and her daughter Maudie brought their crystal radio set around for a demonstration. The family sat in a circle in front of an open-fronted natural gas stove whose bluish flames came through "doughnuts" set into the base of the stove to retain the heat. The reason for being just there, was that you could hook the wispy wire from the radio set onto the metal frame of the stove. The radio itself was a mysterious thing hidden inside a varnished oak box about twelve inches by twelve by ten. It came complete with earphones, and these would be passed around from person to person so that the thrill of hearing Victor George and his friends talking, singing or playing instrumental music on Radio Station CNRA could be shared. KDKA, Pittsburg, and WBZ the Hotel Kimball, Springfield, Mass., and WGY, Schenectady, were the powerful broadcasters, but could be picked up only late on winter evenings and when atmospherical conditions were exactly right.

Moncton moved into the big time of radio broadcasting when CNRA was established for the Canadian National, the main object being to transmit programs to passengers travelling on their trains. Victor George came from Montreal to run the station. Three years later, CNRA joined other stations across Canada for a special broadcast from Ottawa to mark Canada's diamond jubilee of Confederation when Moncton's school children marched in a great parade on July first and were given anniversary coins to mark the occasion.

Except for the local station's Rainbow Melody Boys and Whitey Hains with his orchestra, the programs were not very inspiring for young listeners. Boys and girls soon got used to radio; few were hooked by hearing M. F. "Mose" Tompkins, the C.N.'s regional traffic manager, give an address on the state of the railroad, or listening to such hometown talent as Bessie Wilcox playing piano solos, Dr. Fred E. Burden doing his thing alone on a clarinet, or Ida Bremner Malcolm, J. Edgar O'Brien and Charles Harding with their amateur dramatics. Later, Bob Gander, Katherine Dickson sang and Mrs. George O. Spencer and Mae Rance MacKinnon did readings.

Sometimes there was a little recorded music on the gramaphone. There were some hired vocal performers at first, Desiré Bourque and Alphée Leger, and they weren't very exciting either. Fortunately, it was before television and one did not see the pain in their faces. Then there was Tom Kirby, who in 1979 recalled those years for the newspapers.

He wasn't on staff but he sang a lot in the Knights of Pythias building studio on such programs as "Down Memory Lane." He sang "On the Road to Mandalay" so often that some of his townsfolk hoped he would take it.

Things did get exciting though when the Hawks hockey team went off to play for the Allan Cup and win it in 1933 and Monctonians heard the broadcast direct from Saskatoon, Saskatchewan. Scores of telegrams were shot off, and read by the announcer, and most said "Good luck, Hawks, bring home the bacon." Not a highly original suggestion since the Hawks were playing in the flour-making capital of the country. "Bring home a barrel" might have been more appropriate, for it was Depression "and the times were hard."

When CNRA was taken over by the Canadian Radio Broadcasting Commission in 1923, as part of the national system, its call letters were changed to CRCA but soon it was closed down and for one year Moncton was without radio broadcasting. This didn't bother people too much because wonderful tube sets had come into style with their trumpet-like

Fred. A Lynds

loud-speakers sitting beside them like the picture of the little dog listening to "His Master's Voice" on Victor records. With such powerful sets, you could tune in regularly to WGY, KDKA and WBZ almost anytime (after dark) and often get the New York city stations as well.

    Then young Fred Lynds came out of Mount Allison and was hired as assistant manager of a new radio station company formed by J. L. Black of Sackville, F. R. Sumner, and Herbert M. Wood, of Sackville. Senator C. W. Robinson, of Moncton, came to be top man later. It became CKCW with 100 watts, later to be increased to 10,000. It wasn't long before Lynds became head man and in 1947 he bought the station. In time, he was to create the first television broadcasting station in Moncton, in 1954. How Fred came to be known as "Lionel" isn't quite clear, but "Lionel the Lobster" came to be the station symbol. In his television years an awaited annual event in downtown Toronto was the lobster luncheon. This was held for the advertising and publishing trade and invitations were sought like Grey Cup tickets. As many lobsters as you could eat.

All of that was far ahead of those early years when Fred lived at his boyhood home at the corner of Weldon and Dufferin. As neighbors, we had ridden Moncton's first balloon-tired tricycles together but were out of touch through school or college days.

Then, when Jack K. Grainger became publisher of *The Transcript* (later amalgamated with *The Times* but that's another story) and J. E. Belliveau the city editor, we alternated as news broadcasters for Fred, and did it for free. The custom was to whack out the local and district news after making the morning rounds of railways, city hall, police and the courts, then rush like mad on foot from Main and Westmorland to Bonaccord and Gordon, dash up three flights of stairs and, breathlessly, begin to read the news. With Fred Lynds waving us in and Jim White at the controls, we regaled that "great world out there in radioland" with the latest local tidbits.

Nobody thought there was any conflict of interest between newspaper and radio because the news items were just a few lines long and the fuller versions could be read in the paper a few hours later. Indeed, it was considered that the lunch-hour broadcast only whetted the public appetite for more. Still, a fee would have been appreciated.

Jack K. Grainger and the author (in white) are seen on beach at Pointe du Chene for *Transcript* staff picnic late 1930's. They broadcast news on Lynds' radio station.

F. A. Lynds was ahead of his time in making CKCW a community service station and, as it developed, took over where the local newspapers had left off. Increasingly, they had deserted that area — although they have returned to it to some degree in later decades — and Freddie made the most of it.

You could never be sure with Fred Lynds whether he was happy or sad, because he adopted a glum mien and spoke sparingly. Except when he had a story to tell, and then he surprised you with his unsuspected wit. A clever fellow, Lynds was one of those who could make it in his hometown. By being just a little ahead of his time, he moved into the field which was to become the communications leader of its era, first in radio and then in television. His first wife, Helen, was a lively blonde who herself knew a lot about the business and she proved to be a good "front woman" for the broadcasting companies.

Moncton's early radio provided a wide audience for two of Moncton's most popular and perennial musicians, Arthur and Maude Burbank. Years afterward, Mrs. Burbank's boys' bands even caught national attention.

In her own lifetime, Maude Burbank became a legend but few of its citizens ever knew the colorful career she and her husband, Arthur, had pursued for twenty years before they found a lasting home in Moncton. Maude was born a Danforth in the little northern town of Island Pond, Vermont, and by the time she was eight years old she was playing hymns on an organ. Born to the sound of music, she was given a battered violin by an uncle when she was nine and then Jason Wheeler, an elderly Island Ponder, in four lessons taught her to coax jigs, reels and polkas from the fiddle strings.

As a teen-ager, just out of high school from which she graduated in 1899, she, herself, taught school and decided she could tame some young toughs by teaching them the fiddle. Which she did. It would be a long time until she got back to this first love of teaching music to children. In the meantime, she hit the road.

Tall and on the beautiful and stately side, Maude Danforth met Arthur Burbank at Berlin, N.H., near the Quebec border when she was teaching at East Barre. By this time she had studied violin with competent violinists in Portland, Boston and New York. Arthur Burbank was in town

The Burbanks, Arthur and Maude, when they were on the big-time vaudeville circuit in days before 1920.

with an orchestra, invited Maude to be its leader, and away they went filling engagements all over New England in clubs, at lodge soirees, in halls, dances — wherever they could get a fee. Arthur (and she always called him "Ah-thuh") was a relative of the great botanist Luther Burbank but he worked in a lumber mill when they were married.

Pooling their bank savings, their next step was the Big Apple itself, Manhattan, and dreams of quick theatrical success. They backed a Broadway play, lost $2,000. and were so badly broke they actually went to work for a medicine show. While its slick operator sold "Indian remedies" and snakeoil, they played background music. From there they rose to vaudeville. Arthur played trombone solos and by now Maude was playing piano, violin, trumpet, saxaphone, clarinet, French horn, alto horn, trombone and tuba. She had begun to wear those flowing cloaks which became her trademark in Moncton, and Burbank and Danforth began to pick up steady dates on the famous B.F. Keith circuit. They were contemporaries there of such as the greatest of all juggler-comedians, W. C. Fields and the zany Marx Brothers.

Burbank and Danforth went from town to town and city to city, playing one-night stands, three-night stands and sometimes a whole lovely week. For years they lived out of suitcases and once, long after they were married, a boarding house mistress in New Brunswick and her other guests snubbed them pointedly. Their luggage was marked Burbank and Danforth and the landlady decided they were sharing a room quite improperly.

Good hotels, second-rate hotels, and, more often, boarding houses were their restless homes until 1920. That April, Torrie and Winter booked them into the Grand Opera House in Moncton for $53.33 on a two-day stand when the act had become (for some unexplained reason) Dingley & Norton.

Fred Winter had asked them to stay and strengthen his orchestra but they went on to Halifax where they played a whole week for the immense sum of $160. While there, the Grand Opera's orchestra leader took sick, and Winter was frantic. He wired Dingley and Norton, saying he had booked eight vaudeville acts, his orchestra leader was sick and "all will be ruined unless you come back." They didn't reply and he wired again asking why they didn't reply. Then they came back without notifying him in advance, undecided about what they really wanted to do.

The Burbanks, as Dingley & Norton, were in the midst of an opera house performance when the corpulent Fred Winter appeared in the wings in full sight of the audience and shouted: "Why in the hell didn't you answer my telegram?" Maude used to say that it nearly broke her up but Arthur stamped on her foot while he continued to blow on his trombone and she kept going with a screeching that did not come from the violin strings.

By this time, she and Arthur were playing a bewildering variety of instruments but vaudeville was more and more being relegated to the sticks and they liked it in Moncton. They decided to stay for six months, then a year, and then they never left. In their first years, Arthur started to organize a children's band using his own instruments and then the Burbanks went into real estate. Arthur was a capable carpenter and handyman, so they bought up big old houses and made them into apartments. After a while, Arthur let the band go but Maude wanted kids around, never having had any of their own, and she began tooting horns and trumpets she'd almost forgotten about. She would train a band herself, and the rest is Moncton history.

She began entering the youth bands in festivals and in 1949 at the New Brunswick Music Festival with a band of thirty teenagers, she struck gold. When the British judge commented that "this has been the sort of playing one hears from the best regimental bands in England," Maude had her best reward.

Her custom was to drill the youngsters as if they were her own military regiment, dressing them in jackets and capes and teaching with endless patience. But strict she was and on one famous public occasion she was heard to say through an open mike — "I'll paddle the whole bunch of you....I'll paddle you until you can't sit down."

Maude Burbank kept this sort of thing going when she herself was in her 70's and half the band instruments belonged to her. Sometimes she gave private tuition and Harold Cameron, a veteran local music buff, says he was her first saxophone pupil in 1921. At the age of 71 and feeling she was going rusty on the trumpet, Maude took a course under Ralph Fucillo, trumpet master at the Boston Conservatory. And she drove herself back and forth to Boston, which was nothing for her. In her widowhood, she thought little of driving alone to Florida and even to British Columbia. Maude Burbank was one of a kind.

One of the proudest moments of her life was the acceptance of an honorary doctorate in music from l'Université de Moncton when she was over 80. Even then she continued to teach young players and was rehearsing her band for a festival when she was stricken, ten days before her death. In her hands when she fell was a drawing of a dress she was designing for the festival. It was a red gown with a ball fringe. When she had discussed this one day with her longtime friend, Maizie Read had wondered about the appropriateness of the ball fringe. "But my dear," Maude Burbank replied, "you don't know anything about the stage."

When she was in her seventies and eighties, still vigorous and mentally keen, Mrs. Burbank played in a bridge club with the writer's mother. To a home-visiting exile it was like meeting a living legend remembered from childhood, a star, a celebrity, and now a dear old lady enjoying the last happy years of her life with gently aging cronies who could never, in their wildest moments, imagine performing on a vaudeville circuit. Maude Burbank never smoked or drank, considered it unladylike, but she loved to recount that story of the landlady who thought Arthur and Maude were living in sin. She played her last hand in 1967 and died soon afterward at the age of 87.

The early Moncton years of the Burbanks had also been the first years of "talking pictures." They had been the years of the rise of new businesses in Moncton and the changes in churchly alignments. The first talking picture to reach the city was, of course, "Bulldog Drummond." Then there were such marvels as "The Trial of Mary Dugan" and "Madame X". After that, there would soon be no more accompanists and pit orchestras except for such occasional vaudeville as continued. For such, the Burbanks were always on hand.

Those were the Moncton years when the Rotary Club was inaugurated locally, when Robert K. Buzzell started his battery and auto-electric business, when R.H. Bannon came to town as Eaton's head man to succeed A.H. Grainger, promoted chief of the Maritimes, Newfoundland, Bermuda etc. It was interesting that the sons of these business leaders who had come to Moncton from Toronto and Montreal would not only grow up in the city but remain to succeed in their own fields. And 1921 was when the gruff and able Jess Parsons set up his construction company, having come here originally from the Annapolis Valley to build Eaton's. His son, too, would take over the business and eventually move it on to a third generation, so that the names of Douglas Bannon, Leslie Buzzell, Jack Grainger and Lloyd Parsons would be nearly as well known in town as those of their once-newcomer fathers who inaugurated their particular operations.

Jess Parsons was a tough, driving boss who built a reputation for excellent institutional structures. His only son, Lloyd, a quiet, reserved man much different in temperament from his father, graduated in engineering from the famous Massachussets Institute of Technology. He was one of only four Monctonians known to have taken a degree there. He and his wife, who had been Brenda Burgess of Boston, became deeply interested in the restoration of the Free Meeting House, Moncton's most notable historic building.

Some years before this, in 1921, the Steadman street house of worship had marked its centennial. They with Alexander Pincombe prodded the civic officials into action, Pincombe doing a professional job of researching the House history and the Parsons' researching its architectural origins and setting the work in progress. Even in 1982 the work remains incomplete because civic interest has not matched that of its restoration promoters.

Chapter Seventeen

UP IN THE AIR WITH JENNY

From the day in 1921 when a barnstorming pilot flew his World War One "Jenny" low over the little city, Moncton has carried on a love affair with the air. More than that, as the region's distribution and passenger centre the flight industry has been an important and historic factor in the community's career. Whoever the first barnstormer was or whence he came is lost in the mists of aerial lore but his biplane stays fixed in the mind of a then second-grade schoolboy who is now writing this chronicle.

After he and other pupils of Sister Thomas Aquinas at Mary's Home school had once rushed *en masse* to the wide windows to watch the plane swoop low, the teacher decided one good look was sufficient. However, this one pupil couldn't resist and spent a long while after school writing one hundred times on the blackboard the word "A-E-R-O-P-L-A-N-E." For sixty years since it has been hard to spell it "airplane."

Seven years after that, when a Fairchild Airways skiplane brought down the first airmail on the Fitzsimmons Reservoir between the Irishtown and McLaughlin Roads on a January Saturday, the city surged with excitement. It was the real beginning of the air age. Weather forbade a takeoff for the Magdalens until Monday and the great bird of the air which landed on snow-covered ice was there to be gawked at and touched all day Sunday. Hundreds if not thousands poured out to look at the marvel.

Pioneer commercial flyers in Moncton are seen in front of airmail plane in 1929. Left to right are: H.S. (Junior) Jones, pilot; Arthur Jarvis, air engineer; Burton Trerice, pilot; Walter Flemming, flying club instructor; Romeo Belanger, air engineer; Al. Parker, air engineer; W.H. (Bill) Irvine, superintendent and pilot for Canadian Airways.

— courtesy Moncton Museum.

Another year after that again, on July 1 and July 2 of 1929, a great air pageant drew thousands to the Leger Corner airport on the old George Tingley farm later Moncton Downs Raceway. But perhaps the most extraordinary day in the history of aviation in Moncton was that day late in April of 1939 when the Russians landed. That story may be less important than other air events in the community, but it concerns some of Moncton's first flyers and as such deserves its place.

Before coming to that, there is the summary to be told of the city's air age beginnings. An excellent version of this has been given in the limited circulation and illustrated work edited by Roger Mills of Moncton. It is entitled *Five Decades of Flying — the History of The Moncton Flying Club.* While it is devoted specifically to the history of that remarkable organization which today is reputed as one of the better flight training schools in the world, there are references to Moncton's initial air activities, so that the references in this present work will be concerned only with a sketch of that period.

Assisting Mills in producing the valuable and attractive history were Donald S. McClure, Gordon Ducklow and Peter Fisher. McClure had been associated (and at this writing continues to be) with the Club longer than any of the others.

The club was formally established on July 1, 1929, when the first airport was at Leger Corner, now Dieppe. That was also the date of the first air pageant. One of the originators of the club and airport was Dr. Charles R. Baxter, who had been severely injured in Toronto during flight training for the Canadian Air Force in World War one. Instead of dampening his enthusiasm, he remained a flying buff all of his long life.

Somewhat later in the 1930's, Charley Baxter who was known as one of Moncton's all-time best storytellers, made an historic flight to Miscou Island on a mercy flight. In the dead of winter, he performed an emergency operation on a kitchen table. While he had anaesthetics with him, he had no assistant to administer them until he discovered that a local man had once been a male nurse in Montreal. He had volunteered and as it turned out knew a good deal about operating room procedures, although islanders had not known of it. As Baxter discovered, the fellow never told his fellow islanders that he had been a male nurse out of fear they would call him a sissy.

Dr. Charles R. Baxter's wife was the former Margaret Appleton whose father W.U. Appleton was the C.N.R. vice-president, and it was Baxter's connection with Appleton which influenced the city's most eminent executive to act as interim president when the flying club and airport-development organization got going. The first elected president, however, was Capt. William Dalziel and his executive members were Major Tim H. O'Brien, Capt. Harold N. Price, John W. Humphrey, W.V. Creaghan and R.T. "Dick" McCully. Others who joined the movement for a Moncton airport were A.H. Grainger, the Eaton chief; René Frechet, the architect; P.D. Ayer, a former mayor; C.H. Blakeny, the mayor, and Dr. L.N. Price. Other founders were David Hourston who took a leading role in the first air pageant, Dr. D.J. McLellan, M.F. Tompkins, A.J. Taylor and George Robertson.

The Moncton Airport Ltd. got matching dollars from the city and set up the port at Lakeburn. Its first field had one runway, downhill to facilitate takeoff speed, and the first flying club trainer was a Gypsy Moth.

When it was decided to hold the first and greatest air show in Moncton, it was called the "Monster Air Pageant to Celebrate Growth of Aviation in the East." Two students of the flying club, Reginald Melanson and Leonard Belliveau, were dispatched to tour the Maritime provinces to put out posters and drum up interest. They were chosen because they had the time and an available family car, something few of the students could boast in those years. Touring in the Maritimes was not yet common and they hit a good many backroads over which travel was, to say the least, adventuresome. More than once, in the absence of road maps, they took wrong roads. In the end, their efforts were so successful that when the pageant opened people came streaming in from all parts of the Maritimes. Admission was 50 cents. Parking cost 25 cents in the fields surrounding the aerodrome. There were free flights for lucky ticket-holders and a good many Monctonians had their first aerial thrill on that wondrous occasion. Others paid two dollars a ride.

Mrs. Lloyd W. Steeves, a sister of David Hourston, kept a copy of the pageant program which showed "Moncton's Senior Air Pilots" as being Captain Price, Captain Dalziel,

Miss Ruth C. Wilson, Moncton's first woman flyer, and David Hourston who was then secretary of the Moncton Flying Club and a student pilot.

Ambitious, the pageant's promoters invited the best known flying names in the world to come but, unfortunately, they couldn't make it. However, they sent nice messages and the names were led by Sir Arthur W. Brown, who first bridged the Atlantic by air with Sir John Alcock," (History's famous Alcock and Brown who flew out to Newfoundland non-stop to Ireland in 1919.) Then came the name of Charles Lindbergh, the first man to fly the Atlantic alone, and Lt. Col. W. A. "Billy" Bishop who became Air Vice Marshal Bishop, Canada's greatest war ace then.

Mr. Justice Arthur T. LeBlanc was chairman of the pageant committee and among notables who came were Maj.-Gen. the Hon. H.H. McLean, lieutenant-governor of New Brunswick who officially opened the new airport. The premier, Hon. J.B.M. Baxter, spoke and so did Sir Henry Thornton, president and chairman of the C.N.R., Dr. O.B. Price, M.P. and Mayor Blakeny. Among those mentioned most eminently was Capt. C.R. Troup, who had come from the Royal Air Force in Britain to fly the mail from Moncton to P.E.I. and the Magdalens. "He contributed largely," the promoters said, "to giving Moncton the advanced place it is beginning to take in Canadian air operations."

Aircraft were gathered from many places and were as varied as then existed. Stunts of the barnstorming era were part of the thrill as spectators gasped with excitement. The pageant was repeated in 1931 with limited success and, as Roger Mills has noted, in 1932 with no success at all.

First piloting licenses issued to students of the Flying Club went to Claude Keating, who became a legend in private flying in Moncton, to Arthur Snowdon of Point de Bute, N.B., and Alexander J. "Al" Lilly who was first to receive a commercial license from an instructor at Moncton airport. The instructor was Keating. Lilly, a native of Saskatchewan who had graduated in engineering, had been posted to Moncton by the Royal Canadian Mounted Police. And he was, as it happened, the first in this region to train and handle a tracking dog for the force. He left the force to join Imperial

Airways, (later British Airways) was in the Ferry Command of the R.C.A.F. during the war and later became a test pilot for Canadair. He became a senior executive with Canadair until his retirement to Moncton. He had married Genevieve Parsons of Moncton while he was with the R.C.M.P.

When the Commonwealth Air Training Plan came into existence with the onset of war in 1939, the Department of National Defense in Canada sent trainees to Keating and Snowdon for instruction. Claude Keating became manager for the department of Transport at Lakeburn; Lilly was made chief flying instructor and Snowdon his assistant. After Lilly left, Wylie Weeks came on as Snowdon's assistant. One of the best students the club ever turned out, Weeks later went to Chatham as an R.C.A.F. instructor, and returned to commercial flying with Maritime Central (now Eastern Provincial Airways). As the club left Moncton for Chatham, Donald McClure was able to lease the hangar, fuel house, workshop and office building for $10-a-month. He then bought two old aircraft, stitched them together and began his commercial school and charter service.

As well as training at Chatham, the pioneer Moncton club took over training at Neepawa, Manitoba. In both places it made a major contribution to the Canadian war effort in the air. Afterward, the Club made a comeback and carefully built up at the greatly enlarged Moncton airport a remarkable reputation as a flight training school. Students have come there from all over the world, and private flyers have considered the club's facilities and hospitality the best there are.

One name that should be mentioned in connection with the club is that of Tommy Gallant, a name held by two persons, father and son. Tommy Senior was the club's first chief engineer and came to be known as a man who knew everything there was to be known about private and small commercial aircraft. During the club's more than half century of existence, only he and his son have served in that capacity. If Tommy Sr. was a great mechanic, his son was thought by some to be even greater.

Pilot Walter Flemming flew into Moncton from Saint John one day in January of 1930, and his twenty-minute flight was claimed as a world record for air speed. He had travelled at 270 m.p.h. in a Stearman biplane, and it seemed as if another new age of speed and progress had arrived. Flemming had exceeded the previous record made the year before on "an Upper Canadian airmail route" by 70 m.p.h.

This was too fast altogether, and some experts in Moncton and elsewhere challenged the claim. Several weeks later, while offering proof, Flemming explained that, of course, unusual weather conditions had prevailed. There were "intensely strong tail winds."

It was the year of aviation excitement and in February of 1931, when Walter Fowler, another of the veteran flyers in Moncton, flew Dr. Euclide Leger to Buctouche with a consignment of insulin it was front page news. They took off in 20-below zero F. weather in a Canadian Airways craft and made the trip in twenty minutes, landing on the ice in Buctouche river. Joseph Michaud, a prominent area farmer and father of future Senator Hervé Michaud, was unconscious at home and the mercy mission was on his behalf. He did not survive. (The late Senator Michaud whose widow is the sister of the world-famed author Antonine Maillet, was a student at S. Joseph's university at the time.)

Fowler was to be one of the most successful flyers and executives of the Canadian commercial air age just beginning. A native of Sackville, N.B., he had learned to fly in Hamilton, Ontario, in 1928. After working for a while with Eaton's in Moncton and Montreal, he went to Detroit and in the fall of 1929 returned to Moncton as an aircraft mechanic. He took over from W.H. "Bill" Irvine as instructor for International Airways which later became Canadian Airways and operator of The Moncton Flying Club. The company also flew the mail to the Magdalen Islands.

After Fowler got his flight instructor's license at the Borden, Ontario, R.C.A.F. school, he flew for Canadian Airways until it became Trans-Canada. Among students then in Moncton who trained with him and others, were H.S. "Junior" Jones, Burton Trerice and Joseph Anderson, some of the Moncton flight students who made names for themselves in early Canadian flying. After this period, Walter Fowler transferred to bush operations out of Seneterre, Quebec, then to Winnipeg with T.C.A. which was formed in 1937. He was

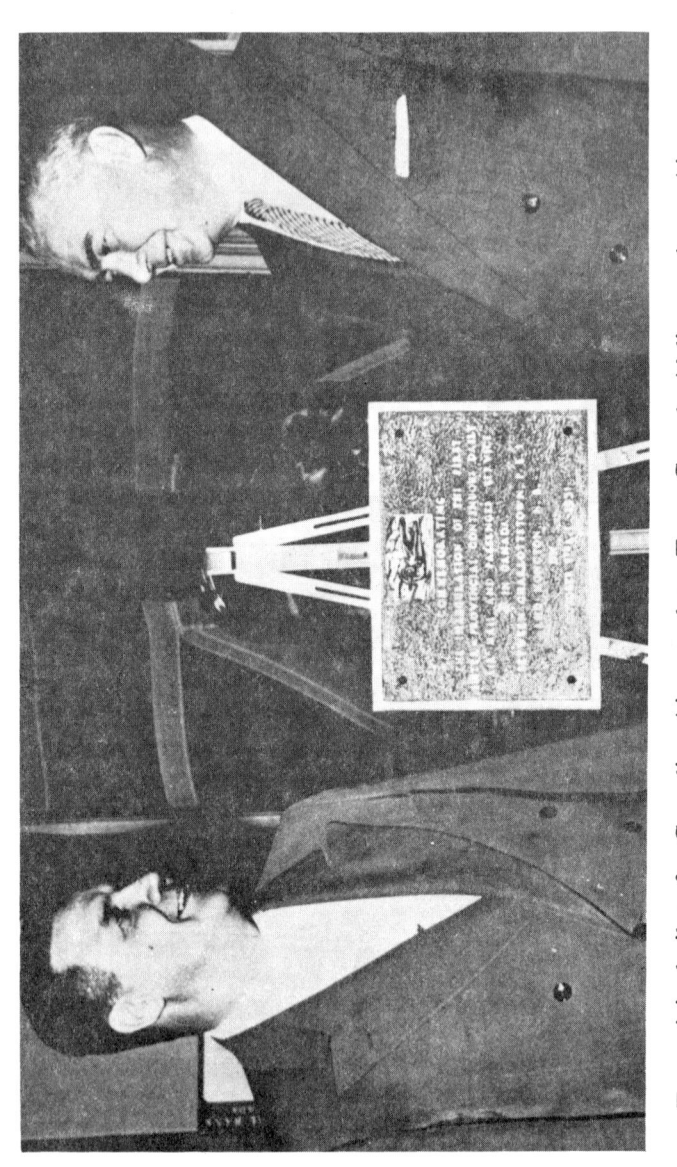

Two original pilots for Canadian Airways, later Trans-Canada Airlines and now Air Canada. At left, H.S. Jones and, right, Walter Fowler. Plaque between men commemorates "First inter-provincial continuous daily air mail and passenger service between Moncton and Charlottetown, Oct. 9, 1931."

— Air Canada photo

next on the Moncton-Montreal run as a pilot, first flying the Lockheed 10A (Vega) and then the Lockheed 14H which carried all of ten passengers.

Fowler left piloting to become assistant to the general manager of T.C.A. in Winnipeg in 1947 and afterward became executive assistant to the president responsible for the Atlantic area. He became general manager for T.C.A. and its successor, Air Canada, in the Atlantic provinces and remained so until he retired in 1971.

In the earliest days of the mail service, when Fowler whipped off to Prince Edward Island and then over the long water stretch to the Magdalens, it was a hazardous business. You flew only when the conditions were suitable, and then without navigation aids. It was 80 miles of open water without radio and nothing but a compass as a guide. Steel runners were attached to floats of the Fairchild 51 aircraft for ice and snow landings in winter. Most of the pilots who at one time or another in the beginning were on that run, Jones, Trerice, Garnet Godfrey, Jimmy Wade and Wiley Weeks are all part of Moncton's aviation history.

The Royal Canadian Air Force had done survey flights in the Moncton area between 1927 and 1931 to map out mail routes, and possible sites for overseas flying boats, and from 1937 had looked closely at Moncton as a prospective air base should war come.

As early as 1938, fearing war in Europe with Canadian participation, Moncton was chosen as the site of an equipment depot. Then, between 1939 and 1945, a total of nineteen air units and formations were established at Moncton and Scoudouc. As a pooling base, the city became known as "home" to tens of thousands of British commonwealth flight trainees, many of them who became famous during the war or afterward.

Soon after war was declared in September of 1939, the R.C.A.F. opened a recruiting station in Moncton. Then came the equipment depot, the service flying training school, the R.A.F. personnel depot, a transport squadron, repair and maintenance station, an inspection station and so on. Between October 1, 1939, and April, 1944, some 7,906 men and women were recruited by the R.C.A.F. in Moncton.

As a Canadian forces base during wartime and as a regional commercial air centre in peacetime, Moncton has been pre-eminent. All of which is worthy of a separate history. It is a story which deserves the knowledge and intimacy which only those involved can tell. Absent from this region during those years, the present writer is unable to do justice to that remarkable period in Moncton history. So it must await an historian who is competent to reconstruct the whole story.

The next big step in air travel for the region found *The Globe and Mail* of Toronto editorializing on the important fact that Moncton and Toronto were joined by an air service taking "only six hours, a saving of 24 hours in train travel." That was on November 13, 1939 when another "three silvery ships of the Trans-Canada Airline had inaugurated a feeder service from Moncton," taking passengers from Toronto and Montreal destined elsewhere in the Maritimes. They came "gliding down the broad runway of the airport at Lakeburn following closely upon one another, then headed for Halifax, Saint John and Charlottetown." This was to be a daily service linking all these cities to Montreal and beyond.

This plane flew first airmail Moncton to Halifax shows Pilot R.T. McCully about 1936.

— Courtesy Moncton Museum

The first T.C.A. plane landed in Moncton on October 5, 1939, to be welcomed by P.G. Johnson, a Trans-Canada executive, and various airline bigwigs from Montreal. There was also Mayor Blakeny and many distinguished local citizens on hand. The plane crew reported fine weather all the way and the flight took two hours and eight minutes in "a big Lockheed 14." The "big" Lockheed 14 carried ten passengers when loaded, flew without today's pressurization but at a low altitude and when the weather was rough it could be very bumpy indeed.

In the jubilee edition of *The Moncton Transcript* of 1975, it is recorded that the first Lockheed from St. Hubert airport, across the river from Montreal, came to Moncton on February 15, 1940, taking two hours and 20 minutes. (The October 5, 1939, flight had made it faster.) There is some confusion on these dates since *The Globe and Mail* set out the service as starting in November of 1939 while the Moncton newspapers indicate that this was when the feeder service out of Montreal was inaugurated. Whatever the case, all of those events were recorded in newspapers during the last months of 1939 so they must all have occurred in that year.

Chapter Eighteen

HARD TIMES AND CADILLACS

As the notorious decade of The Great Depression opened in Moncton on January 1, 1930, a few local people were planning to sail off to the West Indies on the Lady Hawkins out of Halifax. Clara Bow ("ain't she delish!") was at The Capitol movie theatre in "The Saturday Night Kid" fifty years before John Travolta and "Saturday Night Fever." Eaton's offered boys' overcoats for $6.45; men's tweed ulsters for $11.45 and women's fur-trimmed tweed overcoats for $22.45. Mixed chocolates were 19 cents a pound, jellybeans 15.

While phonograph records were very popular with "My Blue Heaven" and "The Two Black Crows," sheet music was still in demand. Favorites for singers standing beside the piano were "When My Dreams Come True" and "Singing in the Rain."

There were only a few ominous storm clouds gathering after the 1929 "Black Friday" stock market crash. Local newspapers reported stock brokers in Montreal and Toronto arrested for fiddling with the market, and soon a Moncton broker would be accused of misusing the investments of widows and orphans, and would eventually go to prison for it. It was the "Ponzi racket," as created by the notorious Boston Ponzi who kept investors happy for a time by paying them off with the new investors' funds which kept coming in. But then the funds stopped coming in.

The New Brunswick Federation of Labor meeting in Moncton in 1930 said that old age pensions, mothers' allowances and a minimum wage for women were among its objectives. They also wanted a minimum wage of 40 cents an hour for men and an eight-hour day. Some layoffs had begun and, early in the year a Moncton C.N. machinist hanged himself in a basement. The inquest report was that he "was mentally deranged."

Just the same, national brokerage houses were "showing widespread unrest" and raids were being made by police while patrons were demanding delivery of stock or their money back. In the summer there would be a federal election, and a New Brunswicker — whose nearest big town in childhood was Moncton — was about to inherit the mantle of Rt. Hon. W.L. Mackenzie King. The Rt. Hon. Richard Bedford Bennett of Hopewell Hill was coming to town to speak to a giant rally at the racetrack. King came to the Capitol. Bennett won.

There was great excitement in Moncton in those days of strong political attachments. Bennett was hailed as a local boy, and even the Liberals turned out to hear him. King, with those peculiar political antennae and crystal balls of his, played it cooler. He got a good house at The Capitol and he was most gracious.

The decade would be hard for many Monctonians but the stable character of railroad employment and the ability of Eaton's to maintain a fairly steady employment record helped keep things on a reasonable level. Old and well-established and well-financed merchants and suppliers like Sumner's and the lumbering companies managed to weather the storms. Because the Maritimes generally had not known the boom times of central Canada and the new West, there was a shorter way to go down.

Still, casual employment was hard to find. Relief rolls grew gradually because there was no such thing as unemployment insurance; no children's allowances. Old age pensions were mere pittances, yet they helped because the old folks lived at home with children and shared what they had. Before the decade was out, the city would be spending what was for then the huge sum of $1,000.00 a week on welfare payments. A good many once-prosperous business and professional people suffered as much as the working-class poor because they had been accustomed to more and now were terribly strapped. Some could not face "going on the dole" or asking for "relief" because they considered "being on relief" a shameful thing. In the end, for some, there was no choice.

At one stage, to get from under some of the burden, Moncton city fathers had the great idea of sending people "back to the land" including a good many who never had been *on* the land. They settled them at Gallagher Ridge, where cabins were provided and it was hoped people could scratch a living from hard scrabble ground. The people there often came close to starvation and struggled even to keep warm, and yet they survived and some even developed decent farms in the area and remained afterward.

In January of 1931 Moncton held a plebiscite to decide whether to keep the street railway going and also whether to reduce electric light rates. The citizens voted decisively against taking off the old cars which had about them a delightful air of Toonerville trolleys. On the other hand, the same citizens actually opposed a cut in lighting rates. Why people ever turned down a reduction is lost in the mists of time. *The Transcript* at the time said it was the result of the work of "two or three agitators who influenced the citizens" but did not explain further.

The New Year was ushered in by the annual ball in the Knights of Pythias Hall sponsored by the Bonar Law Chapter, I.O.D.E. The ball, with Ron Hutchinson's band, was a great success. The orchestra leader is not to be confused with Leverett "Huttie" Hutchinson who was also in the dance orchestra line. The former was son of the police chief, the latter son of the railroad dispatcher.

That year, 1931, was the first in which Monctonians had letters on their automobile license plates. One letter was to precede the numbers for easier identification. The motor car had not only come to stay but was increasing rapidly in numbers but most of them were still put up on blocks for winter, because driving was difficult.

In the Thirties Main street sidewalks were cleared better than roadway. Picture taken probably 1939, looking west.

MAYOR STOREY

Moncton's favorite traffic cop, Stanis ("Stanley") Richard with miniature park made to honor him at corner of Main and Church where he directed traffic for a generation. With him is Mrs. Richard and Foster Keith, a barber whose shop was nearby. Little girl is not identified, perhaps Stan's grand-daughter.
— Photo by H.B. Reid

Cars had trouble in snow because snow was not removed from all streets. Chains were cumbersome things to put over tires and, all in all, winter driving was hardly worth the effort. The Moncton newspapers had been agitating for the opening of highways and a *Transcript* front-page editorial said that "trunk roads in and out of the city should be kept open all winter. Loss of business to Moncton is enormous because of the closing of motor traffic." In Ontario, the editorial pointed out, "even in smaller centres this is being done with success and with heavy tractors now available it could be done here at small expense."

Four years later the paper was still fighting for the same thing and it was not until after the Dysart government was installed in Fredericton in 1935 that the winter openings began in earnest.

When the 1930's had moved into their second year, one of the pleasant Moncton events was the wedding of Jean Attis to Joseph Attis. There were more than 500 guests in the synagogue for the brilliant affair which was attended by all of the city's prominent civic, provincial and federal politicians. Miss Attis was the daughter of Mr. and Mrs. Louis Attis, two of Moncton's earliest and most prominent Jewish families, and her husband was the son of Mr. and Mrs. Harrison Attis, also of Moncton.

If things were getting tough as the depression set in, city councillors found some relief for themselves by voting to pay the mayor $600 a year and themselves $300. Prior to that, they had served voluntarily. At the same time, council reported that $19,000 had been spent on poor relief. This amount for one year would continue to rise until in 1935 it was about $50,000.

Too many non-residents were getting relief, the city councillors said. They called upon other jurisdictions to look after their own. There were, one alderman said, "cases of overlapping." Apparently, some unfortunates had actually been able to draw a pittance from each of two sources, and the righteous alderman couldn't countenance this though they themselves were all well fed.

In spite of the continuing downturn in the economy, J.E. Dodds, of Toronto, a director of Eaton's, arrived in town after touring part of the region and said things were just dandy. He found them "in good financial shape and no lack of evidence of prosperity here." One newspaper reported him as saying "he did not think we Maritimers knew much about hard times."

C. Hanford Blakeny, a former alderman, had been elected mayor in 1929 but in 1930 was defeated by C.W. Redmond. However, he was returned in 1931 and was to stay on the job through the worst four years of the depression. The lawyer, W. Emmett McMonagle, kept trying to knock him off without success but made it in 1936 after a one-year interregnum with Thomas H. King. McMonagle then was re-elected for four terms and proved himself a progressive chief magistrate.

In the meantime, as the early years of the decade went by, general economic conditions worsened and when Blakeny took over the mayor's office in 1934 things were at their lowest.

MAYOR A WHEELER   MAYOR BLAKENY

Unemployment was at its height and relief was confined to a family dole that ranged from $6.00 to $8.00 a week. The city began to operate soup kitchens. Camps were established by the province outside the city for homeless and single men who were given board and $3.00 a week. Then a relief bureau was set up at city hall.

That was the year when Luther T. Tingley became city clerk. He had been secretary to the chief clerk in the C.N.R. offices and was earning $2,700 a year. The city offered him $3,000 and he took it, but very soon he was back to $2,700 because all civic employees were docked 10 percent of their wages and salaries to maintain the welfare office. As he reached his 90th birthday in 1981, the remarkably preserved Tingley recalled those days and the calls of distress which came to city hall. Many people went there directly seeking help. The mayor, Blakeny, worked day and night and the city clerk was on the same shifts. On one winter day in that bleak year of 1934, a cold and hungry crowd gathered at city hall and a riot was feared.

Blakeny was called hurriedly and talked to the shivering and threatening gathering. He told them none would go hungry, without clothing or a place to sleep, and they finally dispersed. That same night he summoned council in emergency session and authorized money for food and clothing depots and to pay overdue rentals. It would also provide work.

Those were distressing days in Moncton and though "Ford" Blakeny would soon go on to higher levels of politics, nothing he afterward achieved did him more credit than his performance at city hall when Moncton was mired in the depths of unemployment before the days of unemployment insurance and family allowances. Tingley remembered how even people who owned Cadillacs would come to city hall for food chits, because they might own the unsalable cars but had no income to buy food, let along run the cars.

Blakeny moved the city's annual budget up to about $150,000 and new bonds were issued to cover the extra expenditures to assist the impoverished.

Lou Tingley had, after World War One, gone to work with the C.N.R. as private secretary to Fred O. Condon, the assistant chief engineer, and stayed with the railway until he went to city hall. He remained there until 1967 when, forced to retire at 66 — having been allowed to stay on an extra year — he accepted a similar post in the new Town of Oromocto. He then retired in 1973 at the age of 72. He had worked with Moncton mayors from Blakeny through Harris Joyce and in his alert 90's had some acute observations.

After Blakeny, the hard-trying W. Emmett McMonagle "was a good mayor and that's why he stayed so long." J. Edward Murphy, the youngest-ever mayor but two, was thought by Tingley to be one of the best, "a good administrator." T. Babbitt Parlee was "a brilliant, clever fellow," and Gregory F.G. Bridges who later became chief justice of New Brunswick, was "solid." To Tingley, Thomas H. King as mayor was "well-meaning" and Arthur Stone "an interim mayor." He considered Harris Joyce the man "who set the stage for the city's modern growth and present extent." For Mayor Frank W. Storey, who was first elected in 1940 and remained until 1945 and returned again in 1949, Tingley had a special affection.

Storey was mayor when the council considered extending the old Moncton Hospital on King street. The plan was to add four storeys for doctors' offices and administration at a cost of $1,000,000. Storey held that this didn't make much sense. What was needed was more hospital beds so he vetoed the move. Then he talked with Donald A. McBeath who owned a tract of land in the northwestern part of the city and McBeath deeded land freely. Storey moved to put out a $2,000,000 bond issue and convinced the County of Westmorland to add $1,000,000 more. Frank Storey then saw the project through and the present Moncton Hospital was the beneficial result.

Storey, a Moncton native, was an early manager for Imperial Oil and the service station his company set up at the corner of St. George and Highfield streets was the first such station uptown. It was leased by Ralph McMichael and Karl Barss, the latter being a son of the first Imperial Oil manager in Moncton.

A jolly and gregarious fellow, Frank Storey was the son of George Storey, a religious railroad engineer who ran between Saint John and Moncton. George was one of the pillars of the Reformed Baptist church on Queen street when the family lived in what was known as the Gunning house on Church street. His son, Frank, joined the oil company in Saint John and came to Moncton as resident manager about 1915, remaining in that post for the rest of his life with a short hiatus in Halifax. Married to Ethel Green of Saint John, he went into politics as an alderman and was eventually chairman of the municipal finance committee before becoming mayor.

In this, he created a still unbeaten record. He was elected more times than any in the city's history, though Leonard C. Jones served longer. Storey was chosen six times for one-year terms, while Jones was elected five times for two-year terms and thus was longest in office.

When Emmett McMonagle was mayor, I had begun writing a daily newspaper column of comment. Though good friends, we carried on a sort of running battle. McMonagle was always helpful to the press at city hall and well liked, but the column attacks got under his skin. One day he said: "Hell's bells, man, isn't there a single thing I can do right?" There was. He was a notably good public speaker with a magnificent voice and a fluency not bettered by anyone in town or beyond.

Once, when he was preparing to honor Moncton's Gordon Drillon, the noted Toronto Maple Leafs hockey player and the N.H.L.'s leading goal scorer, he wanted to be particularly effective. He called me into his office and asked if I'd read the draft. "Do you want me to be candid or candied, Mac?" I asked as he glared hard. "All I want is your opinion — for what it may be worth." The speech was loaded with verbal gardenias, marvellous and mellifluous, almost a work of art, but hardly suited to the welcoming of a hockey player. When I had read it over carefully I said: "Mr. McMonagle, you should be in Chautauqua, on the circuit. You're magnificent. But don't you think it's a little flowery for the occasion?"

Next day, he laid it on, word-for-word as it was written. Maybe he just wanted to show his critics who was boss in town, or maybe it had been just so overpowering to his senses that he couldn't resist.

To return to "Ford" Blakeny who went from city hall to the legislature and cabinet: He was the son of Sherman Blakeny of the old Sunny Brae and Moncton family which had been in the coal and ice business since 1915. C. Hanford Blakeny had been leader of the Conservatives in the mock parliament of Mount Allison in 1914. Later, he worked as a typesetter and then articled in law briefly with C.W. Robinson. He ran the *Busy East* (later the *Atlantic Advocate*) for a few months and then went into business with his father.[1]

After he had been mayor, and having been an active Conservative party worker, he was asked to stand for the Liberal nomination. Blakeny had fallen out with the Tories over the unemployment problem. Then, as he himself wrote in *The Story Of A Business*, his supporters had packed the Liberal nominating meeting before supporters of his rivals, E.A. Fryers, Sr., and James Friel, could get in. He won the nomination and ran against the long-powerful E.A. Reilly, A Tory cabinet minister, to win.

That was in 1935 and, though many of the Liberal old guard never forgave him, he was re-elected in 1939, in 1944 and again in 1948. Defeat came from T. Babbitt Parlee who himself would afterward become a mayor. Blakeny was named Speaker of the legislature in 1939 and later was minister of education.

He would prove to be one of the most effective ever to hold that portfolio.

The provincial school system was in poor shape when he took over and Blakeny's greatest contribution was the establishment of the county unit system of education. Before that, control had been located in local district school boards and this made for much inequality since some districts were poor and others prosperous. Towns and cities could support better facilities and better trained teachers while rural areas were often sadly deprived. The county unit system made the counties responsible for education within their borders and spread opportunity more evenly. As would be seen even forty years later, when the Robichaud government's educational reforms brought about far more radical changes, there was still a long way to go in New Brunswick. But the Blakeny reforms were an essential and valuable first step.

Hon. C. H. Blakeny's governmental example was followed by his son-in-law who had joined him in the business some years after this. He was Lestock G. DesBrisay, the descendant of New Brunswick politicians who had made choppy waves in legislatures of earlier times.

The Hon. L. G. "Dud" DesBrisay represented Moncton in the provincial house. During his entire ten years as a sitting member, he was minister of finance and one of the most notable in the province's history. It was during his terms of office that the Equal Opportunity Program was enacted which, for the first time in New Brunswick history, really did provide a great measure of equality in educational opportunity. Local school taxation was removed from property and centralized to be paid from general revenues; teachers were paid on the basis of training and on the same scale in city or country. That in itself was a revolution.[2]

There was one bright spot in the 1930's and there had been nothing like it in Moncton's long history of sports and entertainment. That was the hockey team that made the city's name famous across Canada, the Moncton Hawks, the original and Allan Cup winners.

The city had built a stadium for them and they became local heroes, though most of the players were from Winnipeg and other points west of New Brunswick. It was Hawk fever, and it was virulent, but it was a blessing for it gave the citizens a lift when everything else was in gloom. It even came to the point that Gordon Dustan, a brilliant local scholar who had been through seven universities and now had time on his hands, wrote of the games in poetically measured stanzas.

Moncton had opened its fine new hockey arena in the fall of 1930 and called it The Stadium. Long a hockey town, there had been the Moncton Victorias — not the originals of Stanley Cup fame but a revived version and they were the first home team for the Stadium. Mostly local players, the team included Frank Quinn, Eddie Kervin, Fred "Fatty" Gould (another Gould was "Niggity") and Wick James, Steve Estabrooks, Tom Radford, Joe Mills, Jack Ingram, Copie LeBlanc, Charley Wilson, Harold Grant and Percy McKenzie. They played in the Southern New Brunswick league. However, it was the formation of the Moncton Hawks which

Famous Moncton Hawks, winners of Allan Cup national amateur hockey title. The 1933 team seen here, starting from top centre and going clockwise: Goaler Jimmy Foster; Bill Gill, Bill Walker, Aubrey Webster, Knucker Irvine, Bert Connolly, Frankie LeBlanc, Trainer "Jigger" Smith, Monty Muckle, Sam McManus, "Duke" McDonald, "Dud" James, Bill Miller, Len Burrage. Man with hat is Coach Percy Nicklin and, at right, Ambrose Wheeler, manager.
— Reid Studio Photo

really inspired the sports fans and, after their first year, inspired everybody for it seemed that all of Moncton had become hockey mad.

The city had never forgotten the original Victorias, the team which won Maritime titles three years in a row in 1907, 1908 and 1909, and with reinforcements went on later to play the Quebec Aces for the Stanley Cup, losing in two straight games. But that was another generation. Now a group of Moncton businessmen centred about Sumner Co. executives supported the idea of importing young hockey players.

The Red Indians

Top Row, left to right: Fred (Fatty) Gould, coach; A. Duddridge and H. Lounsbury representing the sponsors; A.M. (Doc) LeBlanc, manager. The players are, left to right: Len LeBlanc, Harold Ingram, Raymond Malenfant, René Boudreau, Jim Innes, Amedée (Meddy) Cormier, Rheese Dickie, George Wolstenholme, Ernie Carey, Claude Bourque, "Tiki" Gould and Alfred (Babe) LeBlanc. Claude Bourque later played goal for Les Canadiens of Montreal, in the N.H.L. The Junior Red Indians were Maritime champions in 1933 and played for the national championships.

Supposedly amateurs, they were offered jobs in local establishments and some actually worked at these part time. In the Canadian West, economic conditions had produced far worse unemployment than the Maritimes and first-rate hockey players were attracted by the generous offers from Moncton. It was said at the beginning that new Hawks were paid a scandalous $45.00 a week. Since they were called amateurs, this was drawn from the firms which put them on their payrolls. In time, this was considered enough of a scandal that Maclean's Magazine carried a hot exposé which caught national attention.

The splendid new Stadium burned to the ground in October of 1931 but nothing could deter the fever. In the amazingly rapid time of 19 days it was re-built through insurance payments and the initiative of the promoters.

Managed by Ambrose Wheeler, a former mayor and construction company head, the club's business was handled by Budd A. Taylor, another former mayor. Coached by the masterly Percy Nicklin, the team won the amateur championship of Canada and the treasured Allan Cup in 1933 and Monctonians went wild. They did it again in 1934, and Red Burnett, the veteran Toronto Star hockey columnist, years later told this writer the Hawks were probably the best team ever assembled outside the National Hockey League.

The Hawks success inspired younger teams then and for a generation afterward. Gordon Drillon, one of the juniors who began playing on rinks around McAllen's Lane before going to the Toronto Maple Leafs, was the greatest right-winger and highest scorer ever produced in the Maritimes. A Moncton junior team, The Red Indians, once went into national playoffs and their goal-tender, Claude Bourque, starred later with the professional Montreal Canadians.

1. Moncton's first coal merchants were the Winter family, later to be major real-estate holders They followed W. MacKenzie Weldon and J.E. Masters, a retired sea captain whose business was eventually taken over by Isaac Selick & Sons.

2. A detailed story of these reforms is told in *Little Louis and the Giant K.C.* by J. E. Belliveau (Lancelot Press, 1980)

Chapter Nineteen

GRAMMAR, PAPERS and POLITICS

In the hungry years before the Forties, certain old family fortunes took a beating. Some small businesses collapsed, others struggled on, while a few who kept their hands on the levers of finance and industry prospered. And there were new men in town who built up sizeable estates on the earnings of enterprises made possible by the willingness of needful employees to work for very low wages. Among these were the owners of *The Moncton Transcript* and the broadcasting business just getting well into stride.

Otty Ludwick Barbour,[1] of an old Albert County family which became eminent among Saint John business leaders, had been brought in to run the evening newspaper by the heirs of John T. Hawke and other shareholders. He was a lawyer who never practised, had been a newspaper editor in Saint John and with a news service in New England. Barbour was lured in by an arrangement which allowed him to acquire a minority of shares on a pay-as-you-can-earn basis. Senator Robinson, whose father had founded the paper, gave him other shares in trust. Then he bought gradually from the Hawke and Lodge families and eventually held majority control. However, upon his death, the Robinson shares went back to the senator who then assumed financial control until the newspaper was sold to a new group supporting Jack K. Grainger which eventually sold out to the Irving interests.

BARBOUR OF *THE TRANSCRIPT*

Barbour was the first Moncton newspaper publisher to pay more attention to advertising revenues than to news and political partisanship. Because of the newspaper's blatantly Liberal tradition and the fact that other shareholders — especially Clifford Robinson — were important supporters, he could not be quite independent. Still, little by little, he weaned the paper away from the more flagrant political bias. Eaton's had become the biggest advertiser and Barbour catered to them and they were presumed to be politically independent, albeit with strong Conservative leanings. *The Transcript's* circulation was greater than that of *The Daily Times,* the Conservative supporter, and it was concentrated within the city. As an evening newspaper, *The Transcript* was a more attractive advertising medium. Barbour insisted on good news coverage, though he wouldn't spend much to get it. He pushed circulation, promoted advertising, did job printing and book binding which fulfilled good government and railway contracts (when the federal government was Liberal) and did provincial work when the Grits were in charge of the province.

When most citizens were struggling to emerge from the stringencies of mid-Depression, O. L. Barbour in the Thirties was earning some $50,000. a year personally. He lived modestly in a bungalow at the corner of Highfield and Mountain Road and stayed close to his business. A widower, he travelled only once in a while but once during the dreary years he was preparing for a long winter vacation in Nassau, sailing on the "Lady Boats." He didn't much enjoy it because it was very hot in The Bahamas and air conditioning was not invented. On his return, Barbour complained that he'd had to change his shirt four times a day. This didn't win him much sympathy back home where most of his employees had trouble enough paying for appropriate winter wear.

And yet, there was a hidden streak of generosity in Otty Barbour where his own money was concerned as opposed to the company funds. He was charitable but he didn't want it known. However, where business was involved, he was closer than the wainscoting on his old-fashioned office walls. Prying a pay increase from him could be a strenuous trial, especially if you were in the news department which was a cost-factored section and not a profit-generating one.

When this reporter, after a year at work, sought an increase from the eight dollar-a-week starting pay, Barbour would respond by saying there was a lineup of young people awaiting jobs of any kind. Three years later, working as a reporter, teletype news-watcher, proofreader and late-afternoon mail clerk (wrapping papers for the mail circulation), the approach to Barbour was with greater confidence.

Nabbed as he was getting ready to leave for Nassau and could hardly plead poverty, he promised something would be done upon his return. Some months after that he yielded a handsome two dollars-a-week increase.

Ott Hicks who had come up from Sackville some years earlier, was supporting a wife and family on what could not have been more than $18. a week, and he was a senior editor. Bill Hutchinson, the police chief's son, a mature man with a family, a war veteran, was sports editor and was paid no more. However, he knew people at city hall and from them we determined that Barbour had paid income tax on earnings of $50,000. With this information, unified action was considered. There was no immediate result but things did begin to improve.

Barbour had taken on one young fellow from Georgetown (Parkton) as a kind of printer's devil-cum-errand-boy and paid him six dollars-a-week. His name was Eddie White and he had to walk to and from work, arriving early in the morning to get the fires going in the press room. One day the publisher called him into his office and said he would have to dress better. Those tattered mis-matching coats and pants and a mackinaw jacket were not suitable for a young man carrying messages for the august newspaper and pushing a cart up Main street loaded with mail bags headed for the afternoon trains.

"How can I buy clothes?" Eddie asked Barbour. "I have no money for that. I don't have enough money for anything."

Barbour: "Well, I'll lend it to you." He instructed White to save a dollar a week and pay him back when it was accumulated. After a year or so, White said he had the money to repay the loan. "What loan," Barbour asked. "You don't make enough money to make loans. However, you seem to have learned how to save it. Always remember to save something from your earnings." The next week he gave Eddie a dollar more.

A few days after O. L. Barbour died suddenly in May of 1936 on a trip to Fredericton, an elderly resident of Campbell street asked me to come to his home. He was John Doyle, a retired railroader who represented the St. Vincent de Paul Society, a Catholic charitable organization operating without publicity to help the most needful. I was a local newspaper columnist and Doyle wanted to have it made known, now that Barbour was dead, that he had been a major supporter.

He said that the publisher had once invited him to his office and questioned him closely on the work of the society. He was particularly interested in the work being done for families with children and said he would help whenever there were children needing assistance. But it must be on the understanding that no one except Doyle himself would know of his contributions. "There never was a case that I took to him when he did not do whatever was asked. He told me: 'Whenever you have a boy or girl to feed or clothe, just look after them and I'll be good for it.' He was and now I think it should be known. Otty Barbour was a charitable man."

He had no children of his own and his wife, the former Miss Jameson of Saint John, had died in the 'flu epidemic of 1918. He never remarried.

Later, to the surprise of most employees, Barbour included every member of his staff in his will. He left $250,000. to the University of New Brunswick for scholarships to Albert County students. To his managing staff he left sums ranging from $1,000. to $2,000. which in 1936 was substantial. To all employees with him more than a year he left $200. and to those with less service $100. It is indicative of the comparative value of dollars between then and now in 1982 that I used my $200. for a trip through the United States to Louisiana, stayed there for more than a month and returned home by bus via the East coast of the United States. The only additional funds I had were the two-dollars-a-day *The Transcript* paid me for writing a daily column, mailed from wherever I was.

Both Otty Barbour and Bruce Robb, his editor and one of the finest gentlemen ever to work in journalism, had a fetish for the proper use of English. Both had studied law but did not practise it, having been summer reporters on Saint John newspapers who stayed in the craft when law offered little opportunity. Highly literate men, neither allowed a word out of place or a word misspelled and not a typographical error ever got by them. Each afternoon when the first papers were off the presses, they went through the pages with fine-tooth combs and woe betide the writer or proofreader who had committed a grammatical slur, got a fact wrong or spelled a name improperly.

Barbour once recalled that when he was a young man working in Boston he had bought a copy of Meiklejohn's Grammar and every day at lunchtime he would sit in a nearby park and read it. As an editor, he would advise a writer: "You don't write that someone returned *from* a vacation because a vacation is not a place. You return *after* a vacation. You don't write that someone has come home *following* a trip abroad because he wasn't *following* anything. He came home *after* being somewhere. Don't ever write that a dead person's body is lying at its *late* home. The body may be *late* but the home isn't."

Barbour had a strong sense of press freedom and the importance of public business being open to the public. An incident in 1935 soon after Thomas H. King became mayor is an interesting illustration. King, a successful lumber dealer who came to Moncton from his native River Hebert in Nova Scotia, decided it would be more efficient to hold council committee meetings in camera, or at least without benefit of press. The publisher protested but the meetings went on. Then Barbour began a series of front-page editorials written by himself and headed: "Behind Closed Doors." My job was to go to city hall and request admittance to every committee meeting, especially that of the finance committee. On being refused entrance, I was to phone Barbour day or night and tell him. Each time he went back to the editorial. Finally, under the pressure, King opened the meetings.

Years afterward, I met King in the Mount Royal Hotel in Montreal and he wanted to reminisce over coffee. He said that, after the episode, Barbour had ordered his name kept out of the paper and King never forgot the distress the whole affair had brought him.

There was never any doubt of King's sincerity and little question but that he had sought nothing more than efficiency and quick dispatch of civic business. In short, he had acted like a businessman which is always a difficulty in politics. There was a pathetic side of this closed-door story which King related that day in Montreal. "The day after I was elected," he recalled, "I bought a subscription for my mother in River Hebert. She would consider it quite an honor for a boy from a little village to become mayor of the city, but she never saw my name or picture in print while I was mayor. Barbour had given instructions that, because I had opposed him, and was still in office, the paper would refer only to "the mayor, never to Mayor King."

After a year in the post, Tom King returned to his private life, a decent man and a good citizen who had made the mistake of arousing a powerful publisher in a moment of crusading zeal.

After Jack Grainger and his investors bought out *The Transcript* in the late 1930's it fell away rapidly from political partisanship even though its morning rival remained in the Conservative fold. Grainger had no interest in politics nor was newspaper crusading his thing.

After a time, he was able to bring J. C. Keating into a merger. Keating had acquired control of *The Times*. Together, the newspapers for a little while maintained a slight pretext of representing particular political parties but soon they were maintaining what they called a position of independence. But from then until now both papers (They now have the same editorial page content; in fact, it is identical) have a consistently heavy list toward the Conservative side and certainly to conservatism. Grainger eventually bought out Keating and then, in 1948, sold out to the Irving interests.

Increasingly, the newspapers became morning and afternoon versions of the same paper and, having the same editorial views, this was a loss to a community which had a tradition of seeing at least two sides of public issues debated and interpreted.

New Brunswick Publishing Co. Ltd., controlled by the Irving family, negotiated so secretly with Grainger and his backers that even senior employees of the newspapers were

KEATING OF THE *TIMES*

unaware for years of the takeover, since Grainger remained as head man in Moncton. It was said, without confirmation, that the sale had been for $100,000. cash, plus $10,000. yearly for ten years while Grainger as publisher was paid a salary for the position. Actually, he remained well beyond the ten years, and it was only in 1980 that he went permanently to live in Florida and Edward W. Larracey, an old *Times* hand who had been with the amalgamated paper for years, was named publisher.

There was no interference from the new buyers (Irvings) and the business went on as usual except that eventually a general manager responsible to the owners was installed. While Jack Grainger was titular head of the Moncton operation after the papers changed hands, he was so unfamiliar with K. C. Irving that the latter did not know him by sight. When the Irving oil refinery was formally opened at Saint John in 1960, Grainger had to be introduced to Mr. Irving.

Indeed, K. C. Irving was known to visit the newspaper headquarters in Moncton only once; a son attended the annual business meetings. On one occasion, K. C. Irving was waiting outside in a car when the paper's publisher invited him to come inside. It was his first visit; he did not attend the business meeting but reminisced with the publisher about the days when his father, J. D. Irving of Buctouche, and Publisher John T. Hawke were friends.

1. Barbour insisted on use of his initials rather than his given names of Otty Ludwick, his extreme dislike of them probably because their Germanic sound caused embarrassment during World War One. However, as his nephew, W.A. Wilson, a noted Canadian journalist, learned much later, he was called Otty for an Albert County family which originated in Yorkshire not Pennsylvania or Germany. Where the Ludwick name originated is not known.

When circus came to town in late 1930's, parades were held to attract public to performances. Here is the great caliope and elephants going up subway hill on Main street. It was Robinson Brothers Circus.

Chapter Twenty

RISE OF WEALTH AND POWER

If, in the years between 1900 and 1915 "The French question" had been an issue between Irish Catholics and those of French origin, it had become something quite different after 1930. The proportion of Moncton's Acadian population to that of the general population had increased considerably but, what was more important, it was now staking out for itself a much more potent position in the social structure. Still, the argument between the Irish and French within their own ecclesiastical structure had one more vital step to take before a kind of uneasy truce would settle into an acceptable tranquility.

Those reading this now, having noted the many controversal events which arose between 1930 and 1980, will appreciate how strikingly the French-speaking leadership had latterly moved into a secular pattern. They will also have seen in this city, that the linguistic controversies of the Sixties and Seventies were no longer between two groups within one religious community as much as between citizens in general. Moreover, the increase in bilingualism had by the 1980's made the two official Canadian languages common. It had also, perhaps, marked a new maturity where, in the everyday fact of living together, there existed as much linguistic tolerance as anywhere in the country.

Earlier, Moncton had sometimes been branded as "Redneck City North." That period had been one of transition.

By the mid-1920's there had been in the city five French-language societies including l'Alliance Nationale. Of these the most important by far was la Société l'Assomption with its head office in the Banque Provinciale building. Soon after this it would take over much larger quarters in what became known as l'Evangeline Building on Westmorland street next door to *The Transcript.*

The Assumption Society, to use its English name, was neither a Moncton nor Maritime organization in origin but rather an Acadian fraternity which had started among French-speaking New Brunswick expatriates in New England. While Henri P. LeBlanc, of Moncton, Dr. Lucien Belliveau, of Shediac and A. J. Leger, the Moncton lawyer,[1] had been among those who helped set it up, the organization began as a death benefit group. Its first organizer in 1900 was Louis Doucet, a displaced New Brunswicker, at Gardiner, Mass., and it was created as a society at Waltham, Mass., in 1903.

Henri P. LeBlanc, the Moncton orator who had been educated for the priesthood but dropped out before ordination, helped set up the lodges in Massachusetts. Then, in 1902, a scholarship fund was started and from this the fraternal society developed. Most of the Acadians in New England were poor and, while at first the idea of a little sum put aside for sickness or burial was paramount, the understanding that education would be the elevator to a better life soon took strong hold.

The first Canadian branch of the Assumption Society was formed at Buctouche in 1904 and from there it has grown into what today is a major international mutual insurance company based in Moncton. Historians of the Acadian rise after their return from the exile of 1755 to make New Brunswick their new homeland, say that "la Société l'Assomption" may be credited with "la rénaissance Acadienne." There can be little argument with this conclusion.

While it was reorganized in 1960 from an Acadian fraternal and benefit society and then in 1969 became l'Assomption Compagnie Mutuelle d'Assurance Vie (The Assumption Mutual Life Insurance Company) and fully bilingual, the society had been for many decades principal communicator for the Acadians. That was particularly so between 1935 and 1960 because the National Association of Acadians had ceased to function and remained out of the picture until a social and political restructuring took place after 1960.

Left: A view of Moncton's Assomption Place, the city centre. On left is side of Beauséjour Hotel Centre is Assomption office building and, at right, Moncton's city hall. Right: SIMON BUJOLD, president Assumption Mutual Life Insurance Co. (Assomption Compagnie Mutuelle d'Assurance-Vie.)

The society which became an insurance company, by 1980, had assets of $100,000,000. The annual report issued for 1979 showed assets of $97,733,692. with $16,897.00 paid to policy-holders and beneficiaries, revenues of $13,641,693. and net income of $774,478. Furthermore, by then, it was the financier of Moncton's city hall complex.

l'Evangeline, which we have met before in this narrative, started as a weekly, became a bi-weekly, then a weekly again in 1922. It became a daily newspaper in 1931. There had been a drive for funds in 1930 and, supported by the Assumption Society, the paper began a fight for concessions to Acadians. Not only in Moncton, of course, but Moncton was the centre. Demands made by its editor were mainly in the field of education. After fourteen months as a daily, it reverted to a bi-weekly, not becoming a daily again until the first Acadian archbishop had been installed in 1936.[2]

When poverty had hit the French-speaking areas of the Maritimes particularly hard by 1934, and Alfred Roy was editor of *l'Evangeline*, government patronage was the vital source of work. Hon. L. P. D. Tilley, a Conservative, was premier and the newspaper began a series of editorials calling for reform. Some commentators thought of them as jeremiads which demanded, among other things, a French-language normal school. That would be four decades more in coming and, without it, the training of teachers for children of the French language would remain difficult and sparse.

In the same year that Roy began his series, the Assumption Society, acting as the voice of the Acadian people, launched a campaign of its own. This was intended to forge an economic power in Moncton. The Society asked that in all stores French-speaking people use their own language. The society asked for services to be provided in that language, and suggested that Acadians buy where French was available. Eaton's was struck first in a half-hearted boycott (45 years later it seemed to have a preponderance of bilingual clerks) but the campaign had very limited success with small business.

In February of 1935, the Canadian National vice-president and regional general manager instructed his staff to reply in the same language to correspondence received in French. He asked that this policy be rigorously put into effect.[3]

All of this produced a foreseeable backlash and an organization called The English-Speaking League arose to combat the spread and influence of the French language. There was another element excited in Moncton in May of 1935 when, during a radio program marking the jubilee of King George V, French as well as English was used by government leaders in delivering their message of respect and homage.

Rev. A. K. Herman in a series of sermons, along with the English-speaking League, helped build up a feeling of antipathy. On one occasion he advertised that "many priests and bishops will attend a service in Highfield Baptist Church." This brought criticism from the English-language press but Mr. Herman explained that he was using "priests and bishops" in the Biblical sense that all believers were priests and bishops. In the railway offices, despite the vice-president, there were attempts to boycott French and a great deal of disturbance stirred in Moncton. When Anna Malenfant, a Moncton Acadian native who had gained international notice for her voice, appeared in a Moncton Community Concert series, only one hundred members turned out.

It was not a happy period in local history. An Acadian committee, called "servile" by more ardent compatriots, wrote in English a letter to the press blaming the Catholic-French clergy for megalomania and said the French-speaking campaign had misrepresented the true state of affairs between English and French. The letter called for cooperation and understanding. At this stage in Acadian development, some of the French clergy were dominant, even arrogant, a condition which would not serve them well a generation later when a kind of internal backlash developed among the faithful which relegated the clergy to a much lesser position in Acadian society.

The 1935 disruptions, exacerbated in mid-Depression when hardship was endemic in New Brunswick, were reflected in the provincial general election. Together, English and French joined to expel the Conservative Tilley government and in Moncton the vote was dominantly Liberal. Yet when Premier A. A. Dysart formed his government and appointed only one Acadian to the cabinet, the new provincial secretary, Hon. Clovis Richard, some Acadians accused him of "treason." Later, he responded by naming Gaspard Boucher minister without portfolio and chairman of the Hydro Commission.

The Acadian feelings were the more hurt because it was clear that the 1935 Liberal victory had been very much affected by the almost total Liberal support from French constituencies. Dysart, himself of Buctouche, was the English member for the predominantly French constituency of Kent. In Moncton, a few minor jobs went by government patronage to Acadians but otherwise the joy was not exactly unrestrained. What the election had done, in Moncton and elsewhere in the province, however, was to stir French-speaking New Brunswickers politically as they had not been stirred since 1917. They had found their voting power in 1935, and thereafter were more politically active. This culminated a quarter century later in the election of the first Acadian elected as premier.

Those were among the secular manifestations which in Moncton were affecting the social structure as the people of Acadian origin became increasingly more numerous and gradually more influential in the city's life. In the religious sphere, and with Acadians that still then remained the most vital aspect of their society, talk of a new ecclesiastical diocese had been renewed.

On March 20, 1933, Most Rev. Thomas O'Donnell, archbishop of Halifax, was informed by Bishop LeBlanc of Saint John and Bishop P. A. Chiasson of Chatham, that the Pope had been asked to create a third diocese in New Brunswick. Indeed, it would be an archdiocese having for its head an archbishop with the seniority of a metropolitan.

Establishment of the archdiocese of Moncton was announced in December of 1935 and its formal erection designated for March of 1936 by Pope Pius XI. Rev. Louis Joseph Arthur Melanson, a native of Balmoral in Restigouche county, New Brunswick, was named the world's first Acadian archbishop. He had been bishop of Gravelbourg, Saskatchewan, a modest and diplomatic man whose personality helped heal the scars of a long and bitter dispute. His installation was attended by Very Rev. Edward Savage, the old opponent of English-French parish division, on February 22, 1937, along with the fullest representation of priests and hierarchy, both French and Irish.

In his published correspondence, Father Savage concluded by writing: "Roma locuta causa finita" (Rome has spoken, the case is closed).

Most Rev. L.J.A. Melanson, first archbishop of Moncton

Savage had been made a domestic prelate of the papal household in 1934, with the title of monsignor. Four years later, a year after the new archdiocese had been formally installed, he died after 38 years as pastor of St. Bernard's. He had served his new bishop obediently and with respect. Archbishop Melanson presided at his funeral service. Almost all the English-speaking priests and all the French-speaking priests of the new diocese attended along with those of the old, as well as their bishops.

Once established in Moncton, Archbishop Melanson began planning his cathedral. He engaged L. N. Audet, a Sherbrooke, Quebec, architect and together they toured Eastern Europe seeking distinctive ideas. Built on the foundation of the never-completed l'Assomption Church, the cornerstone was laid on June 13, 1939. When the 233-foot-high tower was completed and the cathedral formally opened on November 21, 1940, it was named "Monument de la Réconnaissance" and dedicated to the Assumption of Mary, the Mother of God and patroness of the Acadians. During the preparations for the opening, Archbishop Melanson, in describing the cathedral for a *Transcript* reporter, commented on the tower. "It was modelled on the Kremlin in Moscow," he said. At first, I thought he was joking because the Kremlin on Red Square is the heart of atheistic-communist government.[4]

However in the centre of its Cathedral Square within the 20-towered Kremlin walls stands the magnificent Uspenski Cathedral and "Uspenski" means "Assumption." It was built by the czars in the late 15th century and dedicated to the Assumption into Heaven in bodily form of the Virgin Mary. The archbishop was not joking.

The enhanced spirit among the Acadians quickly resulted in new and strong educational structures. The St. Joseph's presence in Moncton was only temporary and the small college of l'Assomption opened in 1943 under les Fréres de l'Instruction chrétienne (Brothers of Christian instruction). A woman's college, Notre Dame d'Acadie, opened in 1949. By 1953, part of the University of St. Joseph's came permanently to Moncton. Assumption College was discontinued in 1964 and together, all of these became part of the new and full-

Architect's drawing of first Assumption Church, never completed and now site of cathedral for Acadians. The drawing was done before 1914.

facultied University of Moncton which was established in 1963. The story of its founder is for a separate chapter since Rev. Clément Cormier was in his way as important to the city of his birth as the adoptive citizen John T. Hawke, the publisher and public citizen, had been in his time. The one was a promoter and political conciliator between English and French, the other an educator and conciliator between French and English. Their influence combined, and the works they spawned, did as much for the social history of Moncton as any other combination of circumstances.

1. H. P. LeBlanc was born in Moncton in 1879 and died in 1950; he was a railway official; Hon. Antoine J. Leger (1880-1950) a lawyer became N. B. provincial secretary-treasurer, then a senator; Dr. Belliveau, first mayor of Shediac, was born in 1861 and died in 1911.

2. After a 1940 financial campaign the paper was re-established as an independent edited by lay people under the supervision of the archbishop. In 1947 it became a bi-weekly again, in 1948 a tri-weekly and in 1949 a daily under the editorship of Emery LeBlanc, which it has remained since under various editors.

3. The original railway work between Campbellton, in Restigouche county, and St. Leonard, Madawaska, was begun by the Restigouche and Western Railway Co. in 1897. It was taken over in 1906 by the International Railway Co, of New Brunswick, known as the I.N.R. and the whole district took that name, which it holds to this day.

4. The late archbishop did not say, as now recalled, that he and Audet had visited Russia but apparently they did, and to the writer's knowledge this story of the origins of the cathedral front's design has never previously been told.

Chapter Twenty-one

MAY, MURDER AND ABDUCTION

I don't need no prayers. Just bury me deep enough so the birds don't peck my eyes out. — May Bannister

It was a year of extraordinary events, 1936. It was the year in which Bruno Richard Hauptmann[1] was executed for the kidnapping of the Lindbergh child. It was the year of the dramatic rescue in Nova Scotia's Moose River mine when radio came into its maturity.[2] And, in that same year of 1936, when Moncton became the seat of an ecclesiastical archdiocese, it would become as well the focus of international attention for the worst of reasons, a loathsome triple crime.[3]

On the afternoon of January 6, this headline burst out of the evening newspaper: FOUR ARE DEAD IN DOMESTIC TRAGEDY AT PACIFIC JUNCTION.

There were not four, as it would turn out, but three dead and they were Philip Lake, 30; his common-law wife, Bertha, 28, and their son, John, 22-months-old. The fourth, it would be discovered, was six-months-old Elizabeth Ann, the Lakes' tiny daughter. But she was very much alive — kidnapped for purposes of blackmail.

That was how it began, the notorious Bannister murder-kidnap-blackmail case, the most sensational crime in New Brunswick's legal annals. It would be the first time in Canadian history that a kidnapping charge was laid. It ended

"I don't need no prayers," May Bannister said. "Just bury me deep enough so the birds don't peck my eyes out." Here is May Bannister in the first picture ever seen of her in Moncton. Seated outside jail cell in 1936.

— New York Daily News Photo

with Arthur and Daniel Bannister, two semi-moronic youths, dangling from the end of a hangman's noose. That was the last-ever legal execution at Dorchester and, as the boys died, their evil-spirited mother, May, who planned it all, went off to Kingston penitentiary on a reduced charge of harboring a stolen child. She was sentenced to three-and-a half years and came out to live the rest of her life in Berry Mills. She survived 30 years in obscurity, a forgotten pauper among her frightened, shunning neighbors.

Sinister as she may have been, May Bannister was also a kind of twisted victim of the times of deprivation in which she moved. Even now, in the back clearings near Pacific Junction one can sense a kind of malevolence hanging about the place where a family was slain and one of its infants carried away by abductors. It had been May Bannister's nefarious scheme that she could entrap Milton Trites and the innocent Albert Powell into supporting her impoverished family.

They had befriended and helped her, and one at least had shared the favors of her bed. Now, she would blackmail him with an infant she would claim as her own. Failing that, she would blackmail Albert Powell with a baby she would pass off as that of her 13-year-old daughter, Marie, alleging it to be fathered by the hapless Powell. Milton Trites was the second-hand store man who sometimes paid her $2-a-week for part-time housekeeping and occasionally staying overnight. Powell came to teach Sunday school, he said.

It was perhaps no part of May's scheme that murder would be done, though her sons went armed to the shack in the clearing. Their sister, Frances, 15, was tricked by them into carrying a baby away from the cabin, and three human beings lay dead in their wake. For days after the pig-farm hovel of Philip Lake and his young family was burned, one child could not be accounted for. At first, it was thought she had been consumed in the flames but then police found her alive — alive and in the house of the big-bosomed May Bannister who said she was her own.

The times were desperate when Lake and his wife moved as squatters to the Junction in 1933. Their neighbors in cabins and shacks were no better off, and indeed one of them had actually been sheltered by the Lakes. Sometimes Philip worked on the roads, sometimes doing chores for farmers in the Berry Mills district. He trapped rabbits, kept a henhouse, lined his cabin with newspapers to keep out the cold. His only valuable possessions were a hunting rifle and his two gold teeth. He and Bertha had brought into the world two children, a boy Jackie who was 22 months old in January of 1936, and the tiny girl, Betty, who was less than six months old.

They were proud of the children and when a neighbor, Otto Blakeny, came in for supper a few days before the tragedy that wiped them out, they were happy to show off the new baby. And Blakeny noticed a strawberry-shaped birthmark on the infant's forehead. Bertha explained that such birthmarks ran in the family. This, along with Philip's bright identifying gold teeth, were to play vital parts in the investigation to come and the court trials which lay ahead.

In the beginning, when the news came out, it was imagined that the tragedy was just another of those ghastly winter holocausts which engulfed wooden farm homes heated by log-burning stoves. But when Blakeny went out to cut wood, he found the body of a woman and baby outside the demolished Lake home. He had also noticed tracks leading away from the site and a baby's bottle buried in the snow. There were bloodstains in the snow.

He ran to get Omar Lutes, the junction station agent, who called police in Moncton, and bit by bit the real horror of the thing began to reach the public. The charred frame of Philip Lake was found in the ruins of the shack when Royal Canadian Mounted Police went out by rail car to investigate. And it was seen that Bertha, his wife, had fallen or been struck on the forehead as she fled the flames with her little boy in her arms.

When police talked with 18-year-old Earl O'Brien who had visited the Lakes on New Year's eve, he told them how he had been talking rabbit hunting with Otto Blakeny when Arthur Bannister came to the Lake cabin from Berry Mills, six miles away. He was carrying a .22 rifle and said he had been snaring rabbits. It turned out that O'Brien was planning to stay over-night in the henhouse which had been cleared for him and Arthur wanted to stay with him.

Somewhere around midnight, O'Brien had heard Bannister talking with someone outside the place and he went out. Later, he recalled seeing what he thought to be a boy and a girl talking with Arthur. Afterward, Arthur told him it was his brother and sister and they asked him to go home. But he wanted to stay over and go for rabbits in the morning and they left. As trial evidence would later show, this had in fact been a kind of dry run for the hideous crime about to be committed. O'Brien had the idea, long afterward, that if he and Blakeny hadn't been there the whole terrible scheme would have been carried out that same night. Instead, the three Bannisters went to the Lake place five nights later and if it had snowed that night there would have been no tracks left to trace them homeward. When first seen, Bertha's head wound looked as if it might have been caused by a fall on a stump rather than caused by a blunt instrument.

When the remains were eventually brought into Tuttle Brothers' Funeral Parlors in Moncton, a crowd of morbidly curious gathered. Officials and newspaper reporters (This one, 46 years later, still recalls it too vividly) were taken inside where the woman's body, looking otherwise healthy and strong, bore a round red gash on her forehead. The frozen infant with her was unmarked but the blackened man's form was only the legless outline of a skeleton.

Inspector John Bird, head of the Moncton Mounted Police detachment and later to be Canadian commissioner for the famous force, took charge. At first, it was thought that only one murder had been committed and that the others died in a blaze started from an overturned oil lamp. However, the early theory of accidental fire or a fire set after the head of the household had been slain, was quickly discredited.

Arrests of the Bannister boys came within two days of the gruesome discoveries at which time investigators had no idea of the motive for the killings. Police had picked up their sister, Frances Bannister, as a material witness and, later, Maude LeBlanc, the Moncton police matron, went to the Bannister home in Berry Mills — itself no better than the Lake cabin — to pick up Frances' clothes. With her went Gale Swazey of the R.C.M.P. and they were met at the door by May Bannister who gave them a brazen blast: "The Mounties are a damned bunch of murderers," she shouted. They promised to bring the children home (Her sons and daughter). "They're a bunch of liars."

While they were there, Milton Trites, who owned a second-hand store and sometimes brought food to the Bannisters, was reading aloud a newspaper story about the arrest of Arthur and Daniel while their mother and younger sister, Marie, 13, listened. The constable heard him comment that it was mighty hard on May with the boys locked up and her having to look after the baby. Maude LeBlanc wanted to know *what* baby and Trites said he meant May's little girl whom she had just brought home. When Maude tried to look for it, as she told this reporter long afterward, May had barred her way. Later, she went back.

This time with Inspector Herbert V. Harris of the Moncton police and Const. J.K. Randall. The Mounties were new to the district but Harris and Randall had known May Bannister and thought they could get more from her. Harris was an old hand, a native Newfoundlander who still used such delightful outport expressions as "I'se 'll catch 'em" or "I'se the bye as knows what's what." While the three were talking to May, they spotted an infant in the front room of the house and she said it was her son. There were new baby clothes on hand and she told them that Mrs. Cool at the Travellers Aid knew about them and could prove it was her child. When they asked Mrs. Cool she couldn't say. May also said that she had checked into the Windsor Hotel with the baby and they could tell, but they couldn't.

Milton Trites kept the baby when May was taken into custody and until it could be put into the Moncton Hospital for safekeeping. They didn't take May without a struggle, and she was big, a rough customer who cursed and threatened. After an inquest, she was charged with kidnapping. With the story now taking on the color of sensation, newspaper reporters and photographers swarmed into town. Radio was in its news reporting infancy, television had not arrived, so the printed press had the field to itself. Overnight, Moncton became known to people and places which previously had not known it existed.

At the preliminary hearing, H. Murray Lambert, a veteran local lawyer, was engaged to represent the accused mother and her sons while Gregory F.G. Bridges, later to be chief justice of New Brunswick, appeared for the Crown with Harry W. Hickman, clerk of the peace. Marie Bannister, the 13-year-old sister of the accused youths, was sheltered by the Salvation Army in Moncton. The father of them all, George Bannister, had long since left home, now an old man who wandered about and lived hand-to-mouth while his wife, the 43-year-old May, maintained the Berry Mills establishment by means soon to become apparent. While the preliminary hearings went on, the Bannister boys, their mother and sister were kept in police cells on Duke street in Moncton. Frances was held as a material witness only.

The two youths, Daniel and Arthur, were committed for trial in a higher court on February 6 and taken away to the county jail in Dorchester. As they went into the Moncton railway station to be marched aboard a train, an aged and forlorn man sat warming himself. He didn't even look up as the boys passed, nor know they were there. He was George Bannister, their father.

After this, May Bannister was charged with the kidnapping of Betty Lake and the same charge was laid against her sons. As her hearing proceeded, she created a scene in the local courtroom when she objected to the testimony of one Albert Powell.

Powell had testified that he bought clothing for the Bannister boys and girls but not for an infant. A railway freight employee, he said he had conducted Sunday School for some months at the Bannister home and in October of 1935 was told by May Bannister that her daughter, Marie, was soon going to have a baby and told him: "You will be responsible for it." He added that Mrs. Bannister herself had shown no signs of pregnancy at the time.

Before this, she had instructed her daughter, Frances, to write the Protestant Orphanage in Saint John to apply for a baby "under six months old" for adoption. This had been refused. At that time, as it developed, May had planned to charge Milton Trites with fatherhood of an infant and demand his support of it. Then she was told by Albert Powell that he owned Moncton property worth $4,000.00 and her scheme was to find an infant and allege that it was Marie's and he the father.

To produce a child, she had then dispatched Frances to ask the Lakes if the Bannisters could have their new baby and bring it up. When the Lake child was then kidnapped, and the police found it in the Bannister home, May told them it was her own. She said it had been born on November 10, 1935, in a cabin on the Fox Creek Road where she had been attended "by a French woman I did not know." May added that she had been staying at hotels with strangers whose names she did not know and had kept the baby with her.

In his address to the court, Mr. Bridges said "the baby had been kidnapped for the purpose of blackmailing. The same plot was given as the reason for the murder of Philip Lake, and consequently Bertha and Jackie — blackmail."

When May Bannister appeared before the Westmorland Circuit court, she was at first charged not only with kidnapping and abduction, but the murder of Philip and Bertha Lake. In all, seven indictments were made against the woman and her sons. Later, the murder charge against May was dropped.

When Daniel and Arthur faced Chief Justice John Barry in Dorchester, it was the first murder trial held there since 1896 when John Sullivan had been convicted for the slaying of Mrs. Dutcher of Meadow Brook. (That murder had occurred "on the day of the great train wreck at Palmer's Pond" in Dorchester. Sullivan was hanged at the rear of the court house.)

Daniel and Arthur were now charged with double murder and Arthur was tried first. The charge given to the grand jury alleged that they had gone to the Lake cabin at the insistence of their mother. "They had gained it forcibly and carried the child to her and she represented it as one born of herself." Judge Barry called it "a sordid crime," adding that "these poor people living up there in their own humble manner had a perfect right to life. What were those Bannister boys doing prowling around there on the night the Lakes met their violent deaths?"

Just before he died, Arthur Bannister is given farewell by mother, May. Beside them in Dorchester county jail stands I. Newton Killam, high sheriff of Westmorland.

217

This is Daniel Bannister, executed in 1936 for killing of Lake baby's family. His brother, Arthur, was hanged at the same time. Daniel is seen here in county jail.

— N.Y. News Photo

Arthur Bannister was first found guilty of murder and remanded. Next, Mrs. Bannister was found guilty only of harboring a stolen child and acquitted of forcible seizure and abduction. The judge said he was astonished by the jury's decision, and could not understand how they let her off so lightly.

After Daniel's trial and conviction the brothers were sentenced to hang on June 20, 1936, and the 77-year-old chief justice wept. When their mother was sent to Kingston penitentiary the police matron, Maude LeBlanc, breathed a great sigh of relief. She had feared and dreaded May Bannister from the day she had gone with Harris and Randall to bring the baby to Moncton. May had told her: "I'll get you if it's the last thing I do."

Sentences of Arthur and Daniel were appealed but only Daniel's was allowed. In allowing the appeal, the appellate court held that the elderly and deaf Judge Barry had erred in his charge in referring to evidence as corroborative of Frances Bannister, an accomplice, "which did not in any particular confirm that the crime charged had been committed." It was also held that no evidence was produced as to conspiracy.

Daniel Bannister went on trial for his life for the second time. The new judge was Mr. Justice J.A.L. Fairweather, one of the youngest judges in Canada in terms of experience. Evidence was almost wholly similar to that given at the first and, for the second time, Daniel was sentenced to hang. The jury had been out four hours after an 11-day trial.

As the judge donned his black cap and uttered the death sentence, Daniel didn't move a muscle or say a word until Mr. Justice Fairweather commented: "The crime of which full details must be implanted upon his brain......." Then he was interrupted by Daniel who interjected "which I did not do."

On September 23, 1936, a black flag flew from the county courthouse in Dorchester as a signal that two executions had taken place.

The man called Arthur Ellis, Canada's chief hangman, had come from Montreal the day before and chatted with reporters at the Moncton railway depot. He wore a pink shirt, superimposed by a red necktie and his eyes were as bloodshot as the tie was red. For some days, Sheriff I.N. Killam had been badly worried. It was his duty to find an executioner; otherwise the terrifying obligation fell upon himself and as it happened another execution was scheduled for Saskatchewan for Ellis. However, to the sheriff's untold relief, another executioner had been found to go West.

The gallows were erected in the room where the mother of the two had been held during her trial. As William Hutchinson of *The Transcript* wrote the day after: "They went to the gallows defiantly. Daniel, who said from the first he was innocent, persisted in this in the face of his maker." He prayed after asking that the noose be loosened so he could do so, and he asked forgiveness saying he was being hanged for a crime committed by somebody else. Arthur maintained a bravado to the end.

Arthur Ellis returned to the town's only hotel and when the Ocean Limited stopped at the tiny Dorchester station that afternoon, the hangman was "poured into a bunk, so drunk he couldn't get there by himself." Some said he was carried. He had not, after all, retained the sang-froid he had boasted before the event, but had found his release in a bottle.

The famous case and the Bannisters were never forgotten in Berry Mills or Moncton and, one day early in 1981, I had a call from Frank Jones of *The Toronto Star*. He was in Moncton, he said, and doing a series for his newspaper on famous Canadian murder cases. It would, he said, eventually become a book. He had been told, he added, that I too was planning a book on the case. When I explained that my intention was only to include it as a chapter in a book, we agreed to exchange notes. He had gone into R.C.M.P. files in Ottawa and read reports from the original investigation, not all of which had gone into evidence. Then, on a day much like the one on that long-ago January day in 1936, he drove out to Berry Mills and Pacific Junction and talked to older people who remembered the events all too well 45 years afterward.

May Bannister had come back to Berry Mills after serving her time and, as farmer's wife Bessie Horsman told Jones: "She came back as if nothing had happened. I was terrified of her. And then," she added: "Wouldn't you know it?

I ended up in hospital in the same room as her: And she was just as nice as can be to me. She called me 'dear' all the time. She had no time for religion I remember. When the minister would come around she would get rid of him real quick.

"I don't need no prayers," she'd tell him. 'Just bury me deep enough so the birds don't peck my eyes out.' Then she'd give a great big laugh. That was a terrible thing she did and her boys hanged for it. She was capable of anything, yet she walked into Moncton pretty near every day to get things for her kids and her grand-children when they came."

Ernie Little told Jones that once when Frances had "consumption," he had walked into the home and there was no food in the house. Little, who once ran a store at Berry Mills, recalled: "It was bad. I phoned the over-seer of the poor and from that day until she died May Bannister was on welfare." Little said that often he would pick May up on the road "as she walked from Moncton with a bag of bread she'd been given." When Frank Jones, the reporter, noticed that Little was wondering if he'd be thought to sympathize with May, he added: "She should have hanged instead of the boys."

As for the boys, 79-year-old Lee Johnson, an area farmer, said he used to pick them up on the Moncton road when he was hauling firewood and produce to town. "I don't know as you'd call them mentally deficient," he told Jones, "but they had no education. They were simple but I always thought they were harmless."

And the little baby, Betty Lake who had been abducted and never knew her parents? She was blessedly taken away from it all by an aunt and uncle, Bessie and Edwin Cuthbertson, who later adopted her. She had been a lovely, happy baby and she grew up happily in obscurity. That is until 1982, forty-six years later. Through an extraordinary series of events she herself made it known who she now was, how she had found out and what her life had been.

After Frank Jones' book *Trail of Blood, a Canadian Murder Odyssey* was published, she wrote to *The Sunday Star* of Toronto where Jones is a writer, wanting more information about her own past. Then, in a telephone conversation with Jones, she revealed her (until then) unknown story. Until she was 13, the girl had known nothing of her background. One day, she came across a story in the old *Star Weekly* entitled "The Baby Doll Murder Case" which was about the Bannisters and her own abduction.

The sad story had made her cry and when her aunt asked what the trouble was, she showed the story. Mrs. Cuthbertson gasped and said "Oh, God, no," but decided the little girl was old enough to know the story which she might somehow learn in less favorable circumstances. She told Betty the whole story and said later that it was very hard on her. Some years later, Elizabeth married a man named Crossman and together they went to Pacific Junction but could not find the graves of her parents, the Lakes, in an overgrown churchyard.

Living in Saint John as this is written, the Crossmans are both disabled with arthritis and they have two daughters. "I've told them both," Mrs. Crossman told Jones, "so they'll know."

The bad years of the 1930's also marked the end of an era for the western world. Moncton was relaxed, like most of Canada, still little affected by the events shaking the other side of an ocean. War had started in Europe in September. Quickly, Poland was gone and the French who had been considered invulnerable by all but their neighbors, the Germans, were soon over-run. In the same month as the declaration, Clarence Decatur Howe, Canada's minister of transport and later (during the war) minister of almost everything, visited Moncton to announce that Trans-Canada Airlines would be flying mail and passenger service into the city within a month. The Toronto Maple Leaf hockey star, Moncton's hero, Gordon Drillon was engaged to marry Miss Sally Hughes. And in the same week a fire menaced oil-fields near Stoney Creek but came under control before Moncton lost its natural gas supply.

Quietly, and without public knowledge, military guardsmen had been placed at vulnerable area points. A guardsman named Pte. William Milton of the New Brunswick Rangers was shot and killed in an accident at Humphrey station. The bullet which killed him was from the revolver of a fellow guard. The men were so new to wartime duty the weapons were unfamiliar.

Though he was not enlisted in the armed forces, Moncton's first casualty of World War II may have been Thomas Reid, the son of John Reid who lived on Dominion street. He was reported lost on the S.S. Stanholme "believed to have been torpedoed by a German U-Boat two hours out of Sydney, N.S." Because of wartime censorship, the newspapers carried little notice of the event which was reported in December as the first year of the war in Europe ended.

Three years later at least one other Moncton young man would be lost in merchant shipping due to wartime raids. He was Francis Walsh, a son of Mr. and Mrs. Frank Walsh, and brother of Gerald Walsh, the well-known horticulturist. His father, the longtime Moncton merchant, survives as a sprightly 96-year-old as this is written in 1982.

Walter Boudreau, the son of Dr. and Mrs. F. E. Boudreau of Botsford street, Walsh's shipmate, survived the sinking. Their vessel, the barquentine "Angelus" was carrying goods from the Carribbean over the forbidding Atlantic routes when a Nazi submarine torpedoed the "Angelus." The U-boat commander gave warning and allowed time for the crew to get into lifeboats. Several of them, exhausted in the storms which prevailed, lost their lives as Francis Walsh did but Walter Boudreau survived. He has since operated charter vessels out of West Indian Islands.

---

1. Bruno Richard Hauptmann was charged, eventually found guilty and executed for the kidnap-murder of the son of Charles Lindbergh and his wife, Anne Morrow Lindbergh. It was the most sensational ransom kidnapping case in North American history.

2. Alfred Scadding, Dr. D. E. Robertson and Herman Magill were trapped by a cave-in where they searched for gold. On Easter Sunday, 1936, after rescue efforts kept the world on tenterhooks for ten days, two men came out alive. Magill had succumbed in the mine to pneumonia.

3. While the preliminaries went on, King George V. died and the hearings were adjourned. Edward Prince of Wales became King Edward VIII (and later abdicated).

Chapter Twenty-two

THE INCREDIBLE MONCTONIAN

Northrop Frye's nineteenth book, his "masterpiece," is called *The Great Code* and it was published in the spring of 1982 as the first of two volumes. While it may never be a bestseller, it is considered by scholars of the Western world as one of the most important literary events of this century. When Frye graduated from Aberdeen high school in Moncton in 1928, his fellow students knew that he was a scholar. Otherwise, in the town where he grew up, he remained an almost unknown figure.

His latest and greatest work as a literary critic is a study of the extent to which the Bible may be considered a work of literature and the extent to which it has been the source of the rest of Western world literature. Frye's biographer, John Ayre, says the work "may be the pinnacle of his forty-year academic career."

For 30 years, Prof. Herman Northrop Frye has been travelling from Oxford to Peking, from Harvard to Pakistan, lecturing to the learned of the world. He has not entirely lacked honor in his own country since he was the first ever to be given the title of University Professor at the University of Toronto.

And even though his work is on such a high academic level, the book which gained his early fame, *Anatomy of Criticism* published in 1957 by Princeton University Press, still sells a steady 10,000 copies a year. Walter Jackson Bate of

Harvard has called Frye "the most controversial, and probably the most influential critic writing in English since the 1950's." His 1979 lecture tour in Italy won front-page attention in every major newspaper in that country. One of them, "*La Republica*" of Rome, called him "One of the greatest scholars and literary critics in this century."

That was the boy whose Moncton schoolmates called "the professor," and who years later, created the term "garrison mentality" to describe Canadians. It has become part of our cultural language. Perhaps it is not surprising that Frye has not been known in the town where he went to school because he did leave when he was quite young. Still, Aberdeen and the Moncton public library did help such a brilliant student on his way.

His *Anatomy of Criticism* was a forerunner in an entire field of literature. Frye was analyzing written and verbal communications well before McLuhan, his Toronto university colleague. The publishing house of Harcourt, Brace, Jovanovich in New York once spent a million dollars developing a series of textbooks for American schools based on Frye's idea of literature.

There are two men who, in Moncton's history, have made it into the international Encyclopaedias. One is Simon Newcomb, the greatest American astronomer of the 19th century whose story was told in the first volume of this work. The other is Northrop Frye, who has picked up 28 honorary doctorates but never took one himself.

Moncton has never been a hive of intense intellectualism, and yet it has been the home of three of the most remarkable scholars ever to live in New Brunswick. The third member of that extraordinary trio was Mr. Justice Ivan Rand, considered to have been one of the two ablest jurists ever to sit with the Supreme Court of Canada.[1]

Because he practised law in Moncton and then, while chief counsel for the C.N.R. in Montreal and afterward as a judge in Ottawa, Rand always kept close touch with his native place. Unlike Frye, he was not without distinction "in his own house." All of his long summers he spent at The Bluff on Northumberland Strait near Moncton and visited his town friends frequently.

Top is Prof. Northrop Frye and below, Mr. Justice I.C. Rand, Supreme Court of Canada.

It seems proper to tell his story in a chapter with Professor Frye because he, too, was a literary scholar. But first, the story of Frye.

Northrop Frye was born in Sherbrooke, Quebec, in 1913. When his father's hardware business failed and Northrop's only, and much older, brother was killed in France, the family came to Moncton. The brother died when the first bomb ever dropped from an airplane landed on him. Frye senior went on the road as a hardware salesman. His scholarly son's biographers have quoted him as saying that the family was so shocked by his brother's unusual death that "they went into psychological retirement" after they arrived in Moncton in 1918.

Taught by his mother, Northrop had never been inside a schoolroom until he went into Moncton's old Victoria. He was then eight years old and started in the fourth grade. The family lived quietly on Pine street where books included the lugubrious black-bound volumes left by a clerical grandfather.

Understandably, school bored him and he spent his time reading all of Dickens and all of Scott's Waverley novels before he reached high school. By the time he was 14, the Moncton public library had opened and, as a result, he had "a fair grasp of 19th century literature" by the time he was 15. His mother, before marriage had taught at Stanstead College in the Eastern Townships and taught her younger son both to read and play the piano when he was three years old. She was the daughter of an impoverished Methodist circuit-rider in Ontario who, oddly enough, was descended from a Catholic family which settled in Virginia in the 1600's. The family came to Canada in the 1760's and became Methodists. This religion, which has always haunted Northrop Frye's imagination, was deeply grounded in him and in time he became an ordained minister.

When he graduated from high school, Northrop won a scholarship to a local business college and then competed in a national speed-typing championship at Massey Hall in Toronto. He was second speediest, at eighty words a minute. The skill has proved useful in his lifetime of voluminous writing and today he types 150-words-a-minute on his IBM electric. In those days of his Moncton school attendance, I remember the vision of this youngster (exactly my own age, but well ahead in high school) hurrying past our house on his way to Aberdeen. Hatless when few boys were, his wild blonde hair flew in the wind, and under his arm was always a heavy bundle of books. He seemed constantly in deep concentration, was never an athlete and never took part in neighborhood activities. The sons of Frank Gillespie, who lived almost next door on Pine street, hardly knew him at all.

Frye studied piano under Dr. George Ross, a graduate of Royal College of Organists in London, and had a house studio on Archibald street. He credits Ross with giving him his first real education, other than his mother's. Ross gave him, he has said, an appreciation of the arts. His 1928 Aberdeen high graduating classmates never forgot Northrop. Those at the head of the list were the Ramsay brothers Allan and Archie, sons of the Presbyterian minister, Mary Kinnear, an outstanding student who later married Allan Ramsay, and Gertrude Pujolas who married this writer. Nor did Frye forget them as he said in correspondence when this chapter was being researched.

"I grew up," he wrote in one of his books, "in two towns, Sherbrooke and Moncton, where the population was half English and half French, divided by language, education and religion, and living in a state of more or less amiable Apartheid. In the Eastern Townships the English-speaking group formed a northern spur of New England, and had at a much earlier time almost annexed themselves to New England, feeling much more akin to it than to Quebec. The English-speaking Maritimers, also, had much of their cultural and economic ties with New England, but their political connection was with New France, so that culturally, from their point of view, Canada stopped at Fredericton and started again at Westmount. There were also a good many Maritime French families whose native language was English, and so had the same cultural dislocation in reverse."

None of Frye's books is easy reading but *The Bush Garden* is at least slightly autobiographical and perhaps easiest to understand. Eight of his books have been translated and four major publishers in 1980 were locked in battle over rights for his Bible book *The Great Code* — even before it was finished in English.

It was said in the early 1980's that there are "three living Canadians known today as celebrities throughout the world, Northrop Frye, Marshall McLuhan and Pierre Elliott Trudeau." The great paradox is that Trudeau and even McLuhan are well enough known in Moncton where the third grew up, but in his hometown the prophet Frye remains to reach that plateau.

As for Ivan Cleveland Rand, to those who did not know him well he could seem an austere and distant man. Tall, big and almost raw-boned, he was the son of one of Canada's first railway union leaders, Nelson Rand of Moncton and Shediac. He was the descendant of scholars, among them the historian and litterateur, Rev. Silas Rand, an authority of Maritime Indians who wrote a dictionary of the Micmac Indian language.

Ivan Rand's most celebrated public achievement was his invention of The Rand Formula for settling labor disputes, a formula he created after heading a royal commission studying labor disputes in Windsor, Ontario. His ruling, which became law, was that a company employee could remain outside the chosen collective bargaining unit but, since the union contracts benefitted him as well as the others, he should pay union dues. On the bench, Mr. Justice Rand's most famous judgment was the knocking down of the notorious Duplessis "Padlock Law" against Jehovah's Witnesses.

Rand graduated from Mount Allison University, married Iredell Baxter, daughter of a Moncton physician, and studied jurisprudence at Harvard Law School under the great Felix Frankfurter, an advisor to President Franklin D. Roosevelt. In Moncton, he practised with Senator C.W. Robinson until he was appointed railway counsel for the Atlantic Region and then chief counsel for the Canadian National in Canada. From there, he was named to the Supreme Court of Canada. He was kept from being its chief justice by a quirk of timing. Seniority then ruled, as well as competence, and because his appointment had been delayed until Judge Crockett of Fredericton was appointed and served his term, Rand's eventual retirement came just before the death of the chief justice whom he was slated to succeed.

Court authorities in Ottawa, however, maintained that only Sir Lyman P. Duff, a chief justice who had considered Rand his closest confidante, was as great or greater a jurist, in all of Canada's high court history.

In the mid 1920's, through the insistence of his partner Senator Robinson, a former premier who knew his qualities, Rand was named attorney-general of New Brunswick. To sit in the legislature, he had to be elected to a seat and the appointment had come between general elections. At first, as Rand once told this writer with good humor but some rue: "They ran me in Moncton because I was Protestant and English-speaking. I was defeated. (E. A. Reilly defeated him by 980 votes.) Then they arranged for me to go to Gloucester. I had no French, except for reading, but they said go anyway."

Peter Veniot, who was to be leader of the provincial Liberal Party, (and later Postmaster-General of Canada) found a candidate who agreed to step aside until the next general election, and let Rand try for the contested seat. "I had no French at all, so I went across the street from my office," Rand related many years afterward, "and asked my old friend P. A. Belliveau, who was bilingual, to help me out in Gloucester. He did, and I won, and it was the only time I was ever elected to public office. After two years, the general election came and, as agreed, the candidate went back to his own riding. I had to find another seat."

It is difficult to equate the forbiddingly stern and righteous Mr. Justice Rand on Canada's highest court with the young politician. In the famous Reciprocity election of 1911, Rand was already billed in Moncton ahead of the rabidly partisan John T. Hawke at a "Liberal Smoker" in the party club rooms on Robinson street (later the Labor Temple). Then, when he had been elected and served his brief time in the provincial cabinet, he became so reputed as a powerful party politician that the Conservatives in the rough 1925 election called him "Ivan the Terrible." In his book on political corruption in New Brunswick, *Front Benches and Back*

Rooms, Arthur Doyle says the Liberal government of Premier Peter Veniot was "portrayed as an arrogant clique dominated by Veniot, Attorney General Ivan Rand and Dr. William Roberts. The Conservatives nicknamed them 'Peter the Great,' 'Ivan the Terrible' and 'William the Emperor.' "

Rand, who had been elected in Gloucester after being turned down in his home riding, was part of a blatant Liberal attempt in 1925 to woo the Catholic vote at a time when Veniot was being attacked as "Veniot the Frenchman." As Doyle has written: "Rand gave one of the wildest speeches of the campaign." To any one knowing Rand in his days of controlled severity on the bench, this description is almost beyond belief.

But the Conservatives in that election were being associated with the Ku Klux Klan then active in the province, and Rand was stirred to righteous indignation. He referred figuratively to Tory Leader J. B. M. Baxter's regalia as "a white hood and burning cross."

This is the same man who, in later life, would knock down Duplessis' padlock law against Jehovah's witnesses and who, no doubt, would have supported the K.K.K.'s civil right to exist so long as they stayed within the law. And yet his Saint John speech is so out of character it is hard to credit even as that of an ambitious young man. As pointed out, Rand's career in politics was a remarkably short one but all his life he remembered it with affection.

1. Ivan Rand had been an active churchman then, counsel to the United Church of Canada in the union of churches which created The United Church of Canada.

Chapter Twenty-three

A MAN AND HIS UNIVERSITY

When he was Canada's governor-general, the Rt. Hon. Vincent Massey once told a Moncton audience that if he were to choose the ten greatest Canadians of the day one of them would be Clément Cormier. At another time, Hon. Roméo LeBlanc, a federal cabinet minister, said that Father Cormier's contribution to the Acadian people was "incomparable and inestimable."

The man himself had no such notions and when a graduate student's biography of him was published he thought it was "silly." Nevertheless, it could be said of him in truth as Sir Christopher Wren's son had inscribed on a plaque in St. Paul's to commemorate his famed architect father: "Si momentum requiris circumspice." (If you would see the man's monument, look around.) In the history of Moncton only one native son has left such a visible mark, the campus and structures of a great university. It was the first French-language university in Canada established outside Quebec and Rev. Clément Cormier, C.C., C.S.C., was its founder, its first rector and then its chancellor.

For anyone's lifetime that alone would be remarkable. For Clément Cormier it was just one, though certainly the proudest, of the works of a life dedicated to the cultural and material rise of a people, his people, the Acadians of Canada's Atlantic region. To begin with, he was an only child, rarity enough among traditionally prolific Acadian families. He may have been the first-ever Acadian to have studied the social sciences at the noted Laval School of Social Sciences. When he was chosen prefect of studies for his alma mater, St. Joseph's University in Memramcook, he was the youngest ever and when he became head of that university he was the youngest to hold such a position in Canada.

In that role, he was the first French educator to admit Acadian women into higher education. He was the first to develop scientific, commercial and educational courses within the framework of classical French colleges in this region. Much later, he was the founder of the world-renowned Centre d'Etudes acadiennes (Centre for Acadian Studies), creator of the first Acadian Museum and prime mover in the historic Acadian Village in Northern New Brunswick.

Prime Minister Pearson named him as a member of the distinguished and now historic Laurendeau Commission on Biculturism and Bilingualism. Some years afterward, he was made a companion of the Order of Canada, its highest rank, and he had already been elected a member of the prestigious Royal Society, the national academy whose aim is the promotion of learning and research in the arts and sciences in Canada.

Not the least of the quirks in his experience is that, as a young teacher in Quebec, he once taught Claude Ryan, the Quebec Liberal leader who defeated René Lévésque in the Quebec referendum. Back home years later, he led the campaign which brought French-language broadcasting to the region. Then he founded the Acadian Historical Society and, to top it all when he ceased to be chancellor, he wrote a history of the university and its affiliated colleges. By this time, his honorary degrees totalled at least ten.

In retirement, he was busy on his papers, busy with historical documents, busy with a wide correspondence, and busier still fending off demands for participation in a myriad of public activities. In spite of all this, he remained a humble, quiet-spoken, perfectly bilingual citizen who could walk through the malls of his hometown unrecognized by all but the most observant.

Rev. Clément Cormier, C.S.C.

Publicly reserved, he was, in the contemplative spirit of his three score-years-and-ten, still privately angered by the earlier divisions which had once threatened fragmentation of his people. Even so, he himself had not been wholly innocent of the jealousies and controversies which for a time endangered the structure he had worked so hard to erect. Himself as much at home in the English-speaking world as in the French, his aim had been to preserve a traditional Canadian language and culture. He had wanted to see a disadvantaged minority trained to join the main-stream of Canadian life, and he had achieved this to a remarkable degree, but there were some who preferred to hive themselves into separate corners, politically, linguistically and socially. That was what disturbed the educator in his later years though others sometimes said that Clément Cormier had not always been the easiest man to deal with when his own ambitions were crossed.

Yet, to tell the story of the man is to tell the story of the institution he created, the University of Moncton,[1] and the way it came to be. To know the circumstances that made the man is to know something of the dynamic he helped direct among the Acadian community and, primarily, the province of New Brunswick.

In black clericals or casual sports clothes, in retirement he continued to live the religious life to which he had vowed in his twenties when he became a member of the teaching order of Les Péres de Sainte-Croix, known in English North America as the Holy Cross Fathers. His headquarters and home comprised a three-room apartment in a residential keep where retired and other members of the order lived together in Moncton. There, he had more private space for his work than ever in his working career. From the grounds he could see the campus of the university he built, and contemplate with more than a little asperity the things which had gone wrong with his dreams of linguistic and social harmony.

It is difficult to write about Clément Cormier because, after a lifelong acquaintance and years of personal friendship, he remains something of an enigma. Easy to know, he is yet so complex in character that definition becomes confusing. At once humble and retiring, he is at the same time proud and sensitive. Without personal ambition, he has been more than ambitious for others. Still, for all his achievements, he has remained almost unknown as an individual to the community at large.

Sometimes of a summer day when he was in a nostalgic mood, Father Cormier would sit near a little bridge over Murray Creek near Cocagne to meditate on his origins and the influences of his life. It was there he had spent so much time with his father who had been raised by an adoptive grandfather. His father's mother was of Scottish descent, like the Murray neighbors of his childhood, and Father Cormier believed his Scottish grandmother might have had something to do with his own attitudes. She had married a French-Acadian in the United States and their son had returned to New Brunswick to grow up among the French and Scots and Irish of the Cocagne district. Like them, Rev. Clément Cormier had been brought up understanding and appreciating those who might not be of his own racial, linguistic or religious background.

As a schoolboy in Moncton, young Clem attended an Irish-French parochial school where there were French classes depending on the availability of French teachers. When there was a controversy over the division of St. Bernard's Catholic church parish on English-French language lines, his parents remained moderates and took no part in the disruptive and wounding dispute. The family was not nationalistic but interested in preserving the French language and cultural traditions. In his newspaper, Clément Sr. opposed the nationalist elements and this surely influenced his son.

In his grade-school years, the junior Clément spent a lot of time at home reading, with a leaning toward Jules Verne and other science fiction of the period. His father had bought him the 20-volume set of Books of Knowledge and in them he found an encylopaedia of literature, legends and fables but more particularly a glimpse at the scientific world.

The family home was often visited by Acadian and other political leaders, and the young student stayed within ear-shot of their conversations. He learned very early of the movements, both social and political, which were stirring among the Acadian elite. When he was only thirteen, he was sent to St. Joseph's College in Memramcook at a time when the "cours classique" was followed and boys entered at the end of elementary school years. This was a six-year course comprising four years in what now would be considered grades eight, nine, ten and eleven, and two years junior college level. Cormier took his arts baccalaurate in three years, graduating from St. Joseph's University in 1931 at the age of 21.

In his son's college years, Cormier Senior asked Otty Barbour, *The Transcript's* publisher, to take the youth on summer staff without pay to learn the craft. For one season, Clem Junior worked in the newsroom for experience only, but during the next two summers Barbour insisted on paying a modest salary. (All of Barbour's salaries were modest.) A contemporary of the student journalist was Jack Grainger who later acquired the newspaper.

This was a further step in Cormier's bilingual education and it gave him a further sense of awareness of the majority society around him. When he attended St. Joseph's University as a student, it was then a completely bilingual institution and the only successful one in all of Canada. Its students were largely French-speaking and English-speaking Irish boys from all over New Brunswick, a few from Quebec there to learn English, a few from the other Maritime Provinces and here and there a youth from New England. It was only half an hour from Moncton where a mixed population was its inheritance.

When Clem Cormier graduated he took prizes in bilingualism and public speaking. One of his classmates was Hédard Robichaud who would become New Brunswick's first Acadian lieutenant-governor. From there, young Cormier entered the novitiate of la Congrégation Sainte-Croix at Sainte-Genevieve de Pierre-fonds, Quebec. This is the teaching order of Holy Cross Fathers whose football teams at Notre Dame of Indiana became American legends. After a year in the withdrawal of the novitiate, he was admitted to theological studies and was ordained priest at the Grand Seminary in Quebec in 1936.

He then spent two years teaching language courses, English, French and Latin at Collége Ste. Croix and among his pupils was Claude Ryan who was to become editor of Montreal's most prestigious French-language newspaper, *Le*

Devoir and then leader of the Quebec Liberal Party. Given a provincial bursary, Cormier went on to Laval University's school of social sciences, economics and politics, which had then recently been created by the Dominician, Georges-Hénri Lévésque. It was the seedbed of the new Quebec moving out of a rural confessional-school society to a modern, industrial, business and scientific community.

It was there under the liberal intellectual influence of Georges-Hénri Lévésque, who taught a generation that opposed the dictatorial and regressive Duplessis regime, and himself was banished to an African college for it, that Clément Cormier deepened his understanding of the needs of his own people. When they had returned after the exile from Nova Scotia — *le grand Dérangement* — in the 1760's the Acadians in New Brunswick had lived a marginal existence for a century. Then, when the first educational institutions were opened to them, St. Joseph's being the first in higher education, they followed the Quebec French tradition of classical education in the arts, humanities and theology. And they developed a small elite which was concentrated in the priesthood, in medicine and law. Though St. Joseph's had a commercial course strong for its times as early as 1890, few business leaders had emerged, no scientists, no engineers and certainly no social scientists.

It was in this area that strong education must be developed in order to move the French-speaking Maritimers into the mainstream of a modern industrial society. Agriculture was no longer the basic industry and French-speaking New Brunswickers were deserting the farms in thousands, lured to the factories of New England. As a very young man interested in the practical sciences, Father Cormier saw what needed to be done.

Among such emerging young leaders of the new French-Canadian Society as those at Laval, Father Cormier would first demonstrate his ability to make friends and form alliances with those who could influence events. Later, when he was inconspicuously working behind the scenes to finance and create a full university in his native province, this quiet and fore-sighted talent for enlisting powerful aid to his cause was a major key to his success. If Oxford and Cambridge, Harvard and Yale, Toronto and McGill could boast of their old-boy networks, and Upper Canada College and Trinity School at Port Hope could use the old-school tie to achieve their ends, so could Clément Cormier.

When he came to construct his dream of higher education for French-speaking Maritimers, friends like Jules Brillant, the Gaspé transportation and industrial giant; Louis Lévésque the wealthy investor and sportsman, and Paul Desmarais, who built Power Corporation from the base of a local bus franchise in Sudbury, were there to consult. Like Cormier, Desmarais was a non-Quebec Fencch-Canadian who learned to pull the levers of power. Brillant sent sons to St. Joseph's where he had been given a degree.

J. Louis Lévésque who became as famous as a Canadian throughbreed breeder and cup winner as he was in an investor, had a special interest in a Moncton university. His first job had been as a bank clerk there and then he became a broker in Montreal. After 1960, he had become involved in New Brunswick financing and this turned out to be highly lucrative, a stepping-stone to his great fortune. This he remembered by giving, in all, some $3,000,000 in buildings and gifts to the University of Moncton. But it was Clément Cormier's diplomatic skill and timely nudging which awakened the millionaire's interest — with assists from Lévésque's old friends, Mr. Justice Adrien Cormier and Premier Louis J. Robichaud.

Long before that happened, Rev. Clément Cormier was summoned to his alma mater in Memramcook to become its youngest-ever prefect of studies. He was just 30 when he replaced Rev. Louis Guertin who had been teaching at the college since 1886 and this was now 1940. The significance lay not only in the new man's youth but that 52 years of traditionalist influence was about to end. The eventual impact, when Cormier became the university's youngest superior eight years later, would effect as great an impact on French-speaking Maritime society as the founding of the school in 1864.

This was the seminal stage of the turn toward the sciences, and the man and his associates who introduced it lived to see its results within 30 years — results which at last put

French-speaking New Brunswickers in the forefront in the fields of social sciences, engineering, commerce, industry and education.

As a university head at 38, one of Father Cormier's first innovations was the admission of Acadian women into university-level courses. With the agreement of Sister Jeanne de Valois who led the nearby convent of St. Joseph, tradition was broken. It had been customary for French-speaking families to send girls to convent schools for secondary education but those who wanted to go beyond in French had to study outside the province. Or, they might switch to English-language colleges, which only the tiniest few did. Cost and the difficulty of studying in a second language were severe barriers.

Even in Father Cormier's time at St. Joseph's fees were kept as low as $350-a-year for everything. (The college ledger for 1891 has an entry showing that my own father's expenses for the year were $37.17 which included meals but, living nearby, he may have gone home at night. Another entry showed that a student from Cumberland county, Nova Scotia, had brought his own cot and was not to be charged for a bed.) Once when he was walking near the college, Father Cormier was asked by an American visitor, who pulled up his car to comment on the picturesque campus, what the fees were. When told, he wanted to know how it was done. "Well," the prefect of studies told him, "the priest-teachers are unpaid, the nuns do the cooking and housekeeping and are unpaid. The bishops give us a little, the province a trifle. All the rest is dedication."

Like his predecessors in this and other church-related colleges, the young president worked constantly toward some sort of government financial assistance. The St. Laurent government in Ottawa had devised a new formula for helping universities after Premier Maurice Duplessis of Quebec had stymied the original federal plan to give direct aid. The plan was to make funds available through the Canadian University Conference. To benefit by this system, certain conditions had to be met and Cormier set about working toward a university of standing adequate to be qualified. This meant providing faculties and courses in the modern sciences.

For 30 years he had seen the importance of moving St. Joseph's to Moncton from the old rural community of Memramcook. The city was the centre of French society and culture and already had other French institutions. As early as 1948 he had prepared a document to show how it could be done and in 1953 most of its courses were brought to what had been the Church Street Academy, the first large French-language school in Moncton, out of use because other schools had been built where French-speaking population was more concentrated.

A small Collége l'Assomption had been established in Moncton, for which Cormier had set up a course of studies, and for a time it remained. Between 1953 and 1962, Father Cormier had carried on a quiet campaign to make St. Joseph's a full university. L'Assomption and the new girls college, Notre Dame d'Acadie, eventually became part of St. Joseph's. By 1962 it was time to complete the modern university.

Cormier, with his penchant for organizing and seeking counsel from those best equipped to give it, plus their actual help, joined associations of higher education. He travelled widely to study other systems, and he plotted with care after his research. Wherever he went he made friends and when Louis Robichaud was elected privincial premier, he found a new ally.

For his part, Robichaud had been casting about to find a way of raising the whole standard of education in New Brunswick, equally in English and French, to create the same opportunities for youth of his province as existed in other parts of the country. He struck upon the idea of appointing a royal commission to study higher education. It was a stroke of near genius for the premier to seek out John Deutsch as chairman of his royal commission, whose other members were Judge Adrien Cormier (later chief justice) and Prof. Robert Maxwell.

Deutsch was then principal of prestigious Queen's in Kingston, a former professor of economics who had been Canada's brilliant deputy-minister of finance, and would later be chairman of the Canadian Economic Council. He was a rare combination of educator, financier and organizer and he took his task seriously. A native of rural Saskatchewan from a German-speaking home, John Deutsch knew at firsthand of the difficulties faced by a minority-language country child seeking university education.

Deutsch went beyond the standard functions of royal commissions. He drew up a master plan for all New Brunswick institutions of higher education, a new plan of grants and even got down to the details of financing and building. With his recommendations in hand, Cormier and his advisors went ahead with construction on a campus which he himself had had the foresight to acquire for the university when land prices were reasonable.

To create a new university, however, there had to be more than prospective future government grants. A budget of $5,000,000 was set, and Lévésque, Brillant and Désmarais were asked for help. Their contributions were large, especially those of Lévésque, and they brought in others. However, one wealthy and powerful English-speaking New Brunswicker also came into the picture. When the fund-raising committee first approached K.C. Irving it was expected he might donate at least $25,000.

It was a time when the Irving image had been shaded by his controversy with the Robichaud government and some Acadians were turning in their Irving gasoline credit cards. Kenneth C. Irving came with his three sons to a meeting with Judge Adrien Cormier and Father Cormier (no relation). After some discussion, Mr. Irving asked to be excused and went out to talk the matter over with the sons in private. When they returned, K.C. literally shocked the Cormiers by saying the Irvings would contribute half a million dollars — with one proviso, that it be spread over eight years. The plan was accepted with pleasure. For once, the two fund-raisers, long friends and associates in the university development, went out for dinner and a drink to celebrate.

For Clément Cormier, the vision he had nurtured so long became a reality in 1963 when the lieutenant-governor of New Brunswick approved the incorporation of l'Université de Moncton, the first and only French-language university in Canada outside Quebec. Father Cormier became the first rector; St. Joseph's became one of the colleges within the university federation and when it became a non-confessional, secular and state university he became its chancellor. He was

An aerial view of the campus of the University of Moncton (l'Université de Moncton). At right in foreground is tall Taillon Building, administrative headquarters. At extreme right near top may be seen oil tanks at bend of Petitcodiac.

seventeen years in the governance of St. Joseph's University and the new University of Moncton and, as its third rector, Dr. Jean Cadieux said, "all his life was given to one work. He *made* the University of Moncton."

Dr. Deutsch once told this writer that he had recommended a French-language university rather than an expanded and bilingual University of New Brunswick because it was first necessary to allow French-speaking students the chance to develop their skills and improve their knowledge in the familiar mother tongue. For generations, he explained, French-speaking pupils had dropped out of grade schools early because instruction was in English and most textbooks in English while the language of their homes and speech was French. They had thus been at a severe learning disadvantage.

It had seemed logical to Clément Cormier and the Deutsch commission that a federated French-language university would best meet the needs of the French-speaking community of these provinces, but other forces prevailed and this did not quite come off.

In 1966 to complete the transition to a full university, John Deutsch was again asked to chair a committee to chart a course of action. He was joined by Prof. Robert Maxwell of U.N.B., representing English-language universities and Mr. Justice Adrien Cormier as negotiator. The outcome of their deliberations was a recommendation that the university become a secular institution. The next year, the Holy Cross Fathers corporation was dissolved and a new corporation established as a board of regents. Later, a board of governors was named and became the administrative body responsible for ownership of the properties concerned. This resulted in the University of Moncton becoming a state-supported institution. The archbishop resigned as chancellor and Father Cormier as rector in 1967, while Adelard Savoie, a Moncton lawyer, became the first lay rector. Louis Lévésque, who had been its largest financial contributor, was named first chancellor.

One of the most difficult tasks during this period was talking the smaller northern French-language colleges into joining the federation. Mr. Justice Adrien Cormier as a Moncton youth had attended Sacré Coeur at Bathurst, operated by the Eudist Fathers, a teaching order originating in France. He had been among fifty or sixty Moncton boys planning to attend St. Joseph's when Rev. H.D. Cormier, the dictatorial pastor of l'Assomption parish in Moncton, had taken some objection to the Memramcook university. He persuaded the boys' parents to send them to Bathurst. As a result, an important proportion of successful men in public and business life in middle-age during the 1960's and influential in the Acadian community were graduates of the Bathurst College. Like Clément Cormier himself, some had gone on to the Laval School of Social Sciences. They were approached for moral and other support.

Judge Cormier was an effective negotiator, but the going was hard. Neither Bathurst nor the small college of St. Louis at Edmundston, also Eudist-run, wanted to yield their own status, to lose their identity and become just part of a "southern" university. They didn't like the idea of federating with St. Joseph's or of St. Joseph's being the central institution. However, it was the much older, the traditional French-language seat of higher education in the Maritimes and, all else apart, the whole idea had originated and been promoted from the beginning by its rector, Clément Cormier.

The battle now being fought was between the Acadians themselves. Finally, John Deutsch, who was arranging the methods of financing, was blunt: "This is not my affair. Get together or there is no money. It's up to you." They got together.

It had always been the founder's idea that the French university should be a true federation of colleges like Oxford in England, Harvard in Massachusetts or the University of Toronto, all of which had brought confessional or church-related colleges into the overall university. At first, it seemed as if this would prevail but the northern college heads demurred. There was jealousy that the French-speaking southern New Brunswickers and St. Joseph's were getting the better part and already had most of the French-language institutions. The agitation grew and when the university was a fact as the University of Moncton, St. Joseph's remained a distinct college within it but the others remained where they were. That status prevailed until all were absorbed within the

University of Moncton in 1975. Then, the outside colleges of the north were designated as Edmundston and Shippegan campuses of the university, and St. Joseph's disappeared.

A final irony in the situation was that, in 1980, Gilbert Finn, who had for years been the chief officer of the large Acadian mutual insurance company, Assomption Compagnie Mutuelle d'Assurance-vie, (Assumption Mutual) was made rector of the university. He had been one of those originally pressing for more status for the northern colleges. All of which is part of another history and of a later time.

After he had retired as head of the university, a step he knew was necessary to complete the university and make it wholly secular, Clément Cormier was for a time an unhappy man. He had not relished the thought of handing his creation over to others, but concurred fully in the choice of Adelard Savoie. Then, in 1973, Cormier was named chancellor for five years, a ceremonial role which he, in typical fashion, assumed with panache and continued to promote the institution, and do a great deal else, such as to develop a museum and establish a centre of Acadian studies. At the end of his term, he took on other chores connected with the university, carrying through projects which he had begun forty years earlier.

It was only appropriate that in 1980 the Acadian Museum and Art Gallery was opened on the university campus and named the Clément Cormier Building.

The career seemed to have no limits and there is hardly an Acadian development in which he has not had an influential role. Still, when at Savoie's request he wrote the history of the university and its colleges, his own role was never mentioned. There were two generations of young people with talent and ambition who became notably successful in their chosen fields who benefited directly by his encouragement and practical assistance. To mention only two, Antonine Maillet who was the first person outside France to be awarded the prestigious literary Prix Goncourt, and Edith Butler, the folk and popular singer, is an indication of this. Sometimes he went so far as to find material help through his well-placed contacts, and he would never resist an appeal from a talented young person. Always, his help was unobtrusive.

Four presidents of the University of Moncton. Top left is: Adelard Savoie; top right, Father Cormier; bottom left, Jean Cadieux; bottom right, Gilbert Finn.

Apart from the honors and appointments heaped on Clément Cormier, his range of interests can be judged through these positions: Life membership in the Association of New Brunswick Museums, membership in the Canadian Foundation of Human Rights, founding president of the One Hundred Francophone Associates, Knight of the Order of the Pleiad, member of the Canadian Conference of Universities, president of French Language Educators of Canada.

After he had retired and wanted only to live his life, complete his private research, writing and spiritual meditations, he was still sought out. In private conversation, the founder would not hide his disappointment at the direction things had taken away from what was his personal conception of a true university, but he said nothing publicly. He had done what he could and now it was for others to carry on. His whole aim, he maintained, had been to remove the Acadians away from being a folkloric remnant and have them part of a whole society. "Not a splinter of it," as he put it. And yet, within his own lifetime, the divisions he had excoriated were being healed. Once seen as an antagonist of Northern New Brunswick French persuasion, Gilbert Finn, the new president of the university, was proving to be surprisingly healing.

Despite the appeals of friends and associates, Father Cormier refused to write his memoirs. "It's all in my correspondence," he would say. "They can find what they want there," and he had always carried on an extensive correspondence. In the lengthy interviews he permitted this writer for preparation of sections of the university's history and the "French question," he would not talk of his own participation. One thing became clear, however. As an idealist, he found it difficult to accept the idea of professors joining syndicates (unions) "and doing as little as they can for as much as they can get."

He could not forget the decades of unpaid priest-teachers rewarded only by the knowledge of a job well done. "There is no dedication now, and dedication made it all possible."

1. Properly, it is l'Université de Moncton but as this is a history written in English that version is used.

Chapter Twenty-four

A MAYOR IN VIOLENT TIMES

If any one in the history of Moncton epitomized an era in the city's life it was Leonard C. Jones, Jr. who was its mayor longer than any other. And while he brought national attention to the city, some so negative to its image as to imply a kind of stigma, certainly this man born in 1924 and Moncton's chief magistrate for eleven years was the most controversial since his birthplace was first incorporated.

Leonard Jones, whose father and namesake was elected "the boy alderman" the year his son was born, became the focus of national attention in the most acrimonius linguistic and political dispute in regional memory. It even took on national overtones, as Jones' participation almost split the Canadian Progressive Conservative party. In the end, it resulted in his being sent to parliament as the only Independent in local history. The isolation of parliamentary independents in Canada is traditional and the difficulty of achieving anything outside the party ranks is almost insurmountable. As a result, Jones was elected to parliament only once, declining to stand for election a second time.

A much longer perspective will be needed to weigh the merits and effects of Leonard Jones' part in the language controversy that swirled about him. And though the confrontation that marked his career concerned the place of the French language in Moncton, it is less than accurate to

LEONARD C. JONES

attribute to him simple and personal animosity. As mayor, he was, to a degree, representing the unspoken views of a large number of his constituents. What he did was to encourage those only too happy to find a sympathizer who would provide such leadership. He was elected with such majorities, both as mayor and Member of Parliament, that it is impossible to say that he spoke *only* for a minority at the time. There were many non-French citizens who disagreed with him; there were many non-French who thought his positions on bilingualism were dangerous and divisive, but for a long time there was none who would stand up and say so publicly. This left the field to some vocal rednecks and to Jones' first antagonist, the young and fiery Acadian French students and those few older citizens of French orientation who were swung to the students' side by the bitterness of the mayor's response.

Leonard C. Jones was neither the devil he was painted by enemies nor the saint canonized by those who shouted his praises. Like most politicians, he fitted somewhere in between. He played the political game politically and ambitiously. Some might say opportunistically, and what modern politician has escaped that epithet? On the one hand, it hardly seems possible to interpret Jones' attacks on bilingualism as anything but partisan though it may have been strictly political. On the other hand, he argued consistently that he had no objection to French language education and indeed wanted it available in English schools so that English-speaking children could compete on equal terms.

In all of this, Leonard Jones was a product of his times. They were some of the most disturbing and unsettling times in Canadian history. To give some perspective, they should be recalled. Jones was first elected to city council in 1957 at the age of 33 and he became mayor first in 1963. The 1960's were the years of the Vietnamese war. They were the years when Quebec separatism was in its most violent stage. In Moncton, students at the new University of Moncton were in a rebellious mood.

Then, as the Seventies began, six months after Neil Armstrong stepped onto the moon, there was the world's era of mayhem and death. There was the American attack on

Cambodia, condemned by the world; there were the atrocities at Song My; there were unarmed students gunned down by hysterical guards at Kent State in Ohio. In Israel, P.L.O. guerrillas were butchering Israeli schoolchildren. Pierre Laporte was garroted by FLQ terrorists in Quebec, highjackers began to strike around the world and Pope Paul was stabbed with a Bolivian's knife. Then there was Watergate and corruption in the United States.

All of these frightening movements spilled over into Canada, spilled over into even a small and distant province like New Brunswick; spilled over onto the campus at Moncton and into the city hall of an old town which, like all places now linked directly to the world by electronics, could not escape the malevolence that swept over everything. Nothing about Moncton got more attention at home or abroad than Leonard Jones' confrontations with Acadian youth at home and with bilingualism in Ottawa. He became the symbol of antibilingualism to the degree that even his Conservative Party leader, the Hon. Robert Stanfield, disowned him.

Mason Wade, the American historian who is an authority on French Quebec and Acadian history, in the *Journal of Canadian Studies* once referred to "a new militancy abroad in the Acadian world. It is," he wrote, "partly a spillover from events elsewhere, notably in Quebec and France, and partly a product of the times. The Acadians, like the French-speaking minorities elsewhere in Canada, are almost universally opposed to Quebec separatism." Wade referred to the Acadians "traditionally having no great love for the Quebecois. The Acadian is convinced that the Quebecois has usually exploited him while disdaining him as an ignorant and ill-bred poor relation."

As he also wrote, when a few Quebec separatists came to Moncton to agitate, "they were run out of town by Acadians who disapproved their gospel." He and others have said that the troubles which marked the University of Moncton campus "were partly the work of Quebecois or of young Frenchmen who had come to work in Canada to escape military service. They were full of unrest which had shut down the university system in France." In this Wade was not fully informed.

In retrospect, his assessment seems generally true. The provincial separatist political party, Le Parti Acadien, has never gained acceptance and has never elected a member to the legislature. Indeed, if any political phenomenon has occurred in New Brunswick it is that many young Acadians, whose family tradition was Liberal for nearly a century, have tended toward the Conservative party. Partly because it held the power in the province for an extended time and partly because it had become an acceptable thing for an Acadian to do. Normal pragmatism was a factor as was the fact that New Brunswick Conservatives had temporarily become more liberal and the Liberal opposition more conservative.

Quite apart from the national and international disturbances, the Sixties and Seventies coincided with the new sense of identity which had surged through young Acadians. It infected their elders as well. The first-ever elected Acadian had become premier of the province. He fought for reforms which some thought radical, but they were not in the arena of Acadianism itself. The new educational opportunities were for all New Brunswick youth, but especially valuable for those of French-language background who had not previously been able to gain higher education without difficulty and financial sacrifice. As a result, few had then advanced to universities and many could not manage even high school.

So, with a new French university, with high schools of French-language instruction and expanded curricula which for the first time included the sciences, there was a new awakening. There was a surge of pride. This sense of emerging identity, of emerging opportunities for achievement, brought in their wake the natural radicalism that affects students who have felt that now the lid is off old oppression. There were shouts for full equality. In Moncton, spurred by the radicalism that had engulfed a violent element in Quebec, some students began to ask for an extension of bilingualism, for acceptance of bilingual services in Moncton where French-speaking people could count themselves 34 percent of the population.

After the University of Moncton moved into its full stature with various academic faculties in 1963, its student body multiplied rapidly. Many of the new students came with limited means. Many required loans and grants and the university itself was being operated on a careful basis because costs were growing and the increasing student body needing major faculty increases. In February, 1968, students voted to boycott classes to draw attention to the need for larger university funding. They were also protesting the raising of fees, as they had done as early as 1966 when they sought provincial assistance to offset the fee increases.

They barricaded the streets of the campus and held marches through the city. Other student groups supported their protest, including those at Mount Allison in Sackville.

At the same time, four young people from the university of Moncton and French-language area high schools went to Moncton's city council as a delegation to ask for implementation of recommendations of the Royal Commission on Bilingualism and Biculturalism. They were Claude Savoie, of the university, as spokesman (He would later become a conservative construction company owner), Irene Doiron from the university; Yolande Arsenault from Vanier high school, and Bernard Gauvin of the university. Earlier, Claude LeBreton, president of the university's student federation, had asked organizers to call off the protest march which accompanied the delegates. Savoie had disagreed with him and the delegation proceeded to city hall in a peaceful demonstration.

As taped and filmed documentation would later show, Mayor Jones and some members of council gave the students a rude and insulting reception. When they had presented council with a French-language copy of the Royal Commission report, Jones said he would have difficulty reading it. When they asked for bilingual services, he asked where the money would come from. He also said that since only one of the nine council members (Coun. Leonide Cyr) spoke French, they should address council in English. At one point, he suggested to Miss Doiron that since she was so fluently bilingual, she present the case in English.

"You are attending a bilingual university," he told her, "you should be able to speak English." "No," she replied, "it is a French language university."

Then the students suggested that Councillor Cyr interpret for the students and the mayor said that Cyr wasn't paid to be an interpreter. Finally, Jones offered the students what he called "fatherly advice" to return to their studies. However, as reported afterwards by the local newspapers, Leonard Jones acted "like an aggressive crown prosecutor."

When the delegation finally emerged from the council chamber they were cheered by some four hundred marching supporters with banners and placards.

Two days later, a pair of university students from Quebec homes took on the role of delivery men to play a prank which would stir Jones and much of the city's community into a wrathy response. The media made such a big thing of it, with Jones taking it as a terrible insult, that what began as a student prank wound up as a *cause célebre*. The pair, Jacques Bilise of Terrebonne, P.Q., and Jacques Moreau of St. Sauveur, P.Q., went to Jones' home carrying a pig's head in a cardboard box.

In Quebec, a pig's head is a well-known symbol of pigheadedness and the students' idea was to let Leonard Jones know they considered him pig-headed in his opposition to bilingual services. But the symbol was not familiar in New Brunswick, although pig-headedness was a common expression, and it seems likely that many had interpreted it as a bloody reminder of an American gangster ploy. The gangsters, as seen in the Hollywood film, *The Godfather* put a bleeding horse's head into the bed of a moving picture tycoon to horrify him into doing their bidding.

The mayor had flagged a passing police cruiser and had the two students apprehended. They were held on a charge of public mischief. The head had weighed about ten pounds, police said, and was accompanied by a card whose contents they never disclosed. Next morning, Bilise and Moreau appeared before Judge Henry Murphy who delayed the case until Cpl. Robert Rochon, of the R.C.M.P. would be called in to read the charge in French. The young lawyer, Roger Savoie of Moncton, appeared for the two youths and asked for an adjournment. In the meantime, the mayor told newspaper people that he had received a couple of threatening telephone calls from French-speaking students after the city hall episode.

As it developed, Savoie asked that a trial be held in French and the issue was referred to the Supreme Court of New Brunswick to determine whether the French language was legal in the courts. At that time, the Official Languages Act had not come into effect in the province. The case went back to Murphy and the two were tried, convicted and fined $25 which was immediately raised by friends.

The next step in this issue arose when Rheal Drisdelle, a university student, was charged by Jones with loitering outside his home. Savoie represented him as well and again asked for a trial in French. This case became a landmark in Canadian judicial and linguistic history. After Savoie's request, the attorney-general of New Brunswick stayed proceedings because of the question of legality in court language use. The appeal court of New Brunswick ruled that the Official Languages Act made French-language trials valid in New Brunswick. This was appealed to the Supreme Court of Canada by Leonard Jones. By now, there were Official Languages Acts both federally and provincially and the Supreme Court of Canada upheld the New Brunswick decision. Cases could be heard in either English or French in New Brunswick. Drisdelle's case, having been stayed, never came to trial.

A National Film Board crew had been on hand for the various events which marked the university boycott, the city hall bilingualism demands and marches and the pig's head incident. The film which resulted, when shown on television, aroused the students to new heights of anger. Entitled "L'Acadie, L'Acadie" the documentary itself became a cause and caught national attention later. For now, it was enough to create the largest Moncton demonstration yet. This was in January, 1972, and Leonard Jones had been re-elected for the sixth time in the previous year. Various minor events had occurred, such as a spitting charge laid against a student for spitting at the mayor, deliberate parking charges provoked so that the languages of the courts matter could be tested.

There was a great march on city hall involving a large number of Acadian citizens, mostly very young, as well as university students. Estimates of the numbers ran from 400 to 1,000, with the figure of 800 being the most popular.

While Leonard Jones was in the city council chamber casting the deciding vote that Moncton would take no action to create more bilingual services, students were scuffling with police outside in the street. Using French, they asked for a change that would give French its proper place in civic affairs. Jones, going out, told them to speak English. He said later that "it was no good for them to speak French because eight of the nine councillors spoke only English." In an interview with the newspapers afterward, Jones said that, "We were on the verge of a massive riot that night and what I did cooled everything down because there was no riot. The English are great appeasers and they've put up with separatism for so long that the country may be reaching a point of no return. Bilingualism," he added, "could be the death of this city, this province and eventually this country." Of course, separatism had nothing whatever to do with the marchers' requests.

When the decade of the Seventies was over, Jones once told David MacPherson, a *Times-Transcript* reporter, that: "I've suffered over the years because of it. I've been shot at, spit at and assaulted. When they put that pig's head at my door, just imagine the mental anguish my wife and daughter felt." It was necessary sometimes, he recalled, to have police guarding his house 24 hours a day and to teach his family to use a revolver which a city policeman had given Jones, along with a shoulder holster, to carry for his own protection.

Jones told the reporter that "If I had to do it over, I'd do exactly as I did. The problem is not with the Acadians. I have some excellent friends and clients who are Acadians...but they are not separatists." The fact was that Jones and his father and grandfather had always had Acadian clients in the days before loan companies existed. A good many of them, as well as others who had traditionally supported Mayor Jones, continued to vote for him during all the years of controversy.

The mayor seemed to have bitten at every lure sent his way to exacerbate the language issue. At one point, he was sent an honorary Acadian certificate from the university city of Lafayette in Louisiana. Ungraciously, Jones sent it back. And that really soured things. Later, Jones in a radio broadcast heaped coals of fire when he called the twinning idea between Lafayette and Moncton "a low-ley conspiracy to promote bilingualism."

Seven years later, when Roger Savoie stood as a Conservative candidate for a provincial legislature seat in Northumberland county, a whispering campaign was used in an attempt to link him with separatists because he had sought a French language trial for a client. Though the area where he ran, around Rogersville, was primarily French, the English section was normally of Conservative persuasion and they switched their votes. As well, of course, it was a largely traditional Liberal section with some Acadian French objecting to the idea of separatism (which was certainly not Savoie's philosophy) and others simply refusing to vote for a Conservative candidate.

Though Leonard Jones was in no way involved with it, another student event should be described here to provide some background for other events which did. On January 13, 1969, a so-called "rebel student group" took over the administration and sciences building of the University of Moncton and all classes were suspended. About half the student body turned up for classes but returned to their residences. At the campus, normal school classes went on as usual for some 400 students. "Money," headlined the *Telegraph-Journal* of Saint John, "A Root of Occupation." Money *was* the issue but radicalized students had been learning too much from campus events which had been going on in the United States under much different circumstances.

Following their practice in Quebec, undercover agents for the R.C.M.P., kept an eye on a few they considered as dissident students. They had been frightened, as had many in Canada, by the actions of the F.L.Q. in Quebec, but the virus had never seriously penetrated the French communities in New Brunswick. As time would prove, none of the rebellious students gave cause for serious concern. In a very few years, they had gone into conventional adult careers, in business, as conservative lawyers and into Film Board and C.B.C. jobs. As this is written, all of them are ordinary citizens, doing well in their chosen careers and quite the antithesis of rebels.

If the response of Leonard Jones and some supportive city councillors had been as reasonable and understanding of youthful rebelliousness as the campus authorities, it is unlikely if much would have come of the confrontations. The students were maturing in the extraordinary atmosphere of their times, many experiencing for the first time any idea of special social action. The age of confrontation had begun but, in the end, the harsher confrontations and the violence that occurred in so many other places, found no fertile ground among the Acadians. It was really not their style. Furthermore, as this generation, an educated generation — and in a general sense, actually the first full generation of Acadians to have the opportunity of higher education — took over its appropriate place in society, it proved Moncton with a new and ambitious leaven and a more comprehensive outlook.

There were other things besides student confrontations to keep the English-French language pot boiling during Mayor Jones' regime in Moncton. There was to have been a French-language plaque placed on the wall in city hall alongside the English, but Leonard Jones objected. The Societé Nationale des Acadiens had asked that the plaque be hung at the inaugural in December of 1971. The society said that the city's coat of arms, using one language, was an insult to the French-speaking population. Jones led a campaign to return bilingual badges bought for firemen's uniforms.

In the end, Gilbert Finn, president of Assumption Mutual, which had financed the new city centre complex, requested that the unilingual plaque be removed. Jones talked vaguely about moving out of city hall in Assumption Place, but there was the little matter of a forty-year lease. Finn won that skirmish. Then the Dominion of Canada English-Speaking League began distributing a sheet called *Maple Leaf News* in Moncton. It recommended an anglophone backlash against bilingualism.

Finally, there was Councillor Steve Campbell's accusation that Jones had used unauthorized public funds to buy city flags. It was said that the mayor had given the impression that he had paid for them out of his own pocket. Campbell charged that Jones had paid only $360 whereas the total bill was $1,400 and the city paid the difference. After an investigation by the city auditor and city solicitor Jones got a mild rebuke but it was ruled he had done nothing illegal.

It was during Leonard Jones' time in office that moves for amalgamation of Moncton's two suburban towns came to the fore. The original idea was to make one city of eight communities which, in the end, came to be three separate municipalities, Moncton, Riverview and Dieppe. Lewisville and Humphrey were attached to Moncton which much earlier had taken in Georgetown, Sunny Brae and Newton Heights, then Parkton and adjacent lands.

The small provincial grant offered Moncton to accommodate its new residents outraged Jones, who found it easy to be outraged when it came to Fredericton's attitude toward Moncton. On occasion, he would allow rumors to grow that he himself would enter provincial politics as leader of the Conservative Party.

Effectively, the amalgamations creating Dieppe made it an almost wholly French-language municipality. Politically, it constituted a largely Liberal one. Riverview, reflecting the county of its provenance and the preference of many newcomers, became largely Conservative. So far as the federal constituency went, there was a major change with redistribution in 1968 creating the new riding of Moncton.

From its establishment in 1867, the federal riding of Westmorland had been dominantly Liberal. Only on eight occasions out of 31 elections had it sent a Conservative to Ottawa and only once after 1930. Moncton city had been a major part of it, and Moncton's orientation was often Conservative. But the county outside outweighed it because of massive and concentrated Liberal support. Now, beginning with the election of 1968, the balance was changed. The new constituency of Moncton took in both Riverview and Dieppe, with each balancing the other, while an apparently Conservative majority remained in Moncton proper.

Early in 1974, Leonard Jones announced that he would retire from municipal politics and Maclean's magazine named him the worst mayor in Canada. Jones responded by saying he had been called worse, leaving the public to wonder what that might be. He wasn't a bad mayor. Obviously, a majority of voters had thought him a good one, while others considered him misguided, provocative and perhaps naive — though

260

never politically so. He had seen the opportunity of playing on a current right-wing wave of reaction, capitalized on it temporarily but failed to appreciate the long term and wider repercussion of his actions. He did not seem to appreciate the current movement of Canadian history nor interpret and intercept its direction.

He had mounted a bulky steed, one which in Moncton had become spavined and reeking of other time and other morés. He would learn this suddenly after he had gone to the Progressive Conservative nomination meeting in May and gained the local party's approval as federal candidate for Moncton. He won it against a considerable wing of his party but with the strong support of his formidable municipal political machine. Robert L. Stanfield, the leader of the national Progressive Conservative party, was not amused. Jones' reputation had preceded him and Stanfield was in a battle against Pierre Trudeau, a rival in office who may well have been the toughest in Canadian history.

Stanfield was beginning to gain foothold in Quebec. He had learned to speak French passably well; he had ingratiated himself with the party's French-Canadian wing and he had supported the federal policy of bilingualism. To have a candidate with Jones' anti-bilingual reputation would cost him seats in French Canada. So, he made a personal visit to Jones in Moncton, told him abruptly that he could not accept him as an official Conservative candidate. Jones could run, if he wanted, but not under the sponsorship of the Progressive Conservative Party of Canada.

So, Leonard C. Jones decided to run as an Independent, and his machine went to work. His opponents split the opposing vote badly, with Charles Thomas, the official P.C. candidate getting 6,456 votes, Leonide Cyr, the Liberal candidate getting 16,199, David Britton, N.D.P. 1,496 and Robert M. Taylor, Social Credit, 342. Jones topped them all with a massive 20,671. It was much less than half the vote cast, but it was impressive even if he ran against weak candidates. It was revenge for the former mayor but in the end it lost Jones a career at the national and provincial political levels. He could no longer aspire to provincial leadership and he soon discovered that, in Ottawa, independents count for little. Few countries have a party system so entrenched as Canada, unlike Britian M.P.'s they cannot with impunity cross the floor to leave a party. Nor, unlike the United States Congress, can they vote independently from their parties and get away with it.

It's a lonely life and one that led to Leonard Jones' early retirement in 1978 and the accession of a Liberal M.P. for Moncton, in 1979. He was Gary Francis McCauley, an Anglican pastor, born in Cochrane, Ontario, and a resident of Riverview, N.B.

Chapter Twenty-five

NEW MAYOR BITES THE DUST

It is necessary now to return to that year of 1974 when the mayoral seat was vacated and a young construction engineer decided to fill it. He was Gary Wheeler and he was opposed by Dr. Michael Cripton, a one-time Montrealer, an orthodontist and bilingual. The bitterness of the Jones linguistic battles had not subsided and when Cripton used the French language at city hall, it hindered rather than helped him. Wheeler won the contest by 1,700 votes and began a moderate regime calculated to heal wounds so nastily exposed in the previous ten years.

He began on a solid note but, before his term was out, Wheeler ran into trouble of a kind Jones had never experienced. More than that, during his time Moncton was to experience one of its darkest moments in a generation. It arose out of a kidnapping which ended in the ruthless slaying of two Moncton police officers in the line of duty. It was early in December of 1974 that 14-year-old Raymond Stein, son of the prosperous and prominent restaurateur Cy Stein, was kidnapped and a ransom demanded. An arrangement was made to pay the sum and the boy was released.

The arrangement had been completed in Riverview and, afterward two Moncton policemen, Corporal Aurele Bourgeois, 47, and Constable Michael O'Leary, 33, were

GARY WHEELER
— Ahearn Studio Photo

checking a suspicious automobile near the Riverview Mall when last heard from. Then they disappeared. Their abandoned car and an ominous shovel were found five hours later and the city shivered with the fear that something dreadful had happened. Two suspects were apprehended within hours and Richard Ambrose was held. For two days a frantic search went on for the police officers, with every hour becoming more desperately gloomy. Finally, before noon on Sunday, December 15, their bodies were found in a shallow grave near the Cape Breton Road beyond Irishtown. They had been manacled and shot.

Not only Moncton and its sister towns were shocked and troubled but the affair had taken national attention. Everywhere police were dismayed and disturbed. Hours after the bodies were discovered, Royal Canadian Mounted Police under a search team led by Sgt. Gregory Cohoon, went looking for James Lawrence Hutchinson. Roadblocks went up, house searches were made with guns drawn..Hutchinson was spotted several times and then gave himself up to the police. Eventually, he and Ambrose were tried, convicted and sentenced to hang. However, the death sentence was abolished before they were due to hang and their sentences were commuted to life in prison. It had been the first time in this century that a Moncton policeman had been killed on duty.

There was a great out-pouring of sympathy for the families of the victims. A huge funeral at the Assumption Cathedral conducted by the archbishop of Moncton was attended not only by citizens but by representatives of police forces from across Canada. Then, when a fund was begun to give practical recognition to a city's grief, a remarkable total of $400,000. was quickly subscribed for the families of the victims. Contributions came from all over Canada and from many in the United States.

There was more violence in 1974 and two rival groups got themselves into a minor gang war in Moncton. Thomas Meredith, 24, was gunned down as he stepped out of a Main street restaurant. Only two days later, police found the body of Francis Bastarache, 26, beaten and with three shots in the head. Six men were charged in the affair and three were convicted.

One effect of the police slayings was the attention given the remarkable police work of Sergeant Gregory Cohoon, who had been in charge of the R.C.M.P. Newcastle detachment. When, in 1975 Moncton decided to reorganize its police force (partly because of its handling of the kidnap case) Cohoon was brought in as Moncton's new police chief. A professional, and a most competent and determined one, he quickly set about giving the city a modern, well chosen and well trained protective force. It was the one good thing which had come out of the tragic series of events which marked the mid term of the decade. All in all, it would prove to be one of Moncton's most disturbing in a century.

This was not the only change wrought by the new broom sweeping city hall. Wheeler fired some department heads, reorganized other departments and established a new community services section. Council committees were abolished and a city manager, Robert Boxwell, was hired. The former police chief, C.M.(Moody) Weldon, went into early retirement when that department was about to be reorganized.

Under Cohoon, what began to happen might be called a station revolution and, when it was over, the highly competent new chief had done what he had set out to do with Wheeler's approval. This was the establishment of a modern city police force from what had been essentially a holdover of smalltown cops. The force had gone feeble after improvements and strengthening had been achieved after World War One by Leonard Hutchinson, a chief who came with excellent credentials.

He in his time had introduced professional policing methods to the city, but the force was small, resources limited and, after he retired, nothing much happened for a long time.

Between Hutchinson's time and Cohoon's, the department had deteriorated with a succession of politically-chosen chiefs. As for. Hutchinson, a native of Sackville, before coming to Moncton, he had been chief keeper at Dorchester penitentiary for 22 years. As well, he had been provost-marshal during World War One at the army's Camp Aldershot in Nova Scotia. Later he had been in army intelligence at Halifax.

CHIEF G. COHOON

CHIEF HUTCHINSON

Hutchinson came to Moncton in 1920 and remained as chief from then until his retirement in 1946. During his first years, he had introduced Moncton's first traffic control measures. These included traffic lights and stop streets. His arrival had coincided with the change from left-hand (British) driving to right hand (American) driving, in 1922. For a while this caused a great deal of confusion.

One of the chief's first apprehensions was of his cousin, Bill Chapman of Dorchester, when the first stop signs were put up. Chapman had slowed up but not stopped and when the chief ordered him to pull over, he said: "You and I went to school together, Bill, and I learned that S-T-O-P- doesn't spell 'hesitate.' How come you didn't?" With that, he let Chapman off with a warning.

Hutchinson's military police experience was valuable to the city during World War Two when as many as 20,000 service men could be in Moncton at one time. Working in harmony with military police, he kept the city notably crime-free and peaceful during that whole period.

For his services, Hutchinson was recommended for the Order of the British Empire, but before it could be awarded, Prime Minister Mackenzie King had titles and British orders abolished in Canada, so that Hutchinson's honor remained only a recommendation.

Returning to the 1970's and Mayor Gary Wheeler, it could be said that his term of office brought a gradual shift in English-French relations. He cooled out the heat generated during the Jones era and got on with the job of reorganizing the city's administrative structure. It was long overdue. Moncton had grown but mayors and councils hadn't noticed. However, by 1976, there were some on council whispering that Wheeler was associated with companies doing business with the city. Sylvio Savoie, a young lawyer, had become chairman of a citizen's committee which called for a provincial inquiry in early 1977. This was rejected by the provincial department of municipal affairs but Charles J. Gillespie, a lawyer and councillor-at-large, would not let the matter drop. He raised his voice in council and out, maintaining that there were conflicts of interest at city hall. He demanded that the Provincial Supreme Court remove Wheeler from office for conflict of interest.

CHARLES J. GILLESPIE
— Ahearn Studio Photo

Just days before the city election, the court found dissatisfaction with conflict-of-interest legislation but ruled Wheeler was being unjustly pursued and, in any case, he was returned to the mayoralty with a narrow majority.

Both Gillespie and Gerald Carson, who had been involved in the controversy because of business connections, lost their council seats in that election. Carson was replaced by a young school teacher, Dennis Cochrane (one of six new councillors).

After his defeat, Charles Gillespie continued his fight against conflict-of-interest, taking the case on appeal from the Supreme Court of New Brunswick to the Supreme Court of Canada. The case developed extraordinary interest among lawyers and public servants all across Canada, although at the time the public took it calmly. It stirred talk in Moncton but few believed that Gillespie's application would be successful. However, he and Savoie had done their homework and they presented a carefully argued case to the court.

As such cases do this one took considerable time to reach decision and, in the meantime, Wheeler carried on the civic affairs for which he had been elected. And he had problems there, too. A theft ring was discovered in the police department and seven constables were dismissed. Cohoon's strong hand was showing well. The dismissed policemen were charged but given suspended sentences or conditional discharges by Provincial Court Judge Henry Murphy who said that they were good men who had slipped in moments of weakness.

Then, another shock for the city's administration. A former fire chief who had become fire prevention officer, was found to have been setting fire to local buildings. Charged with arson, he was convicted and sentenced to prison. Later, he was transferred to a mental institution. It was a tragic case of personal destruction.

The Supreme Court of Canada ruled in the Wheeler matter in 1979 and that ended the regime he had established at city hall. He was ordered to be removed from office. Wheeler had been following the New Brunswick Municipalities Act as his guideline in conflict of interest concerns. However, the

Supreme Court of Canada ruled that Moncton's own more restrictive Consolidation Act took precedence over the provincial act. The court noted that Wheeler had not attempted to conceal his business interests but that did not make the matters legal. The mayor and the city were stunned. The decision became a Canadian legal landmark. Gary Wheeler resigned as mayor and decided to try federal politics.

When the Conservative nomination convention was held, he won on the first ballot. But his campaign was haunted by the Supreme Court decision and Leonard Jones, by then retired from national politics for reasons of health (and severe Independence malaise) opposed Wheeler openly, though he did not again become a candidate for the federal seat. With the Moncton Conservative Party suffering from the series of blows that lowered esteem, the Anglican clergyman, Gary McCauley, who lived in Riverview, served a parish in Moncton and had become a celebrity as a broadcast commentator, easily took the seat for the Liberals.

Five years earlier, in a provincial election, Liberals had shown revived strength in the city and much of it had arisen out of the antagonism Leonard Jones had raised among French-language voters. In this 1974 New Brunswick election, the citizens chose Councillor Ray Frenette and Rev. Michael McKee, both bilingual. At the time, Father McKee was a practising Catholic priest, the first ever elected to the provincial legislature. At the same time, another Acadian, Hon. Jean-Paul LeBlanc who had been in the cabinet as treasury board chairman, was defeated because he was a Conservative and the voters of the day had equated Conservatism locally with anti-Acadianism. (Premier Richard Hatfield would spend the next eight years in an effort to prove otherwise). Another Moncton Conservative who lost in the post-Jones provincial contest was Arthur Buck. It was not hard to see that year's poll result as a reflection of the Acadian antipathy toward city hall than straight partisan politics.

Chapter Twenty-six

NO FIDDLERS ON THE ROOF

If the history of Moncton's Jewish community were to be romanticized, one might imagine the little village of Dorobjny in Lithuania as a locale for that beautiful production "Fiddler-On-The-Roof." It was from this Old Country shtetl that most of Moncton's original Jewry came. They came out of hardship and it might be said that they prospered in this new and welcoming town.

That would be accurate in two respects: Most of the first Moncton Jewish settlers did come from Dorobjny and many have prospered here; some exceedingly well. Truth, however, is never quite that simple. The Dorobjny people did not leave Lithuania because of persecution; they left because of financial deprivation and perhaps even oppression. But when the first of them reached the new railroad town of Moncton, they were not exactly greeted with open arms. Still, they were all related one way or another, each family helping another in its turn, and they managed.

The unromantic fact is that, not for eleven years after the pioneer Jacob Baig arrived in 1898, was the little Judaic community able to support a rabbi, who even then could be only a part-time leader. And it was 26 years before the adherents could gather enough through contributions of ten-cents-a-week to build a synagogue.

When they bought land on Steadman street for the building, the auction price of $650.00 was forced up unreasonably by those who objected to such a place of worship going into one of Moncton's choice residential streets. As it developed, this objection favored Jewish families because adjoining homes were sold to them and they could be close to the temple. Further, it was just a block away from Telegraph (now Lewis street) street where many of the first settlers lived, and the orthodox could observe the sabbath custom of walking to the synagogue without difficulty.

It was a long time before even trained and talented members of the community could find employment, except as they made it themselves in commercial pursuits. The railroad was the biggest employer, but no Jews need apply. There was nothing for them. It was the same, after 1920, when Eaton's came to town. Catholics might complain that they could not rise to managerial positions there but for the Jewish applicants there was nothing at all.

Historically, it is worth recording that bright and highly competent daughters of Jewish families found employment locally more difficult than did their brothers. It was not until Ruth Selick, a high school and business college graduate, was hired by Calvin I. Mills, of the Record Foundry, about 1930, that a Jewish woman in Moncton found office employment. During the 1930's as a new generation was finishing high school and going on to university, Monctonians began to appreciate the competence and sometimes brilliance of their fellow-citizens in the academic sphere.

In all these things, Moncton was no different from most other Canadian and American communities. Of course, ignorance was at the base of the prejudice — as it is of all prejudice. The people of Hebraic faith and of Polish-Lithuanian or Russian-Lithuanian extraction were exotics to the isolated local citizenry. They were "different," spoke alien tongues, observed a different sabbath and preferred foods sanctified by ritual law. So it is only historically true to say that they were shunned by the majority in the first years of this century.

Today, of course, a more sophisticated population sees things differently. The Jewish population which is one of the largest in the Maritimes, is, by and large, prosperous and sophisticated itself and the community has produced some of Moncton's most outstanding achievers. Though he stayed only briefly before moving on to Amherst, its first Jewish resident, Jake Baig, was to be the uncle of Moncton's first and, so far, only Jewish mayor, Mike Baig, whose death occurred in August, 1981, at the age of 79.

The one romantic thing which might be ascribed to the Moncton Jewish community is perhaps that, in business, in science and in finance, it has contributed out of proportion to its size.

The family of Mr. and Mrs. Isaac Selick, while not one of the first among Jewry settling in Moncton, could nevertheless be said to have given that community an important lift. They had come from Hillsboro where Isaac and his brother Samuel had developed a successful business. They had begun as peddlers and were known and respected in Albert County. As soon as Isaac and Bessie Selick (She was a sister of the merchant Harry Kirsh) set up in Moncton, they became immediately active in Jewish affairs. Isaac bought the Cassidy and Belliveau hardware store, went into groceries first and expanded quickly into general supplies, catering particularly to the needs of farmers and woods operators and later in the fuel business. That original business site is now covered by the Beauséjour hotel on Main street at the foot of Alma.

Mr. Selick was elected first president of Tiferes Israel synagogue and Mrs. Selick was a leader in women's groups. They built a house on School Street, beside Aberdeen High, and were among the first Moncton Jews to move a short way from the Telegraph-Steadman enclave and form a warm association with their Gentile neighbors. For many of us, the Selick home was the first Jewish home ever visited and it was a hospitable one.

Another Monctonian who was an innovator in merchandising was Abe Levine who established Moncton's first real super-market for groceries. This expanded into the St. George Food Market, modelled somewhat on the great Steinberg chain founded in Montreal. Eventually, Levine sold out his operation to the Sobey chain.

Writing in 1982 when at least three children of the Moncton synagogue have made their mark on the national and international scene as financier, scientist and author, it is difficult to recall the community's harsher beginnings. Difficult except for the fact that the writer grew up in Moncton at a time when most of the original Jewish residents were still around and one could see the emergence of a new Moncton-born generation. Their scholarship, drive and application was a challenge to those whose opportunities had been more favorable.

Among the earliest of local arrivals was Morris Gorber, who in his eighties in the 1980's could still regale his listeners with stories of the hégira from Lithuania. He himself had got as far as Antwerp in Belgium, with long-saved money carefully put aside for his passage and visa. However the city's bright lights intrigued him as he waited for his ship and he began to sample the delights of a kind he had never before known. By sailing time, his little hoard was gone and he was left behind. But his friend, Solomon Jake, had reached Moncton and he sent Gorber the money to continue his journey. (Solomon Jake was the father of Freda Selick, Sara Block and Morris Jake.)

Mr. Gorber also remembered how Frank Mendelson, his wife and their children, had come on the same boat to Canada. Their worldly possessions were gathered into a down-filled comforter but, tragically, it had split open while their goods were strewn onto the deck to their consternation but to the amusement of fellow-passengers. Three-quarters of a century later, Morris Gorber could still see the confusion.

By 1926 there were still only 26 Jewish families in Moncton and in that year a cornerstone for a synagogue was laid. Tiferes Israel was completed in 1927 for $7,000.00 and the contractor, Ambrose Wheeler, lost money on the contract as Rabbi Joshua Spiro noted at the time. A sometime mayor of Moncton, Wheeler had come here from Newfoundland and was particularly prominent in the 1930's when he managed the Moncton Hawks hockey team and the Moncton Stadium.

It was about 1930 when a small plot of land was purchased for a Jewish cemetery; before that, burials were in Saint John. But no one wanted to be first to be buried in the new cemetery (No one wants to be first in any cemetery of course, or second or third) and some continued to request burial in Saint John. However, Aaron Coleman before his death in 1931 asked to buried in the Chartersville location.

A white-bearded patriarch whose wife's bagels were famous in Moncton, he was the father of Lizzie who married Morris Gorber, the community's current patriarch. His grandson, Oscar Coleman, is an air traffic controller as this is written. Later, Isaac Selick donated more land for an extended cemetery, a Chevra Kiddisha (or Burial) Society was formed and Jake Lampert served as first president and continued for several years.

Moncton's first rabbi was Jacob Hans who, though not ordained, had some rabbinical background such as teaching and ritual slaughtering. This was in 1909 when the community was large enough to support a rabbi. By 1914 when there were some 15 families, Nathan Schelew served for a time as rabbi. Later, he was widely known in Moncton's business community and in politics. Jacob Hans did much to mold the community and maintain the Hebraic traditions. After a time, he gave this up and went to live in the Gorge area becoming a cattle buyer for Swift's packing company. His life ended when he was killed in an automobile accident around 1960. His brother, Harry Hans, himself a local tradition, lives in retirement on Church street in Moncton as this is written. He operated a grocery store for 60 years and knew more about the Jewish community than anyone else.

One of the first ordained rabbis of Tiferes Israel was Joshua Spiro who came from Poland, and it was he who was instrumental in organizing the building of a synagogue in 1926. He was still living in Toronto at the time of writing.

Notable among the rabbis was Rabbi Harry Bronstein, who had come to Moncton from Sydney Pier in the late 1930's. Some years after his service in Moncton, Rabbi Bronstein went to New York where he became nationally known for his scholarship in Jewish ritual and then even more famous for his work helping to bring Jews out of Russia. At the time of writing he was president of Al Tidom, an organization dedicated to providing Jews in Russia with materials to maintain their Jewish religious life.

No local rabbi came to be so well known to the general population in Moncton, nor to participate so frequently in public activities, as Rabbi Lippa Medjuck. More than that, he served longer than any other, coming to the congregation in 1940 and remaining until his death in 1971.

A later rabbi, who remained for six years from 1971 to 1977 was the Hungarian-born Menachem G. Kitziner who had come to Canada after World War II. Rabbi Stanley Greenberg, born a New Yorker, had the distinction of being a "reborn Jew" in that he came to religion during college years. He was also unusual in Moncton since Tiferes Israel was his first pulpit. It is a remarkable coincidence that both Rabbi Kutziner and Rabbi Greenberg were killed in tragic automobile accidents.

Another New Yorker was Rabbi Philip Lefkowitz who was born in Brooklyn. Arriving in Moncton in 1979, he brought to the congregation a strong tone of Orthodoxy. His early training had been in the Conservative movement of Judaism but later rejected its theology and entered Orthodoxy. (Judaism has four denominations and, going from fundamentalism to "liberalism" they are, in that order, Orthodox, Conservative, Reconstructionist and Reform. The Tiferes Israel congregation was Orthodox under Rabbi Lefkowitz.) Studying under Rabbi Israel Jacobson, dean of the Lubavitch Rabbinical Seminary for eight years, Rabbi Lefkowitz was ordained in 1968 and served congregations in New York, Pennsylvania, New Jersey before being invited to Moncton.

Because he was mayor of Moncton from 1957 to 1961, Michael M. Baig was known personally and by name to more Monctonians than others of the Jewish community. However, in the long term and on a national level, that of H. Reuben Cohen was certainly the most eminent.

Baig had come from Saint John in 1939 to set up a furniture business but Reuben Cohen was born in Moncton and never lived anywhere else. In the world of finance, he had come by the 1970's to be among the country's most successful investors. At the same time, he had maintained a lifelong association with Moncton affairs, was fascinated by local history and sometimes talked nostalgically of a boyhood when adherents of the synogogue were largely concentrated in the city's East End.

A soft-spoken and reticent man, Cohen enjoyed the practice of law but gradually and through local real estate investments, he had become more and more involved in the financial field. This would grow so important that he no longer had time for law, leaving that to his partners, while becoming the first Monctonian in history to reach a position of national stature in finance.

In his youth, he had as many friends among the Acadian-French of that area as in the Hebrew schule and remembers only one incident of religious discrimination. In a backyard rink near Queen and Alma streets, a doctor's son told him he could not play there, and said why. Cohen remembered half a century afterward that his pal, Ernie Richard, and all of his friends left the rink with him, leaving the doctor's boy to play by himself.

Reuben Cohen linked with Leonard Ellen as a partner in finance in the 1960's when the Quebec-based lumber wholesaler was buying and selling the product for domestic and export markets. Ellen had made a good deal of money, lived in a fashionable Westmount home in Montreal and invested in such companies as Central & Nova Scotia Trust (later merged with Eastern Canada Savings & Loan to form Central & Eastern Trust Co., and now with Central Trust.)

Together, the partners invested in the Maritime Life Insurance Co., later sold to John Hancock Mutual Life Insurance Co. Cohen was on Maritime's board of directors and by 1981 was the oldest serving director. Then Cohen and Ellen moved into United Financial Management Ltd., and bought a part of Crown Trust, an important national company.

In Toronto and Montreal, Reuben Cohen was known as the largest shareholder in Central Trust, itself the largest trust company in Atlantic Canada. He became a director and member of the executive management committee of the Mortgage Insurance Company of Canada, whose other directors form a cross-section of the elite of English and

H. REUBEN COHEN, Q.C.

French Canada's older financial establishment. In this and other affairs, he was so often in Toronto that he maintained a residence there, as well as a home in Palm Beach. His widespread financial interests made him a constant traveller on the North American continent and beyond.

Once inside the exclusive portals of Canadian higher finance, the movement was straight upward for H. Reuben Cohen. His name became one with which to conjure in the realms of national investments. And yet, while his business associations had made him a citizen of a wider world and an eminence in his home town, he remained always faithfully attached to the city's Jewish community. A traditional observer of its Orthodox rites, he was the only member of the Maritime Provinces Jewry to be honored with the Order of Canada.

As his own corporate and personal interests expanded, there was one voluntary project to which he became particularly dedicated. That was the endowment and pension fund of Dalhousie University in Halifax. As chairman of the investment committee of the board of governors, of which he was a member, Cohen devoted much of his time and concern to keeping that $100,000,000. fund healthy and growing.

Neither casual nor eclectic, he and his wife Louise were patrons of the arts, especially in painting and music, and built a collection of paintings worthy of a respectable museum. In all of this, they were something new in the history of Moncton's affluent families who had rarely breached the walls of culture and even more rarely supported them. And there were few so attached as Reuben Cohen to the history and memories of the hometown which had given him his career and his distinction. More than most, he had remained a part of it even though his business affairs had grown far beyond it.

Nearly half a century after the event, Reuben Cohen remembered with justified pride that he had led his high school graduating class in 1938, but he recalled with even more enthusiasm what happened the year before and the year after. His friends, Jayson Greenblatt and Myer Mendelson, each led his own class in 1939 and 1937. Like Cohen, Greenblatt and Mendelson went on to Dalhousie with scholarships, and all three have become outstandingly successful in their chosen fields. Only Cohen, the lawyer, remained in Moncton.

Myer Mendelson was born in Lithuania, was brought to Moncton as an infant. He and his sister, Anne, who is now the wife of Dr. Jayson Greenblatt, were raised by their maternal uncle, Jake Marks. As this was written, Mendelson was head of psychiatry at the University of Pennsylvania, an expert on depression psychology. He is author of the authoritative "Psycho-analytic Concepts of Depression" and other books. He is a fellow of the Royal College of Physicians and Surgeons of Canada ano professor of clinical psychology. He married Miss Margaret Algie, of Moncton, whose father, Robert Algie, came to Moncton with the Eaton's in 1920.

Aberdeen High School's 1928 graduation class was exceptional in including Prof. Northrop Frye, Canada's most renowned literary scholar, and for three years running in the 1930's the exceptional three of this chapter led the School's graduates. The third of these, Dr. Jayson Greenblatt, is even more reticent about his achievements than the so-nearly invisible Cohen. His father, Moses Aaron, had come to Moncton in 1931, from Thetford Mines, P.Q. His mother and the family followed later. From Quebec, they spoke French, an accomplishment few non-Acadians of New Brunswick then enjoyed. M.A. Greenblatt opened the Maritime Instalment Co., and was the founder of credit stores in Moncton.

His daughter, who married the Moncton merchant Isadore Fine when he came from Montreal, was in her turn at the top of Moncton High's graduating class. Jayson Greenblatt took a master's degree in chemistry at Dalhousie and earned his doctorate at McGill. From there he went to the National Research Council in Ottawa. Greenblatt was a specialist in defense chemistry and was during World War II sent to Washington as a liaison scientist. He chaired the Commonwealth defense staff and for some years, he was Canadian deputy in Washington, responsible for the management of technical co-operative defense program involving commonwealth countries. Later, he was chief of the Canadian Navy laboratory in Halifax where he now lives, retired from the Navy but a busy consultant.

Chapter Twenty-seven

THE TAMMANY TWINS

Moncton in its time has produced some interesting politicians but not many of them made it to the national capital. O.B. Price and Henry Murphy, Sherwood Rideout and his widow, Margaret Rideout, and W.L. Creaghan went as M.P.'s though none stayed all that long. Gary McCauley was on his second term as this was written. However, when the Liberals held their leadership convention in 1958 which chose Hon. Lester Bowles Pearson as federal chieftain, a couple of ardent Moncton party men took it upon themselves to be on hand. They had no federal ambitions for themselves, only a desire to help their candidate.

As it happened, the writer was also there, as a newspaper man, and was intrigued by the operations conducted by the two self-appointed helpers from the old hometown. They were Ernie O'Brien and Laurie Williams, and the former had been a schoolmate, the latter familiar for his associations around and about Moncton's city hall. They had, as it chanced, been introduced to Pearson while he was in Moncton (then as minister of external affairs) campaigning during the general election of 1953.

Walter Gordon, later to become a short-lived minister of finance, was running Lester B. Pearson's campaign for leadership. To him, Ernie and Laurie introduced themselves as friends of the candidate, willing to do anything he might bid.

They then took up posts as inner and outer guardians of the door to Pearson's suite in the Chateau Laurier hotel. In a *Toronto Star* political column, they were dubbed "The Tammany Twins; from a part of the country where politics is still politics." Unconcerned with the sometimes unsavoury connotations of Tammany, they were indeed delighted with the description and showed the article about as the very few early supporters dribbled up to the Pearson convention headquarters.

Before Ernie and Laurie had arrived on the scene, there really were few supporters around. They had come before most other delegates. There was work to be done at this headquarters and no politicians on hand to do it. At least, not until the Tammany Twins took hold of the reins. They had, they told Gordon and Pearson, experience in such things. They knew where to find the bodies and how to lure them into such hospitality suites as this. They were there in Ottawa to help, and Mike Pearson was their boy. For themselves they wanted nothing, but if any merit should attach itself to their unselfish services it ought to fall to Henry Murphy, M.P. for Westmorland (as the riding then was) their local member aspiring to re-election.

Now, as has been said, they did not arrive unequipped, for Laurie had been an alderman and Ernest ran the concessions at a race-track — professions in which one gets to know the people at the very roots of grass.

Furthermore, they once had taken a course in practical politics and in the art of public relations in the most useful sense. And even furthermore, again, Ernest had once been in the debt of a man who owed him some thousands of dollars. The man couldn't pay but he had a service station in Boston, Mass., and Ernie went there to work for the man and, to that extent at least, get some of his money back.

While in that hive of practical politics, Boston, the home of Mayor Jim Curley of "The Last Hurrah," Ernest missed no opportunity to further himself in the field of political science. Once he went to hear Boss Curley speak and as he remembered: "Boy, I really learned something about politics from that guy."

In addition to his other attributes, Ernest in his youth learned to speak colloquial French the way it was spoken in the streets and in the meeting halls of East-End Moncton. In addition to this advantage in the Tammany twins, Laurie Williams despite his name was an Acadian-French Nova Scotian who learned English as his second tongue.

They believed with a deep conviction that Mr. Pearson was one of the world's great men and they believed with equal conviction that he hadn't had time to get into the field of grass roots, practical backroom politics. To remedy this deficiency they were now on hand.

So they stationed themselves near the outer door of Pearson's suite and welcomed one and all. Welcomed them in two languages. Welcomed them with a warmth and an understanding hard to find in the coldness of a national capital.

If there was an errand to run, one of them ran it; if there was a chore to be performed, one of them performed it. If there was a touchy bit of diplomatic wooing to be done on the vote-getting level, they did it.

No one passed those portals without becoming clearly aware that Mike Pearson, winner of the Nobel Prize, the diplomat of world renown, was likewise and par excellence the greatest politician who ever lived and breathed. The twins told them so.

"Lester B.," they called him if the visitor seemed particularly dignified; otherwise it was just plain "Mike."

Now there were some who did not reach the portals and Laurie and Ernie had *their* concerns at heart as well. They went out, from time to time, to seek these lost sheep and guide them homeward.

It must now be obvious to the most careless reader that Ernest and Laurie were not without effect, for Lester Bowles Pearson won the title and he won it big.

"How did you like that?" they said in unison after Ernie grabbed my coat lapel when Lester B. had been acclaimed the winner. "Did we do a job or did we do a job?"

So I went over then to shake the hand of Mr. Pearson and I asked him: "What's your version of the hometown now?

How do you like the way those boys from Moncton propelled you into leadership?"

And this is what Mike said: "Weren't they wonderful?...Weren't they something?"

Pearson never afterward went through Moncton without inquiring about Ernie....who eventually became president of the local Liberal association, and about Laurie, his partner in politics.

Chapter Twenty-eight

THE OLD (BUT NEW) NEIGHBORS

Because it was one of Canada's first railroad towns, Moncton developed into a city of commuters earlier than most. At first, people came from surrounding places daily to work in the railway shops but as motor roads were opened for winter traffic after 1935 increasing numbers of non-residents came into the city for varied employment. Then, from 1950 onward, two communities which had not been merged with the city itself took on a new growth and new stature. By 1973, two full-scale satellite communities had been incorporated as towns.

They themselves came into being through their amalgamation of old and traditional villages along the opposite banks of the Petitcodiac. Oddly enough, in their origins, each had been settled by French-speaking inhabitants but after the mergers one became fundamentally "English" and the other basically "French" in their linguistic orientation.

Dieppe, the new town with a new name, had grown so quickly that in the first year of the 1980's it had as many elementary schools (and one secondary) as Moncton had in 1920. Riverview, on the other hand, had attracted so many newcomers from the 1960's onward that it talked about gaining city status.

Because the village was no longer a "Corner," it would have been inappropriate to have left Dieppe with its old name of Leger Corner. More than that, when the new town was fully incorporated, it combined several villages so that a new overall title was needed. Its nucleus, Leger Corner, had first been called French Village by its predominantly English neighbors around the turn of the last century.

By itself, the tiny community was a village lying between the old settlement of Lewisville now a part of Moncton, and Chartersville and St. Anselme on the Memramcook side. Today, the place once known as Leger Corner is settled mainly by descendants of Acadians who had escaped deportation in the Expulsion of 1755-58. They had managed to survive as refugees in hidden encampments of Albert County where pursuers like Major Scott were unable to rout them out. When their civil rights were restored and New Brunswick created a province separate from Nova Scotia, those who had been at Le Cran (Stoney Creek), at La Rosetta (Edgett's Landing) and Babineau Village at the head of the Coverdale river, took land grants and moved over into Fox Creek (Ruisseau des Renards), St. Anselme and Dover-Pré d'en Haut district. All of which, except for the last named, are now part of Dieppe.

Town records of Dieppe mention one Honoré Leger as heading the prominent local family for which Leger Corner was named. However, other information suggests differently. The descendants of Joseph Leger, known as "P'tite Houppe,"[1] maintain that his offspring were the first settlers. There is good evidence to believe that this is so, although the Honoré Leger family may have been at the Corner when it got a formal post office name.

This Joseph Leger was born in 1750 at the village of Rosette on the West side of the Petitcodiac near what is now Edgett's Landing. He survived the peregrinations of the Exile period and in 1775 married Marguerite Maillet at Memramcook. A son, Amable, was born at St. Anselme in 1785, and fathered a large family. Most of them went to the Barachois-Shediac area. Mrs. Kathleen Doyle, who is in her hundredth year as this is written in 1982, was a daughter of

Peter Leger and his wife, Catherine Anketell, and she recalls that it was his grandfather, Jean (usually known as John), whose sons actually first settled at Leger Corner. She knew Jean to have been a son of Joseph ("Houppe") who lived until 1815.

In any case, she recalls that the sons of John were her father, Peter, engineer at the Moncton sugar refinery; Olivier, Calixte, Amable, Ferdinand, Sevére, Thaddee and Simon. If her recollection is correct, Joseph-Armand Leger, of Shediac, who is said to be the first Acadian medical doctor, was the son of Amable. In any case, her family has always maintained that it was John (Jean) and his sons who founded Leger Corner. The family was notable for the longevity of its members, and the widow of Amable, on her hundredth birthday in 1889, spent the day visiting her children, grandchildren, and great-grandchildren. By the time she was 100, she had 357 descendants.

Leger Corner was renamed Dieppe in 1946 to commemorate the Canadian soldiers killed in the Dieppe Raid in France in World War Two, and it became incorporated as a village. Six years later, it was incorporated as a town and has grown steadily since. A section of Lakeburn (the site of the Moncton airport) was annexed in 1948, and in 1973 the villages of St. Anselme, and Chartersville and the unincorporated areas of Fox Creek and Dover became parts of the enlarged town of Dieppe.

Dover was a natural cutoff point, for it was there the vast estates of Governor Frederick Wallet DesBarres began. They followed the river and at one time took in the whole Memramcook peninsula between the Petitcodiac and Memramcook rivers and extended into Minudie, Nova Scotia. Long and historic confrontations and legal battles went on until 1840 involving these lands and the rights of returning Acadians who had been given land grants and took up occupancy.

On the Moncton side, however, Fox Creek known to the Acadians by its French name, Ruisseau des Renards, is a very old community and was already settled in 1774. St. Anselme dates about the same time. As for Chartersville, it has a special distinction in being a small English enclave in a French district. The Charters family is an old Norman-English one and the brick family homestead which stood until recent years was said by some to have quartered British-Canadian soldiers summoned for defense in the War of 1812 with the Americans. Howard D. Charters was enumerator for the census of Moncton in 1861 as town clerk. Later he and his family were long in business in Moncton.

Dieppe's recent development began with the expropriation in 1972 of 400 acres of land for industrial purposes. Before that, Simpson Sears had opened a large store in the Champlain Mall on the marsh between the old Leger Corner and Moncton. Protected by early dykes, the marsh had been divided by what was once the very large Hall's Creek and the Creek itself was considered the city's eastern boundary at the river.

By 1981, Dieppe's population had grown to approximately 10,000, having risen from 3,402 twenty years earlier. Back in 1909, the unofficial census gave the community of Leger Corner 395 residents. This included a few farmers such as George Tingley whose lands extended to what became the Moncton Downs racetrack and the first local airport.

Sifroi LeBlanc was named chairman of the first village council in 1946, succeeded by Arthur LeBlanc in 1948 and Cecil Dawson in 1950. When Dieppe became a town in 1952, it chose as its first council chairman and mayor a distinguished citizen, Adelard Savoie, a lawyer who became first lay president of the University of Moncton. His successors have been: Alphée LeBlanc, J. Regis LeBlanc, William Malenfant and Clarence Cormier. As of 1982, Mr. Cormier has remained and become a prominent figure in the affairs of Greater Moncton. So far, no Leger has been chosen for the chief magistracy but the Cormier family has a long connection with the community and its immediate neighbors.

Charles Cormier, who lived near the Lewisville boundary, was a county councillor for Westmorland for many years representing the district. His father, Patrick, had been associated with Bliss Thibodeau in a brickyard[2] in Leger

RALPH CASELEY   CLARENCE CORMIER

Corner. Like many of the "Acadians" of the area, Charley Cormier was of mixed Irish and French descent. His mother, Nell, was the daughter of James Alexander who was one of the first residents of the Sunny Brae-Irishtown section. Two nieces of this Charles Cormier, the Misses Marie and Pauline Cormier, still reside in Moncton as this is written. It was Marie Cormier who recalled the early Leger Corner industry of brickmaking. She also remembered that a treasurer of the company named LeBlanc ran off to Paris with the company funds, which brought about its ruin. He eventually returned but a feud broke out between the Thibodeau and that particular LeBlanc family which lasted for two generations.

Clarence Cormier, the mayor of Dieppe in 1981 and other years, is not related to the above-mentioned Cormier family but a son of Guillaume (Willie) Cormier of Ste. Marie de-Kent.

The larger town of Riverview is newer as an incorporated town than Dieppe and its rapid growth had given it a population of 14,177 in 1981 which was an increase of some 3,000 since its incorporation on July 9, 1973. Indeed, there was consideration of an application for city status during 1981 though this was laid aside some months later.

When it was first named, the new town was called "Coverdale" by the lieutenant-governor-in-council. However, at the request of the minister of municipal affairs, it was formally called "Riverview" nine days afterward. Some new-town residents even had the idea that it might be called "Gunnriverbridge" — an impossible mouthful taking in the names of the three villages being merged, Gunningsville, Riverview Heights and Bridgedale. Fortunately for the first mayor, Harold B. Findlay and the first administrator, George E. Hamilton, they were rescued from having to emboss stationery with such an unwieldy name as "Gunnriverbridge."

When the mayor in 1981, Ralph E. Caseley, was considering city status for Riverview, he pointed out that it had become the fifth largest municipality in the province including those which already held city status.

Located as it is on the south side of the Petitcodiac, Riverview is in Albert County which was once part of Westmorland but cut off in 1845. Until the establishment of the town, it had been traditionally rural with a few villages but no towns. Still, the riverbank area which became the town had long been settled. At nearby Stoney Creek, then known as Le Cran, there had been an Acadian settlement during the French Regime before 1755. Behind the present town there had been another French settlement, a refugee encampment really, at Fourche-a-crapaud which later settlers called Turtle Creek. ("Crapaud" is French for "toad" rather than turtle although, oddly, the place on Prince Edward Island called Crapaud is said to refer to eels rather than toads.)

Turtle Creek, which is just outside the boundaries of Riverview but flows to the Petitcodiac at its boundary, was in earlier times known as the Coverdale River.[3] An English settler named Horsman (probably Christopher) was in the place around 1785. However, the villages which became the town were all part of original land grants and extensions of settlements which had spilled over from Salisbury and Hillsborough where the Stief dynasty was all-important. Many of those who settled were descendants of the patriarch Heinrich Stief (Steeves) and his seven sons or of families connected with the Steeveses.

On a survey map drawn and engraved under the direction of H.F. Walling and published by Baker in New York in 1862, land grants are set out as surveyed by D.J. Lake and H.S. Peck. Those included in what is now the entire Riverview area included: B. Wilbur, E.S. Outhouse, several Trites and Steeves families, A. Gaskin, J. O'Conner, G.T. Mitchell, W. Colpitts, J. Ryan, S.B. Weldon, A. Mitten, J.N. Chapman, G. Geldart, J. Wallace, S. Chisholm, J. Barry, J. Jonah, E. Duffy, J. Rodgers, A.P. Smith. The last four names were actually in the Stoney Creek district beyond the present town limits. (Spellings above follow the survey map's usage).

What may be of interest to present-day readers is the fact that in 1862 the Turtle Creek river had an oat mill, a grist mill and a sawmill. Families of Fillmore, Jonah, Graham, Kelly and Mitten were settled on the river and at the top of the river was the Gross Hotel and post office.

Coverdale, from Stoney Creek at Salisbury, in 1862, had a total population of 1,233 and the entire population of Albert County, at 9,444, was far smaller than the present Town of Riverview itself.

It was always a bit difficult to define the boundaries of communities within the general old name of Coverdale. But a century ago they were known simply as Lower Coverdale which comprised the section from Gunningsville to Mill Creek; Middle Coverdale, which ran from the later Bridgedale, and Gunningsville near the river bridge westward toward Upper Coverdale (or just plain Coverdale). This is today the district of the causeway, shopping malls, Pine Glen Road and westward to the boundary of Ritchie Road. Presumably, when the ardent Baptist and Methodist Bible-readers named the general river district opposite The Bend it was all just Coverdale named for the translator of the New Testament.

As 1982 began, Riverview was having difficulty coming to terms with itself, in the words of Ray Tupper, the president of a new Riverview Business Association. He said the town "was in an identity crisis," because in the telephone directory Riverview numbers were mixed with those of Moncton City. Large as it was (and the Moncton newspapers mentioned a population of 16,000 while the town administrator made it 1,823 less) the town was still without its own post office. This had been a constant source of irritation, especially since village post offices had served the district from 1855.

As mentioned, Coverdale is believed named for the Englishman, Miles Coverdale, the churchman and reformer who translated the Bible,[4] or at least the New Testament — into English and died in 1569. Though he had been an Augustinian friar and later a bishop, he was dismissed by Queen Mary the Catholic. He was a follower of some of the German Protestant theologians and therefore would be approved by the Pennsylvania Germans who first settled Albert County after the French period. The settlement of Coverdale became a postal district in 1855.

It is thought that Bridgedale may have been named for the bridge over Mill Creek and it achieved postal distinction in 1885. Gunningsville got its postal name in 1910 and was named for Hazen Gunning, its first settler. Presumably he was a descendant of John Gunning, an Englishman who was lost when the vessel "Sophie" went down in the Bay of Fundy in 1828. On early maps, names of James Watson, a Sproule and a Ludlow were found in the Lower Coverdale and Coverdale districts where grants went to Joseph Gray, a Maugher and a Stief. John Gunning had married a daughter of Matthias Stief, a son of Heinrich the patriarch.

The Geldarts of Coverdale are descended from Joshua Gildart, (sic) a Yorkshireman, who was an early Hillsborough settler. One of the most prominent of first Coverdale families was that of the Wallaces who were also at Hillsborough. A romantic figure in this family was a thrice-married woman who is part of the Steeves family lore. She was said to have been a young lady of high rank in Quebec named Govang (Gauvin) who had married Charles Smith of Hillsborough where she had come in 1775 as the wife of Robert Crossman, who died soon afterward. At this time some of the noted Pierre Thibadeau clan were still living in the area. When Smith too died, Suzanne Govang married a Wallace from Coverdale. Her daughters married into the Stief and other German families.

Esther Clark Wright, the historian of the Steeves family and the Petitcodiac, in her book *Samphire Greens* quotes old settlers as saying of Suzanne that "she was one who could dress in her silks." And silks were rare at that time in the primitive settlements.

Other early names in Coverdale included descendants of Robert Colpitts and his wife Margaret Wade who had come to found Colpitts Settlement from Norton, Durham County, England on the *Albion* in 1775. And there were Triteses of the family which became the first Moncton inhabitants, and John and Charles Lutz who were at Turtle Creek around 1820 also gave descendants to the district now included in Riverview.

After the turn of the present century, the farm of Woodrow (Will) Wallace a little distance from the Pine Glen Road, was sold to Fred H. Walsh. This was in 1911 and Walsh, an interesting man who had been an overseer in the Moncton cotton mill and left the weaving trade to study scientific farming, developed one of the most advanced agricultural operations in the province. He had come to Valleyfield, P.Q., from England as a boss weaver, then removed to Moncton where he decided that trade was not for him. The Coverdale farm was carried on after his death by his son, Jack Walsh, who became a leader in the farm cooperative movement. Another son, F.Waldo Walsh, retired as Nova Scotia's deputy minister of agriculture and marketing.

Neighboring farm families were recalled by Waldo Walsh in his book, "We Fought for the Little Man," a story of cooperatives in the Maritimes. They were those of Charles Wilson, Albert Wood and Mrs. Barbara Fownes who farmed with her son Fen for a few years on the Wallace land. Edson Wallace had an adjoining farm and nearby was the McDonald farm owned by the McDonald Construction Co., of Moncton.

Ewart B. Gaskin, living in Moncton in 1982, a retired railroad engine man once president for New Brunswick of the

Canadian Council of Labor, also recalled families who lived in what is now Riverview in his boyhood. A dapper man of 87 with a remarkably lively mind, Mr. Gaskin was a son of William Dixon Gaskin who came to the district in 1816 from Canterbury, England. He was born William Dixon but took his mother's name, Gaskin, when he served in the Napoleonic wars. As a member of the British marines, he crossed the Atlantic four times before staying on this side.

Inheriting some means from his sister who had married a wealthy husband, Gaskin took up land grants in both the Lower Coverdale district near Stoney Creek and at Turtle Creek. His daughter married James Renton, joining another early Albert County family. Not far from the Gaskin farm was the historic Outhouse Point farm, opposite Moncton's Bendview Square, and an aged Mr. Outhouse was still in occupancy. Mr. Gaskin says, however, that the farm was originally that of the Rickers, whose forebear Jacob Ricker was one of the original Pennsylvania German settlers. George Ricker, long Moncton's city court clerk, was of the same family. For some years in the present century, the farm was occupied by Thomas Nowlan and his family who had come from Buctouche and operated it as a large piggery.

One of the more colorful figures at Coverdale in the early part of the present century was Sanford Ryan, a member of the New Brunswick legislature and one of the few Liberals to have represented that part of the province. He owned a farm near the Coverdale church and the present Pine Glen Road, but his personal prosperity depended more on his political contacts. At one point, he had gained a contract for supplying semaphore poles for the Intercolonial Railway and it was said that Ryan benefitted to the extent of eight dollars a pole. It appears that a great many semaphore poles were required in the region and Ryan prospered. The Ryans (James T. and his son, Tilley) who operated the fine-food store on Main street, Moncton, near Church, were cousins of the politician and equally ardent Liberals.

The tradition of having important legislature members from Coverdale district and now Riverview has been carried into the present and at two levels. Mrs. Brenda Robertson who, like a majority of residents was born outside the town (in her case, Sussex, N.B.) held three cabinet posts in the Hatfield government. Gary F. McCauley, M.P. for Moncton federal constituency, is also typical of the new town in having been born elsewhere. (Cochrane, Ontario). He had been pastor of St. James Anglican church in Moncton and a radio-television commentator. He was promoted to being a parliamentary secretary, a post in which the holder speaks for a minister of the Crown in the Commons.[5]

Hon. Lewis Smith, a Conservative minister of agriculture for New Brunswick in the Baxter, Richards and Tilley governments of the 1920's and 1930's, farmed in what is known as Lower Coverdale. Another Conservative provincial cabinet minister from Coverdale was the Hon. Claude Taylor who served in the government of Premier Hugh John Flemming.

Ralph Caseley, the mayor of Riverview in 1982, was another resident coming from elsewhere. A native of Wilmot Valley near Summerside, P.E.I., he is a retired manager for a farm feed company but not one to retire wholly. At the time of writing, he was fulltime chairman of the provincial Welfare Appeals Board. It was no small coincidence that his fellow town mayor, Clarence Cormier, was director of another provincial agency, the Alcoholic and Drug Dependency Commission.

Riverview had come a long way since its amalgamation, Caseley once told a service club audience as he referred to a decision of town council to ask the province for city status. A lot of things had come at one time, he maintained, "and too many people think the government is a pit with no bottom." People wanted everything at once, a large police force, a cleanup of the polluted river, an industrial park, having already achieved a new town hall, a police force, an ambulance and garbage collection. "People," the mayor said at the time, "are spoiled."

Spoiled or unspoiled, the truth was that the townfolk had moved the community forward rapidly in its initial decade. It was not only a dormitory suburb but inevitably it did serve as the domicile of a majority whose employment was in the adjacent City of Moncton.

If one name is associated with the development of Riverview more than any other it is that of Byron Dobson, and Byron Dobson *was* its great developer. Over the years, the Dobson family name has become almost synonymous with Coverdale and Albert County but the Dobsons were not among the first settlers. An English Yorkshire family, they had first homesteaded in the Port Elgin area in Botsford parish. Later, a son Joseph took up a farm in Stoney Creek and expanded. He did so well with lumbering and farming that when he gave Harold, one of his three sons, the family farm and moved into Moncton he bought more properties. To another son, Byron, he turned over a 100-acre farm near the Pine Glen Road, which had been the extensive holdings of Sanford Ryan the politician. In time, Byron greatly extended his holdings. A third son, the late Joseph W., practised as a medical doctor in Moncton for many years but never lost his interest in his native Albert County and its woodland trails. Harold Dobson was killed during an electrical storm at the family farm while Byron, the youngest brother, survived to become — in a sense — the physical founder of Riverview.

While he had lived on the Ryan farm, Byron Dobson had always been a builder and specialized first in small houses. During World War Two, he gained a contract for a housing development for air force families in Moncton and this became Acadia Park in the city's New West End. His major venture afterward was to sub-divide his farm land in Coverdale and begin the development of sub-divisions which became the basis of the modern town.

Dobson's daughter, Virginia, in later years became associated with her father in the huge business which had grown from its modest beginnings. A son, Wayne, was also connected with the firm while another son who had studied operatic music and was the possessor of an extraordinary voice, planned to enter the construction business.

In the mid-1960's and having taken advantage of the boom times, Byron Dobson had extended his operations to the extent that in one major deal he sold 54 houses to J.A. Keefe of Moncton. Keefe later sold some 20 of these and became a rental landlord with the rest. In true entrepreneurial style, Dobson went on to develop new streets and courts and built some 2,000 or more houses to make himself and his family the biggest land and housing developers in the entire history of Greater Moncton.

Unlike some of the early Moncton developers such as Oliver Jones, Byron Dobson was no business buccaneer but a solid and energetic construction boss and real estate operator. He carried out his operations from the woods to the finished product, to financing arrangements and sales.

Across the river in Moncton, Jack Keefe, who had made his success out of the fuel oil trade and in real estate and insurance, was more than a landlord. A notably public-spirited citizen, and a particularly generous one, Keefe came to Moncton from Sydney, N.S., in 1924, having been transferred in the banking business. Soon afterward, he bought out the W. McK. Weldon & Son coal business, an old Moncton firm, and later moved into insurance in the 1940's, going into real estate some ten years later.

J.A. Keefe's public service began in a substantial way when he became president of Moncton's Children's Aid Society in the 1940's and held that post for many years. He was later president of the original Moncton Community Chest, forerunner of the United Way fund. Between 1947 and 1952, he was on city council and when the University of Moncton was in its expansionary period, Keefe was involved in fund drives and notable as one of the few English-speaking Monctonians so actively concerned. For 14 years he was on the board of Pine Hill Divinity school (now part of the Atlantic School of Theology), on the board of the Maritime School of Social Work for a dozen years, president of the Greater Moncton Y.M.C.A. and for years president of the Moncton Real Estate Board.

In 1980, J.A. Keefe made an offer of $100,000. to establish what is known as The Greater Moncton Foundation, providing contributions of $10,000. annually until his gift was complete. Purpose of the Foundation was to set up a permanent fund whose capital would yield earnings for cultural and social services. It allows contributors to designate their capital contributions' earnings for specific purposes and, if desired, create institutions or services which will bear their names in perpetuity.

1. P'tite Houppe may have been known for a tufty beard or for wearing a toque with a tassle since "houppe" means a tuft of hair or a crest of hair on the head. It also refers to a tassle which suggests the habitant-like toque.

2. Brick houses were rare in the district and no doubt the Cormier house benefitted by the brickyard. Nearby in Lewisville the Cummins family operated another brick plant as a very large local industry.

3. Ewart Gaskin recalled both wild turtles and eels in Turtle Creek. "There were always eels in the Petitcodiac."

4. A rare and original set of Coverdale's Bibles is among the treasures of Longleat, the great estate of the Marquis of Bath in Somerset where it was found by the present author in 1982.

5. Margaret Rideout, a previous Moncton politician representing Westmorland as a Member of Parliament in Ottawa, had been parliamentary secretary to the minister of health and welfare. Having the ear of Prime Minister Pearson, she was one of the most effective M.P.'s in half a century but Moncton did not continue to support her and she lost the election of 1968 when Moncton became a separate riding.

Chapter Twenty-nine

A CITY COME OF AGE

A new cast of personalities was taking hold of the city's destiny as Moncton entered the 1980's. The face of the community had been much altered since the halfway mark of the present century. Now, it had become the centrepiece of a small metropolis known as Greater Moncton. And it was indicative of a new thrust that the man at its helm was the youngest mayor ever elected.

Dennis Cochrane, a school teacher whose previous political experience had consisted of two years as a councillor, was also the only academic ever to have achieved the mayoralty. There had been other scholarly occupants of the chair but he was the first teacher and the first to have taken degrees at both the University of Moncton and the University of New Brunswick. He was assuredly the only one who had studied French toward a Master's level and therefore perhaps the first whose preparation mirrored the duality of Moncton's culture.

That Cochrane should also bear the name, with a slight variation in spelling, of Moncton's first schoolteacher, Thomas Corcoran, was a coincidence as well as a mark of continuity.

Mayor Dennis Cochrane, Youngest ever.

Something else had pointed to that same factor of continuity in the city's career earlier when it entered the 1960's. Always, Moncton had been a commercial centre, a geographical hub from which people came and went and goods were made and distributed to the region about it. Michael Baig was the mayor when the first major industrial park was planned in 1959 as the city council and the Board of Trade established a subsidiary company of the corporation known as the Moncton Industrial Development Limited. It was a forward-looking idea, a creature of its time actually, but it took tne foresight and voluntary effort of cooperating business and industrial leaders and the council itself to make it work.

A provisional board of directors put it on foot. They were Mayor Baig, Leonard C. Jones, then an alderman; A. MacDonald Cooke, the city clerk; Orley W. Fowler, a business man who headed the venerable Lounsbury mercantile company; Bennett W. Isner, who had come to be general manager of the Moncton Publishing Co.; and Albert E. Eagles, a civil engineer. In 1982 George T. Urquhart retired as president of the M.I.D., having served thirteen years as president and doing so as a volunteer effort for his hometown where he had himself achieved outstanding business success. It had been a most effective period of local development and Urquhart had proved himself an inspiring business leader.

Winston A. Steeves had been one of the prime movers in the development which by 1982 could count some 150 Maritime, national and international companies participating in the parks. A. George English, who had come to Moncton in the 1930's with General Motors Acceptance Corporation and remained until his death a distinguished and progressive business leader, was the first president of M.I.D. as it was formally inaugurated in 1960. Succeeding him were E.A. Rooney, W.A. Steeves, Russell H. Miller, F.A. Lynds, F. Patrick Driscoll, Aurele Arsenault and George Urquhart. During the years under review, some 140 citizens had given freely of their time to act as directors and officers. For some of them, like Mr. Driscoll who had been president of the Board of Trade, there were streets named. It was the insistence of Mr. Driscoll and his supporters that resulted in the unusual attractiveness of the entire park. In drawing up and executing the plans, they refused to accept anything but what would enhance the appearance and keep it that way permanently.

Fifteen years after its start, the Park was given a $3,500,000 facelift with new rail facilities, roads, utilities and other integrated services. The companies occupying the sites are engaged primarily in manufacturing, distribution or transportation, employing more than 3,400 of the labor force. Tax assessments for 1981 reached more than $53,000,000. Only the Canadian National Railways employed more.

A dozen years after the first park opened, a 1,300-acre tract of land near the Trans-Canada Highway between the Irishtown and Shediac roads was set aside at a cost of a million dollars. This was given the name of Caledonia Industrial Estates and at the time of writing is being developed in 100-acre-block stages. By 1981, more than $4,000,000 had been assessed there alone.

As this was happening, the old Moncton which had been entered by rail, water and roads that wandered out of the surrounding countryside since the first military track was opened from Shediac in 1816, was assuming a different aspect. Sweeping modern highways with their interchanges were finally giving easy access to a greatly enlarged community. To the north, Mayor Gary Wheeler's dream was taking the form of a boulevard with his name, a bypass highway joining Eastern boundaries to Western outskirts and beyond. The marsh around historic Hall's Creek, already holding a massive shopping mall named for the explorer Samuel de Champlain (He'd never come up the Petitcodiac but he'd sailed past its mouth) became a network of interchanges. The modern development would have been almost inconceivable even to a generation still alive and aging in Moncton. To one remembering the creeks and the windswept margin between the river and Lewisville it seemed as remarkable as the draining of the Pontine marshes of Rome centuries and centuries ago.

A causeway had been built across the river to the new town of Riverview. When it opened to traffic in 1969, its service to the flow of vehicles was cheered. A lake was created but few, if any, had foreseen what a causeway would do to the river. It had been a river among world rivers with its daily surge of tidal waters, called a bore. Moncton had been known by it, had lived by it, profited by it and gloried in its triumphant power. Some men had dreamed of harnessing this power for energy; now, backed up by a man-made causeway the river silted with startling speed. It narrowed as its banks moved outward to allow only a tiny channel. The splendor of the tide-rush was lost. Navigation was forgotten. No longer would boys hurry down to its mucky, chocolate-colored edge to dangle lines for tom-cod. The odd salmon might find its errant way upward but the river had filled with effluent.

People in the later decades, as they had before, talked about railway relocation, with Main street subway and Mountain Road bridge removal. They talked and did nothing. Plans were made and begun to renovate the downtown core of the city, and some things were done, but without the subway removal perhaps all other efforts would be frustrated. When he was publisher of *The Transcript* before 1920, John T. Hawke had argued for the movement of rail lines along the river front to the station of the old Moncton and Buctouche Railway near what used to be Marven's Biscuit factory, and thence over the marshes and then eastward to Nova Scotia and westward and northward to wherever the lines would run.

Nothing was done. He was too far ahead of his time. He had fought against the construction of a railroad overhead passage known as a subway (Horse and car traffic *did* go *under* the bridge, so they moved sub-surface and therefore it *was* a subway). But Hawke was defeated by a railroader named Gutelius and a mayor named Sumner and Main street was forever saddled with an ugly, troublesome, divisive and water-catching "catastrophe," as Zorba the Greek would have called it.

Up on Mountain Road, where once smokestacked locomotives needed height to get under overpasses, a crazy bridge remains with its hump in the middle long made unnecessary by diesel engines with flat tops. Still, the nuisance remains. Perhaps now it should stay, a monument to the inability of a city and a dominating railroad to come to simple terms. City Hall continues to say, as one writes, that an engineering group and the C.N.R. has "plans." They've always had plans but nothing happens.

By stages, from its first incorporation in 1855, Moncton's boundaries had been extended until in 1912 it took in what had been known as Georgetown at its northwestern edge. Thirty-eight years later, in 1950, Newton Heights at the southwest corner had been added and in 1954 the wartime area of homes known as Acadia Park in "the New West End." After that, just a year later, the Sunny Brae sector which in fact if not in name was as old as The Bend itself, joined the expanding city. One more year brought one more area into the fold including Parkton which was an offshoot of the original Georgetown and the Moncton Industrial Park.

In another year 1957, Humphrey school district came in bringing the long-settled woollen mill community and, finally, in 1973, an amalgamation giving the city boundaries that, half a century earlier, had been considered "away out in the country." These new areas comprised Lewisville, the Magnetic Hill section, what was known as Salisbury Road, and open lands to the north and east of the city. The amalgamation of 1973 took in 43 square miles, the biggest swath the municipality had ever cut and made the total Moncton city area 58.06 square miles. It meant that by 1981 the city had 237 miles of streets as compared with 48 miles it called its own in 1928. At that time the little city covered just 3.7 square miles and that included Georgetown.

As Moncton entered the 1980's in a period of national and international recession, it was facing some business difficulties. The closing of Eaton's catalogue division in 1976 had been a traumatic shock, taking more than 1,000 jobs. Still, this appeared to have been overcome without serious disruption. Later, automobile agencies long connected with the city were wound up and a few other businesses ended their careers. Small railway layoffs were seen as portents of worse but the Canadian National had more than 4,500 employees at work and some 2,000 rail cars were being handled at the Gordon Yard on an average day with more than 1,000 workers there. Another 1,300 were employed in the shops and 600 at regional headquarters. Thus, the railway remained as it had for a century the city's lifestream of industry.

If there had been setbacks, the motto of the city was still "Resurgo" (I Rise Again) and Moncton was moving to overcome them in the 1980's as it had done so often in the past.

While the old downtown had deteriorated gradually as large and prosperous retail shopping malls took business elsewhere, a foreward-looking new generation was working toward its restoration. The Moncton Central Business Development Corporation, in energetic young hands, was moving with city council and the young mayor to revitalize the old city core. Various imaginative ideas were studied, including a plan to cover a portion of Main street. While meeting traditional objections from the over-cautious elements which had always been part of Moncton's social fabric — and has always been overcome by its more progressive citizens — Dennis Cochrane had led his council to begin major improvements.

Meanwhile, so-called mega-projects were being set in motion along New Brunswick's eastern and north shores with government installations at Shediac, a large high-tech industry in place at Buctouche. All of these would benefit Moncton, the supply and service centre of the region, and the most important retail trading city on the east side of the province. It was easy for Moncton's less optimistic citizens to forget that so much of the city's trade came from the coast and from western Nova Scotia and Prince Edward Island.

The fact was that in 1981 Moncton sold more industrial land — indeed three times as much — than the total of all industrial parks in the province. It already had three times as much occupied and productive industrial park space occupied as the rest of New Brunswick combined. This was hardly a depressed outlook.

Recognizing the reality of The Maritimes' central city's continuing role as a distribution centre, there had already been notable expansion in hotel facilities. A first-class sports Coliseum had been housing a professional hockey team and other sports and exhibition features including an Agrena which had begun to make Moncton the exhibition and agricultural exposition preference for the region. Convention dollars were coming to the city in increasing volume and an energetic mayor was spreading his philosophy of optimism.

The community had become a substantial educational locale with eleven new schools built since 1950 for a total of 22. The Community College established in 1974 supplanted the New Brunswick vocational and technical school and had an enrolment of close to 1,400 and a staff of 200 while the university, with its normal school affiliate and full academic and research and library-archival departments, could count 2,600 students and a staff of 600 in teaching and office personnel.

The superb university library with its research facilities was available to the general public and the city's public library was bursting its bounds with services in both official languages. It was a far cry from the years before 1962 when Moncton's only library was contained in a made-over family residence. A civic museum opened in 1973 was on the verge of expansion and beginning under professional and dedicated management to serve its intended purpose.

While some other forms of employment had fallen off, few recognized that Greater Moncton by 1982 was home to something in the vicinity of 4,000 civil servants in various levels of government. The city's biggest taxpayers were in fact the federal government, the provincial government, Assumption Place the city's showpiece and civic centre with its enlarged Beauséjour Hotel and office units, Highfield Square and the New Brunswick Telephone Co.

Moncton still remained a city of private homeowners with 23,730 private dwellings and, new for the community, more than 8,000 apartment and duplex units.

The years of conflict in matters of language seemed to have faded into a less happy past with a recognition that two basic language groups could live and prosper together in the same environment. In each department of the city's government efforts were being made to provide essential services in both English and French. Dennis Cochrane was influencing a council toward orderly change where a positive attitude prevailed in these once heat-freighted issues.

What was even more indicative of the winds of change was the emergence of a multiculture in a community where traditionally only a handful of citizens were outside the Anglo-Saxon and French tradition. There had been three or four families of Italian origin early in the 20th century, one or two Greek families, the Lithuanian and Russian-Polish Jews, a handful of Chinese, here and there a family from the Ukraine, and practically no others.

In a modern Canadian city which had grown from a little settlement of German-speaking Pennsylvanians, a beginning of Yorkshire English, a few Scots traders, a remnant of Acadian French and then a flush of immigrant Irish, something fresh was developing. When an organization calling itself the Multicultural Association of Greater Moncton Area held an international dinner early in 1982, some 200 people attended representing a wide variety of cultures and nationalities. There were Ukrainians, Italians, Spanish, East Indians, people from Pakistan and Vietnam. There were prominent Chinese, a group whose people had been in Moncton longer than most; there were Turks, Koreans, Arabs and Europeans of almost every modern nation. Skin tints varied from Russian white to Haitian black and languages covered the linguistic spectrum.

This was a city which had grown into a minor metropolis with a slight flavor of cosmopolitanism. It was a city aware of its roots and heritage. It had become an amalgam of Twentieth Century Canadianism.

Le Coude, The Bend, Moncton and now Greater Moncton, where Canada's two founding races had lived together, grew together and welcomed these other and newer Canadians, had come of age.

INDEX

Aberdeen High 120, 143, 224, 225, 228, 275, 282
Abrams and Son 131
Acadian 14, 15, 19, 41, 47
Acadian Expulsion 46
Acadian Historical Society 233
Acadian Museum 233, 246
Acadia Park 298, 305
Acadia Sugar 22
Acadian Village 233
Acadien 53, 95
Agrena 307
Ahern Studio 270
Air Canada 107, 170, 171
Albert County 28, 30, 37, 38, 39, 87, 88, 106, 112, 189, 193, 197, 288 et seq.
Albert County Museum 37
Alberta 30
Albion, The 295
Alcock, Sir John 167
Aldershot 266
Alexander, James 291
Alexander, Nell 291
Algie, Margaret 282
Algie, Robert 282
Allan Cup 154, 188
Allen, Austin 73
Allen, Roscoe 140
Allen, T. J. 61
Alliance Nationale 200
Alma 139
Al Tidom 277
Alward 93
Ambrose, Richard 265
American Hotel 21
Amherst 275
"Anatomy of Criticism" 224, 225
Ancient Order of Foresters 151
Anderson, Joseph 169

Anderson, S. Boyd 91, 92
Anketell, Catherine 289
Anketell, Richard 289
Annapolis Valley 101, 162
Antwerp 276
Appleton, Margaret 166
Appleton, Mrs. 104
Appleton, W.U. 61, 101, 102, 103, 104, 135, 166
Archibald house 113
Arena Rink 129
Arizona 125
Armstrong, Neil 251
Armistice 93
Arsenault, Aurele 303
Arsenault, Yolande 154
Association of N.B. Museums 148
Assomption Compagnie Mutuelle 200
Assomption Parish 55, 245
Assomption Place 201, 259
Assumption Band 32
Assumption Church 58
Assumption College 206
Assumption Mutual 46, 200
Atlantic Advocate 184
Atlantic Underwear Ltd. 142
Athens, Nick 121
Atkins, Daddy 23
Attis, Harrison 179
Attis, Mrs. H. 179
Attis, Jean 179
Attis, Joseph 179
Attis, Louis 179
Attis, Mrs. L. 179
Ave Maris Stella 47
Audet, L.N. 206, 208
Augustinian Friar 294
Australia 77
Ayer, H. H. 49
Ayer, Percy D. 32, 96, 166

The man who abuses his partner is as likely to be a lawyer as a labourer. He may have learned this by observing abuse between his own parents, through his own experience as a victim of abuse, or as a result of social conditioning.

Some men are not able to express their feelings constructively. They tend to hold in hurt and frustration. At some point, these feelings must be released and often come out as anger directed at wife and family.

For these men, for the women who are abused, and for the children who live in fear, violence is often a terrible secret. Frequently each person feels alone and hopeless.

communment to work through the problem from you.

To learn more about our service, telephone to speak to an *OPTION THERAPIST*

(506) 857-3258

This service is funded N.B. Health and Community Services community donations

commitment to work through the prob[lem]
from you.

To learn more about our service, tele[phone]
to speak to an *OPTION THERAPIS*[T]

(506) 857-3258

This service is funded
N.B. Health and Community Serv[ices]
community donation[s]

The man who abuses his partner is as likely to be a lawyer as a labourer. He may have learned this by observing abuse between his own parents, through his own experience as a victim of abuse, or as a result of social conditioning.

Some men are not able to express their feelings constructively. They tend to hold in hurt and frustration. At some point, these feelings must be released and often come out as anger directed at wife and family.

For these men, for the women who are abused, and for the children who live in fear, violence is often a terrible secret. Frequently each person feels alone and hopeless.

Ayer, Lloyd 127
Ayre, John 224

Babineau Village 288
Baig, Jacob 273, 275
Baig, Mike 175, 178, 302
Baie Ste. Anne 47
Baird, Victoria 35
Baker 293
Bank of Nova Scotia 70
Banque Provinciale 200
Balbo, Italo 87
Balmoral 204
Bannister, Arthur 211 et seq.
Bannister, Daniel 211 et seq.
Bannister, Frances 211 et seq.
Bannister, George 215
Bannister, Marie 211 et seq.
Bannister, May 209, 210 et seq.
Bannister Murder 68
Bannon, Douglas 162
Bannon, R. H. 162
Baptist Convention (Maritimes) 27
Baptist Congress of Canada 27
Barachois 288
Barbour, O.L. 110, 112, 189, 190 et seq.
Barker House 125
Barquentine Angelus 223
Barry. Mr. Justice J. 216, 219 et seq.
Barss 64
Barss, Karl 182
Barton, Capt. A. 92
Bastarache, Francis 265
Bath, Marquis of 300
Bathurst 135, 244, 245
Bathurst College 245
Baxter, Dr. C. R. 165, 166
Baxter, Hon. J.B.M. 95
Baxter, Iredell 229
Baxter, Margaret 165
Beaton, Norman 32
Beauséjour, Centre Catholique 45
Beauséjour Club 46
Beauséjour Hotel 85, 89, 201, 308

Beauséjour Societé la Jeunesse 45
Bedfords 62
Belanger, Romeo 164
Belgium 276
Bell, H. Seeley 49
Belliveau, Albert 151
Belliveau, André 151
Belliveau, Anna 149
Belliveau, Beach 128
Belliveau, Catherine 149
Belliveau, J. E. 156, 188
Belliveau, John 128
Belliveau, Leonard 166
Belliveau, Dr. Lucien 200, 208
Belliveau, P.A. 34, 36, 57, 96, 147, et seq.
Bend, The 16, 81, 93, 106
Bend View Square 296
Bennett, Rt. Hon. R.B. 140, 141, 175
Berlin, N.H. 157
Berlinquette, Louis 35
Bermuda 88, 162
Berry, J. E. 120
Berry Mills 211, 212, 215 et seq.
Bible, The 224, 229
Big Apple 159
Bilise, Jacques 255
Billy Jackson 152
Bingham 93
Binney, Stephen 81, 90
Bird, Insp. J. 213
Bishop, Lottie 113
Bishop, Col. W.A. 167
Black, J. L. 155
Black, Friday 174
Blakeny, Hon. C. H. 20, 127, 166, 167, 173, 180 et seq.
Blakeny, Otto 212, 213
Blakeny, Sherman 20, 184
Block, Sarah 276
Bluff, The 225
Board of Trade 66, 84, 131, 303
Boer War 14
Books of Knowledge 236
Borden, Ont. 169
Borden, R. A. 70
Borden, Sir Robert 18, 70

Boston, 116, 157, 162, 194
Boston Bridge Works 116
Boston Sunday Advertiser 130
Botsford, Judge 69, 110
Botsford Parish 298
Boucher, Gaspard 203
Boudreau, Dr. F.E. 223
Boudreau, Mrs. F.E. 223
Boudreau, René 187
Boudreau, Walter 223
Bourg, Abbé Mathurin 47
Boundary Creek 65
Bourgeois, Cpl. Aurele 263
Bourgeois, B.A. 42, 57, 95
Bourgeois, J.J. 42, 44
Bourgeois, Joseph 44, 127
Bourque 93
Bourque, Claude 187, 188
Bourque, Desiré 154
Bourque, Dr. L. N. 42, 49
Bourque, Phyllis 144
Bouzaine 59
Bow, Clara 174
Bowness, C. 32
Bowness, F. 32
Bowness, S. 32
Bowness, W. 32
Boxwell, Robert 266
Boyer, R. F. 93
Brentwood Motors 67
Brewster, Herbert 61
Bridges, Judge G.F.G. 182, 215, 216
Bridgedale 292 et seq.
Brillant, Jules 239, 242
Bristol 76
Britain 76, 167
British Columbia 161
British West Indies 77
Britton, David 261
Bronstein, Rabbi Harry 277
Brooklyn 278
Brothers of Christian Instruction 206
Brown 93
Brown, Sir A. W. 167
Brown, Frank 35, 60
Brown F. M. 77, 78, 79, 80
Brown. Harold 79, 80

Brown-Holder 79
Brown, Jack 35
Brunswick Hotel 65, 89, 101, 117, 134
Brydges 115
Buck, Arthur 272
Buckingham Palace 92
Bucksport 140
Buctouche 169, 200, 307
Bujold, Simon 201
Bulmer, Rufus 116
Burbank, Arthur 157, 158, 159, 160, 162
Burbank, Luther 159
Burbank, Maude 157, 158, 159, 160, 161, 162
Burden, Cecil 21
Burden, Dr. F. E. 154
Burden, Isaac 21
Burden, William 21
Burgess, Brenda 162
Burnett, Red 188
Burns, C.F.W. 69
Burns, Herbert 70
Burns, O. P. 122
Burrage, Len 186
Bush Garden, The 228
Busy East 184
Butler, Edith 246
Buzzell, Leslie 162
Buzzell, R. K. 59, 162

Cadieux, Dr. Jean 244, 247
Caledonia Industrial Estates 303
California 81, 94
Calkin 93
Cambodia 252
Cambridge University 238
Cameron, Harold 161
Campbell, Steve 259
Campbellton 208
Canadair 168
Canada Biscuit Co. 77, 78
Canada Temperance Act 23, 131, 119
Canadian Airways 169, 170
Canadian Air Force 165

Canadian Army 92
Can. Bank of Commerce 67
Can. Broadcasting Co. 258
Can. Conference of Universities 248
Can. Council of Labor 296
Can. Economic Council 241
Can. Foundation of Human Rights 248
Can. Gov't Railways 22, 95, 98, 99, 104, 107
Canada House 73
Can. National Railways 19, 61, 89, 96, et seq. 106, 107, 112, 153, 154, 167, 175, 182, 202, 235, 229, 303 et seq.
Canadian Navy 282
Canadian Northern 116
Canadian Pacific 89, 99, 101
Can. Radio Broadcasting 154
Canadian Rockies 116
Canadiens, Les 187, 188
Candy Girl 152
Canterbury, Eng. 296
Cape Breton Coal & Ice 20
Cape Breton Rd. 265
Capitol Records 62
Cargaric 112
Caribbean 223
Carey, Ernie 187
Carroll, F. 60
Carrol, G. 60
Carroll, H. 60
Carroll, Jack 34, 60
Carmen, Gerald 271
Catherine B. 151
Caseley, Mayor R.E. 10, 291, 292 et seq.
Casey, Rt. Rev. Thomas 51
Caseys 64
Cassidy 93
Cassidy & Belliveau 275
Cavour, Count 69
Central & Eastern Trust 279
Central & Nova Scotia 279
Central Trust 70, 116, 279
Centre d'Etudes acadiennes 54, 233
Centre of Acadian Studies 233
Chamberlain, Charley 61

Champlain Mall 290
Champlain, Samuel 304
Chandler, Dave 86
Chandler, Lorraine 56
Chapman, Bill 269
Chapman, Cavour 69, 129
Chapman, J.N. 193
Charlottetown 81, 82, 172
Charters, 290
Charters, Howard B. 290
Chartersville 277, 288, 289
Chateau Laurier 284
Chatham, N.B. 168, 204
Chatham, Ont. 141
Chautauqua 183
Chevra Kiddisha 277
Chiasson, Bishop P.A. 204
Chicago 130
Chinese 308
Chisholm, S. 293
Church Point 47
Church, Mayor Tommy 134
Church St. Academy 241
Citizens Band 32
City Hall 305
City Land Co. 113
Clare Shore 61
Clifford, David 80
Clydeside 28
Cocagne 47, 141, 236
Cocagne River 83
Cochata 152
Cochrane, Dennis 10, 111, 271, 301, 302, 306, 308
Cochrane, Hon. F. 98
Cochrane, Ont. 162
Coffey 93
Cohen, Louise 281
Cohen, Reuben 278, 279
Cohoon, Gregory 265, 266, 271
Cole, E.C. 69, 74
Coleman, Aaron, 277
Coleman, Lizzie 277
Coleman, Oscar 277
Coles 93
Col. Drake's Well 28
Coliseum 307
Collége Ste. Croix 237

313

Colleens 144
Collins, Tom 36 et seq.
Colonial Theatre 67
Colpitts, Lorne 21
Colpitts, Margaret 295
Colpitts, Robert 106
Colpitts, R.R. 21
Colpitts Settlement 295
Colpitts, W. 293
Columbia Farm 105
Comeau 93
Comeau, Adolphe 61
Comeau, Arthur 92
Commonwealth Air Plan 168
Community College 307
Connaught, Duke and Duchess 75
Condon, Betty 113
Condon, F.O. 182
Congrégation Ste. Croix 237
Confederation 76, 77, 154
Consolidation Act 272
Connecticut 83
Connolly 64
Connolly, Bert 186
Connolly, J.B. 143
Connolly, Mrs. 102
Conservative Election 95
Cooke, J. McD. 69, 125, 302
Cook's Brook 105
Cool, Mrs. 214
Copp, Hon. A.B. 19, 52
Corcoran, Thomas 301
Cormier, Mr. Justice Adrien 239, 241, 242, 244
Cormier, Dr. A.J. 55
Cormier, Alvina 55
Cormier, Amedée 187
Cormier, Charles 290, 291
Cormier, Mayor Clarence 10, 290, 291
Cormier, Rev. Dr. Clément 11, 49, 53, 208, 232 et seq.
Cormier, Clément Sr. 42, 44, 52, 53, 237
Cormier, Rev. F.X. 47, 56
Cormier, Guillaume 291
Cormier, Rev. H.D. 54, 55, 245
Cormier, Lorraine 35

Cormier, Marie 291
Cormier, Patrick 290
Cormier, Pauline 291
Cormier, Zoel 141
Cosman, Fred 32
Cosman, Y.C. 32
Coté, Paul 145
Coverdale 106, 292, et seq.
Coverdale Church 296
Coverdale, Miles 294
Coverdale River 288
Crandall Studio 72
Crawford, Lindsay 132
Creaghan, W.D. 166
Creaghan, W.L. 283
Crichton, Alexander 29, 62
Cripps 93
Cripton, Michael 263
Croasdale family 114
Croasdale, Sarah 110
Crockett (Victorias) 35
Crockett, Mr. Justice 230
Cross, J. 34
Crossman 222
Cumberland County 83, 110, 240
Cummins family 17, 300
Cunningham, E.H. 115
Cunningham, Lauchlan 115
Cushing (Victorias) 35
Cuthbertson 93
Cuthbertson, Bessie 221, 222
Cuthbertson, Edwin 221
Cyr, Leonid 254, 255, 261
Cy's Seafood 139

Daley, Bill 151
Dalhousie University 44
Dann, Ray 22
Dare Industries 80
"David Harum" 151
Dayton, F.M. 148
Dawson, Cecil 290
Danforth, Maude 157, 159
Dalziell, Capt. William 166
Davis 93

DeNiverville, Janet 117
Densmore 93
Department of National Defense 168
Department of Transport 168
DesBarres, F.W. 289
DesBrisay, Hon. L.G. 20, 185
DesBrisay, R.B. 20
Depression 174, 203
Detroit 169
Deutsch, John 241, 242, 244, 245 et seq.
Devoir, Le 238
Desmarais, Paul 239, 243
DeValois, Sr. Jeanne 240
DeVona, Alvina 120
DeVona, Bill 121
DeVona, Daisy 120
DeVona, Dominick 120
DeVona, John 121
Dickie, Rheese 187
Dickens, Charles 227
Dickson, Katherine 154
Dieppe 10, 106, 165, 260, 287, 288 et seq.
Dieppe Raid 289
Digby 44, 140
Dingley & Norton 159, 160
Diocese of Chatham 51
Diocese of Saint John 51
Dobson, Byron 298, 299
Dobson family 298
Dobson, Joseph 298
Dobson, Harold 298
Dobson, Dr. J.W. 298
Dobson, Virginia 298
Dobson, Wayne 298
Dodds, J.E. 179
Doherty (Victorias) 35
Doiron, Irene 254
Dorobjny 273
Doncaster, V. 60
Donnelly 93
Dorchester 13, 15, 16, 23, 27, 39, 69, 70, 97, 106, 148, 211 et seq.
Dorchester Cape 106
Dorchester Island 106
Doucet, Louis 200

Douglas, Burel 32
Douglas, Gordon 32
Douglas, Wayne 32
Dominion of Canada 259
Dover 288, 289
Doyle, Arthur 231
Doyle, James 49
Doyle, Mrs. Kathleen 288
Doyle, Dr. L.F. 92
Doyle, John 193
Dreamland 130
Drillon, Gordon 183, 188, 222
Driscoll, 93
Driscoll, Patrick 303
Drisdelle, Rheal 256
Ducklow, Gordon 165
Duddridge, A. 187
Duff, Sir Lyman 230
Duffy, E. 293
Dunkleman, David 123
Dunlap, Jack 22
Dunlap wharf 105
Duplessis 93
Duplessis Padlock Law 229, 231
Duplessis regime 238
Duplessis, Maurice 240
Dustan, Gordon 185
Dutcher, Mrs. 216
Dysart, A.A. Hon. 203, 204
Dysart government 179
Dysart, Mrs. R.A. 11

Eagles, A.E. 302
East Barre, Vt. 157
East Indians 308
Eastern Amusement Ltd. 71, 73
Eastern Canada Savings & Loan 279
Eastern Canada Track Record 151
Eastern Provincial Airways 168
Eastern Townships 227, 228
Eastman, Elbridge 35
Eaton's 93, 97 101, 116, 121, 129, et seq., 162, 169, 174, 175, 179, 274, 282
Eaton, Sir John 134

315

Eaton, R.Y 134
Eddy, Mrs. 141
Eddy Paper family 141
Edgett, J.F. 70, 111, 139
Edgett's Landing 288
Edinburgh 28, 112
Edith Cavell School 84
Eighth Battery 92
Edmundston 148, 245, 246
Edward, James 69, 75
Edward VIII 223
Edward Prince of Wales 223
Elgin 37
Ellen, Leonard 279 et seq.
Elliott, Jumbo 66
Ellis, Arthur 219, 220
Elmwood cemetery 27
Emmerson 93
Emmerson, Emily 26
Emmerson, Hon. H.R. 13, 17 et seq. 23, 25, 26, 27
Employment Service of Canada 121
Empress Theatre 130
England 92, 123
English, A.G. 303
English, George 66
English and Scotch Wollen Co. 123
English-Speaking League 259
Equal Opportunity Program 185
Estabrooks 76
Estabrooks, Steve 185
Eudist Fathers 245
Europe 91, 171
European 309
Evangeline (see also L'Evangeline) 200, 202
Expulsion of Acadians 288
Ewart, Dr. E.W. 110

Fairchild Airways 163
Fairweather, Mr. Justice J.A.L. 219
Far East 77
Father Point 112
Fergusson Atlantic Underwear Ltd. (see also Atlantic Underwear) 22

Ferguson, Elmer 25, 35, 36, 37
Ferguson, Dr. W.A. 70, 125
Fiddler on the Roof 173
Fields, W.C. 159
Field Battery 91, 92
Fillmores 64
Film Board 258
Fine, Isadore 282
Findlay, H.B. 292
Finn, Gilbert 246 et seq., 259, 351
First Baptist Church 33, 59, 64
Fisher, Peter 165
Fitzsimmons reservoir 163
"Five Decades of Flying" 165
Flannagan, J. 49
Flannery, J. 60
Flatiron Gang 110
Fleming, Walter 164, 168, 169
Flemming, Hon. H.J. 297
Flett family 145
Flewelling 145
Flying Club 167
Florida 128, 161, 196
Forbes, Iris 144
Forbes, S. 129
Fort Cumberland IODE 113
Foster, Jimmy 186
Fowler, Orley 302
Fowler, Walter 169 et seq.
Fourche-à-Crapaud 292
Fownes, Barbara 295
Fox Creek 188, 289
Fox Creek Road 216
F.L.Q. 252, 258
France 77, 92, 227
Frankfurter, Felix 229
Fraser, Clarence B. 78
Frechet, René 166
Fredericton 84, 120, 127, 193, 228, 260
Fredericton Road 37
Free Baptist Church 64
Free Meeting House 162
Free Speech (newspaper) 25
French Village 288
Frenette, Ray 272
Friel, James 73, 184
Fréres d'Instruction Chrétien 206

"Front Benches and Back Rooms" 230, 231
Frye, Northrop 224, 225, et seq.
Fryers, E.A. Sr. 184
Fryers, E.A. & Co. 65
Fryers, Ernest A. 172
Fucillo, Ralph 161

Gallagher 93
Gallagher, Bill 124
Gallagher, Florence 123
Gallagher, Patrick 125
Gallagher, Patrick, Jr. 123
Gallagher Ridge 176
Gallagher, Thomas 123, 125
Gallagher Twins 125
Gallant, J.O. 46, 52
Gallant, Rolande 10
Gallant, Tom. Jr. 168
Gallant, Tom Sr. 168
Gander, Bob 154
Gas & Oilfields Co. 31
Gaskin, A. 293
Gaskin, Ewart B. 11, 295, 296, 300
Gaskin, W. Dixon 296
Gaudet, A. 32
Gaudet, Adlophe 32
Gaudet, Will 32
Gauvin, Bernard 254
Geary, James 69
Geldart family 294
Geldart, G. 293
General Motors Acceptance 303
George, Victor 153
Georgetown 93, 192, 260, 305
George V. 203, 223
Germans 91, 197, 222
German Protestants 294
Gideons of Canada 67
Gilbert and Sullivan 33
Gildart, Joshua 294
Gill, Bill 186
Gillespie, Blanche (Mackasey) 107
Gillespie, C.J. 269, 270, 271
Gillespie, Frank 228

Girouard 93
Girouard, Edward 32
Girvan 64
Gish, Dorothy 130
Givan, Ern 73
Givan Steam Laundry 75
Gleaner, The 151
Globe and Mail 172, 173
Gloucester 230
"Godfather, The" 255
Godfrey, Garnet 171
Goguen, Laurence 127
Goodall 93
Gorbell's 94
Gorber, Lizzie 277
Gorber, Morris 276, 277
Gordon, Walter 283, 284
Gordon Yard 306
Gorman, Charles 33
Goshen, N.Y. 151
Gould, Fred 185, 187
Gould, Niggidy 185
Gould, Tiki 187
Govang, Suzanne 294, 295
Graham family 293
Grainger, A.H. 135, 166
Grainger, J.K. 110, 156, 162, 189, 195, 196, 197, 237
Grand Dérangement 238
Grand Opera House 159
Grand Seminare 44
Grand Trunk Rly. 69, 101, 107
Grant, Harold 185
Gravelbourg 204
Gray, Bessie 137
Grey Dort 141
Greater Moncton Foundation 299
Great Code, The 324, 329
Gregory, Chester 35
Greig, David 65
Green, Rev. Bowley 59, 61
Green, Ethel 183
Greenberg, Rabbi S. 278
Greenblatt, Jason 281, 182
Greenblatt, Moses A. 282
Grey, Edward 91
Grey Cup 155

317

Gross Hotel 293
Gross, William 34
Gueguen, Joseph 47
Guertin, Rev. Louis 239
Guiles, F.L. 124
Gunning, Hazen 294
Gunning, John 294
Gunning house 183
Gunriverbridge 292
Gunningsville 292, 293, 294
Gunter, W.D. 84
Gutelius, F.P. 22, 98, 99, 305

Hagerty 93
Hains, Georgie 62
Hains, Sterling 61, 62, 64
Haitian 308
Halifax 22, 35, 70, 79, 81, 82, 84, 95, 107, 125, 143, 159, 172, 174, 204, 266
Halifax Exhibition 151
Hall, Edward 20
Hall, Frank 20
Hall's Creek 22, 290, 304
Hamilton 169
Hamilton, G.E. 292
Hamilton, Hugh
Hamm, P.N. 22, 76
Hannigan 59
Hans, Harry 277
Hans, Jacob 277
Harcourt-Brace-Jovanovich 225
Harding, Charles 154

Harris 69
Harris, Christopher 108
Harris, Insp. H.V. 214, 219 et seq.
Harris, J.H. 49, 70
Harvard 111, 225, 238, 245
Harvard Law School 229
Hatfield, Hon. R. 272
Hatheway & Co. 76
Hauptmann, Bruno 209, 223

Hawke, Admiral E. 99
Hawke, John T. 15, 18, 37, 39, 49, 97, 98, 110, 120, 188, 189, 197, 208, 230, 305
Hawks, The 35, 154, 185, 186
Hayes 61
Hayward, C.C. 62
Hazen, Hon J.D.
Henderson, J.A.L. 28, 29
Herman, Rev. A.K. 61, 203
Hewson, R.W. 38
Hickman, H.W. 215
Hicks, O.H. 192
Higgins, Lester
Highfield Baptist Church 61, 203
Highfield Square 308
Hill 70, 92
Hillsborough 87, 106, 275, 293, 294 et seq.
Holder, S.L. 77, 79
Holstead's 131, 132, 133
Holstead, Al. 133
Holy Cross Fathers 235, 237
Holy Name Society 59
Home Guard 82, 148
Hong Kong 59
Hopewell Cape 37, 38, 106
Hopewell Hill 175
Horsman 93
Horsman, Bessie 220
Horsman, Christopher 292
Hourston, David 166, 167
House of Commons 26, 27, 107
Howe, Hon. C.D. 222
Hughes, Sally 222
Hughes, Sam 91
Humphrey 17, 260
Humphrey, Helen 87
Humphrey, Jimmy 35, 36
Humphrey, J. W. 166
Humphrey's Mill 22, 93
Humphrey Station 222
Humphrey school district 305
Hungerford, S. J. 102
Hutchinson, J. L. 265
Hutchinson, Leverett 166
Hutchinson, Chief, L.H. 266, 268, 269

Hutchinson, Ron 176
Hutchinson, William 192, 220
Hydro Commission 203

I.C.R. 22, 296
I.C.R. Shops 17
Imperial Airways 167, 168
Imperial Oil 182
Independent (Political) 261
Independent Hockey League 60
India 29
Ingram, Harold 187
Ingram, Jack 60
Innes, Jim 187
Intercolonial Railway 15, 96 et seq, 101, 104
International Airways 169
International Auto Co. 71
International Rly. Co. of N.B. 208
I.O.D.E. (Bonar Law) 176
Ireland 47, 167
Irishtown 265
Irishtown Road 93, 141, 163, 303
Irvine, Knucker 186
Irving family 195
Irving Interests 189
Irving, J.D. 197
Irving, K.C. 197, 242
Irving Oil Co. 31
Irving, W. H. 164, 169
Island Pond, Vt. 157
Isner, B.W. 302
Israel 252
Italian 308

Jacobson, Rabbi Israel 278
Jake, Freda (Selick) 276
Jake, Morris 276
Jake, Sarah (Block) 276
Jake, Solomon 276
James, Dud 186
James, Wick 185
Jameson, Miss 196

Jardineville 105
Jarvis, Arthur 164
Jean K., The 139, 140
Jeffersons 64
Jefferson, H. B. 23, 25, 99
Jeffrey, Evelyn 144
Jehovah's Witnesses 229, 231
Jenny, World War One 163
Jewish 19, 273 et seq.
John A. Hal 151
John Hancock Mutual 279
Johnson, Hon. J.M. 140
Johnson, Lee 221
Johnson, Peter C. 140, 141
Johnston, P. G. 173
Jonah, J. 293
Jones, F.C. 69
Jones, Frank 220, 221, 222
Jones, H.S. 164, 169, 171
Jones, Leonard C. 183, 249, 251 et seq., 272, 302
Jones Line 105, 106
Jones, Oliver 73, 106, 116, 117
Journal of Canadian Studies 41, 252
Joyce, Harris 88, 89, 90, 139, 182
Judaism 278

Kansis City 151
Keating, Claude 167
Keating, J.C. 162
Keefe, J.A. 298, 299
Keith, B.F. 159, 178
Keirstead's 131
Kelly family 293
Kennedy (Victorias) 35
Kent County 52, 105, 204
Kent Theatre 67
Kent State Univ. 252
Keogh 134
Kierans, Eric 88
Killam, Sheriff I.N. 217, 220
King, J.B. 97, 98, 99
Kingsclear 56
King, Thomas H. 139, 180, 182, 194, 195

319

King, Rt. Hon. W.L.M. 175, 269
Kingston Penitentiary 211
Kingston, Ont. 241
Kinnear, Dick 151
Kinnear, Mary 228
Kirsh, Bessie 275
Kirsh, Harry 275
Kitchener 80
Kitziner, Menachem 278
Knights of Columbus 46, 64, 151
Knights of Pythias 113, 143, 154, 176
Kirvan, Eddie 185
Kool, Jean K. 193
Kool, Molly 138, 139, 140
Kool, Capt. Paul 139
Korean 308
Kremlin 206
Ku Klux Klan 57, 231
Kyle, A. 34

Labrador 89
L'Acadie, L'Acadie 256
Lacopia 151
Lady Hawkins 174
Lafayette, La. 257
Lake, Bertha 209, 212 et seq.
Lake, D.J. 293
Lake, Elizabeth Ann (Betty) 209, 212 et seq.
Lake, John 209, 212
Lake, Philip 209, 211 et seq.
Lakeburn 166, 168, 172, 289
Lakeside 123
Lakeville 105
Lambert, H.M. 215
Lampert, Jake 277
Lancelot Press 188
Landers, J. 34
Landry 93
Landry, Sir P.A. 15, 95
Landry, Valentin 15, 42, 44, 46, 52
Lane's Bakery 67
Lane, Corrigan 68
Lane, Francis 67, 68
Lane Hall 68

Lane, Joseph 68
Lane, Leo 68
Lane, Mary L. 68
Lane, W. F. 68
Laporte, Pierre 252
Larracey, W.E. 150, 196
Laurier, Sir. W. 26, 148
LaRosetta 288 et seq.
"Last Hurrah" 284
Laurendeau Commission 233
Laval School Social Sciences 233, 238, 245
Lea, Paul 81, et seq., 90
Leaman 93
LeBlanc 93
LeBlanc, Alfred 187
LeBlanc
LeBlanc, Alyre 32
LeBlanc, A.M. 187
LeBlanc
LeBlanc, Arthur 290
LeBlanc, Judge A.T. 167
LeBlanc, Copie (Aurele) 185
LeBlanc, Rt. Rev. E.A. 204
LeBlanc, E.A. 54
LeBlanc, Emery 208
LeBlanc, Frankie 186
LeBlanc, Henri P. 15, 42 et seq. 141, 200, 208
LeBlanc, James D. 62
LeBlanc, Jean-Paul 272
LeBlanc, Len 187
LeBlanc, J. Regis 290
LeBlanc, Marjorie 144
LeBlanc, Maude 213, et seq
LeBlanc, Minerva 144
LeBlanc, P.N. 85
LeBlanc, Hon. Romeo 232
LeBlanc, Sifroi 290
LeBreton, Claude 254
Le Coude 93, 309
LeCran 288 et seq.
Lefkowitz, Rabbi P. 278
Legers 61
Leger, Hon. A.J. 127, 200, 208
Leger, Alfred 154, 190
Leger, Alyre 32

Leger, Amable 288, 289
Leger, Azime 132
Leger, Calixte 289
Leger, C.I.L. 127, 128
Leger Corner 93, 165, 288 et seq.
Leger, Dr. Euclide 169
Leger, Ferdinand 289
Leger Hardware 132
Leger, Honoré 288
Leger, Maj. J.A. 95
Leger, Jean (John) 289
Leger, Joseph (P'tite Houppe) 288, 289
Leger, Joseph-Armand 289
Leger, Leo 32
Leger, Olivier 289
Leger, Peter 289
Leger, Sevére 289
Leger, Simon 289
Leger, Thaddee Sr. 289
Leger, Thaddee 132
Leicester 83
Leonard, Henry (Ben) 84
Lemieux, Biff 61
Lent, Mrs. Adrienne Brown 60
L'Evangeline 44, 52, 95
Levesque, Rev. George-Henri 238
Levesque, René 233
Levesque, Louis 239, 242, 244, et seq.
Levesque, René 233
Levine, Abe 275
Liberty Ships 141
Lincoln, Ont. 107
Lilly, A.J. 167, 168
Lithuania 273, 274, 276
Little, Ernie 221
Little Louis and the Giant K.C. 188
Lindbergh, Ann Morrow 223
Lindbergh, Charles 167, 109, 223
Lockhart, Charles E. 82
Lockhart, Henry d. 83
Lockhart, Henry D. 83
Lockhart, Jane (Murphy) 83
Lockhart, James 87
Lockhart, Leonard, Sr. 82, 84, 87, 88
Lockhart, Leonard Jr. 83, 87
Lockhart, Marks 87

Lockhart, Mary 84
Lockhart, Melvin 105
Lockhart's 81, 83, 87
Lockhart, S.J. 101, 104, et seq.
Lockhart Woodworkers 87
Lock-Wood Ltd. 87
Lodge family 189
Lodge, Harry 120
Lodge house 114
Lodge, Mathew 69, 108 et seq.
Lodge, Mrs. 112
Lodge, Mathew Cabot 115
Lodge, W.W. 120
London, Eng. 46, 71, 75, 91
London, Ont. 36, 59
Lounsbury's 20
Lounsbury, H. 187
Lounsbury's store 62, 302
Longleat 300
Louisiana 257
Lower Coverdale 296
Lubovich Rabbinical Seminary 278
Lutes 93
Lutes, Omar 212
Lutz, Charles 295
Lutz, John 295
Lynds, F.A. 64, 155, 156, 157
Lynds, Helen 157
Lynds, Leslie 62
Lynds, Sheriff 38

Machum, Lloyd 91, 148
Mackie Bob 34
Mackasey, Andrew 107
Mackasey, Bryce 107
Mackasey, Frank 107
Mackasey, Reginald 107
Maddison, George 38
Magdalens 116, 167, 169, 171
Magill, Herman 223
Magnetic Hill 306
Mahoney family 67
Maillet, Antonine 47, 169, 146
Maillet, Marguerite 288
Maine 116

321

Malcolm, Ida B. 154
Malden 67
Malenfant, Anna 203
Malenfant, Ferdinand 32
Malenfant, John 32
Malenfant, Raymond 187
Malenfant, Robert 32
Malenfant, William 290
Manitoba 168
Maple Leaf Bakery 68
Maple Leaf News 259
Marconi 130
Marks Bros. 159
Marks, Jake 282
Maritime Bakeries Ltd. 68
Maritime Central Airways 168
Maritime Oilfields Ltd. 28
Maritime Instalment Co. 282
Maritime Life 279
Maritime Hat & Cap Co. 93
Maritime Paint & Chemical Co. 88
Marven's Biscuits 77 et seq., 305
Marven, J.A. 76 et seq., 221
Mary's Home 20, 51, 49, 110, 163
Massachusetts Institute of Tech. 116, 162
Massey Hall 227
Massey, Rt. Hon. Vincent 232
Masters, Capt. J.E. 21, 22 108, 111, 188
Masters wharf 105
Maxwell, Prof. R. 241, 244
Meadowbrook 216
Memramcook 47, 89, 97, 148, 233
Memramcook River 115, 289
Meiklejohn's Grammar 194
Melanson, Mrs. A.H. 145
Melanson, Archbishop L.J.A. 56, 204, 206
Melanson, H.H. 74
Melanson O.M. 15
Melanson, Ozite Richard 53
Melanson, Reginald 166
Melanson, Simon 15, 42, 51, 56
Melanson, W.A.S. 32, 115
Medjuck, Rabbi Lippa 278
Melrose 44, 68, 129

Mendelson, Anne 282
Mendelson, Frank 276
Mendelson, Myer 281, 282
Meredith, Thomas 265
Merrill 28
Messer, Don 61
Methodists 23, 227
Michaud, Joseph 169
Michaud, Senator H. 169
Micmac Indians 15, 229
Middle Coverdale 193
Mill Creek 293
Miller, Bill 186
Miller, R.H. 303
Mills, C.I. 274
Mills, Roger 165, 167
Milton, Pte. W. 222
Minto 80
Minto Hotel 123, 125
Minudie 289
Miscou Island 165
Miscouche 47
Mitchell, G.T. 293
Mitton, A. 293
Mitton family 293
Modern Enterprises Ltd. 66
Monckton, Col. Robert 21
Moncton Airport 289
Moncton Airport Ltd. 289
Moncton Amateur Athletic Assoc. 33
Moncton & Buctouche Rly. 305
Moncton Central Bus. Dev't. Corp. 306
Moncton Children's Aid Soc. 299
Moncton Club 69, 73, 151
Moncton Community Chest 203, 299
Moncton Conservative Party 272
Moncton Cotton Co. 88, 111
Moncton Curling Club 151
Moncton Downs 165, 290
Moncton Electricity & Gas. Co. 30
Moncton Flying Club 165 et seq.
Moncton Gas, Light & Water Co. 112
Moncton General Hospital 73
Moncton High School 123
Moncton Hospital 21, 87, 182, 214
Moncton Industrial Dev't. Co. 66, 302

et seq.
Moncton Lumber Co. 88, 139
Moncton Manufacturing Co. 88
Moncton Publishing Co. 302
Moncton Speedway 147, 150
Moncton Sugar Refining Co. 112
Moncton Urban Dev't. Commission 87
Moncton Utility Gas. Ltd. 31
Moncton Victorias 34, 35
Moniteur Acadien 44, 48, 95
Montgomerys 61
Montreal 19, 26, 36, 78 et seq., 104, 107, 115, 117, 162, 165, 169, 172, 173, 225
Montreal Herald 36
Montreal Star 36
Monument de la Réconnaissance 206
Moores 64
Moore, Mrs. Berdia 113
Moose River 209
Moran, Evelyn 128
Moreau, Jacques 255
Morley, Robert 29
Morrell, Caleb 137
Morris, Jerome 40
Morrissey, James 32
Mortgage Ins. Co. of Can. 279
Mount Allison 108, 112, 115, 184, 229, 254
Mount Royal Hotel 194
Moscow 206
Muckle, Monty 186
Mulgrave 97
Multicultural Assoc. 308
Murphy, F.P. 67
Murphy, Dr. Fred. 68
Murphy, Judge Henry 68, 255, 271, 283, 284
Murphy, J. Edward 68, 83
Murphy, Dr. Patrick 68
Murray Creek 236
Murray, James A. 111
MacBeath, Alexander 73
MacBeath, D.A. 73, 74, 182
MacBeath, Ronald 73
MacDonald, Billy 78

MacDonald, John 32
MacDonald, J.M. 31
MacKinnon, May Rance 154
Maclean's Magazine 188, 260
MacLeod family 59
MacLeod Junior 71
MacNeillie, Supt'd. 98
MacPherson, David 257
McAfee, H. 64
McAllister, W.O. 102
McAnn, L.W. 96
McAuley, Rev. E. 37, 39
McAuley, Mary-Anne 36, 37
McCarthys 62
McCarthy, Adelaide 110
McCarthy, Edward 110
McCauley, Gary F. 262, 272, 283, 297
McCully 49
McCully, R.T. 166, 172
McClure, D.F. 165, 168
McCormick's 78
McCormick, F.A. 78
McDonald, Charley 99
McDonald Construction 295
McDonald, J.L. 142
McDonald, Margaret M. 166
McDougall, Bruce 25, 26, 27
McDougall, Fulton 69
McDougall, W.A. 138, 139
McGee, Agnes 144
McGee, Harry 135
McGill University 238, 282
McGregor, W. 34
McGowan, Mary 102
McHaffie 101
McHugh 93
McHugh, Mary 123
McKay, Robert 122
McKee, Michael 272
McKenzie, Percy 185
McKinnon 93
McLaughlin Road 163
McLellan, Dr. D.J. 166
McLean, Hon. H.H. 167
McLuhan, Marshall 225
McManus, Catherine 117
McManus, Frances 117

323

McManus, Edward 115, 117
McManus, Janet 117
McManus, John 116, 117
McManus, John W. Ltd. 116
McManus, Margaret 117
McManus, Mary 117
McManus, Reid 115, 116, 117
McManus, Reid (Memramcook) 117
McManus, Sam 186
McMichael, Ralph 182
McMonagle, W.E. 180 et seq.
McQuinn, Roy 32
McStay, Will 32
McSweeney 52
McSweeney, A.E. 69, 111
McSweeney, Agnes and Jo 62
McSweeney Brothers 69
McSweeney, Peter 21

Nassau 191, 192
National Association of Acadians 200
National Film Board 256
National Hockey League 36
National Research Cncl. 282
National Transcontinental Rly. 89, 97, 99
N.B. Conservatives 253
N.B. Federation Labor 175
N.B. Gas & Oil Fields 29, 113
N.B. Lumber Dealers Assoc. 84
N.B. Municipalities Act 271
N.B. Music Festival 160
N.B. Petroleum Co. 110
N.B. Power Corp. 67, 70
N.B. Publishing Co. 195
N.B. Rangers 222
N.B. Telephone Co. 87, 308
N.D.P. 261
Neepewa 168
New Brunswick 81, 119, 167, 184, 185, 200, 203
Newcastle 125
Newcastle RCMP 266
Newcomb, Simon 235
New England 130, 159, 189, 200, 228

Newfoundland 80, 89, 164, 167
New France 228
New Jersey 278
New Ireland 36, et seq.
New Shops 97
New Testament 293
Newton Heights 93, 260, 305
New West End 305
New York 71, 123, 151, 157, 225, 278
New Yorker 118
N.H.L. 183, 188
Nicklin, Percy 186, 188
Nobel Prize 285
Noble's Garage 67
Norman (Victorias) 35
Northern Ireland 83
"Northern Magus" 53
North River 87
Northumberland County 258
Northumberland Strait 225
Notre Dame 83, 84
Notre Dame d'Acadie 89, 206, 241
Nova Scotia 81, 83, 87, 194, 209
Nowlan, Thomas 296
N.Y. Daily News 210

O'Blenis, Amos 61
O'Brien 93
O'Brien, Earl 212, 213
O'Brien, Ernie 283, 284
O'Brien, J.E. 154
O'Brien, Ned 32
O'Brien, Tim H. 166
Ocean Limited 220
O'Connor, J. 293
O'Donnell, Rev. T. 204
Official Languages Act 256
Oklahoma 112
Old Home Week 71, 73, 75
Old Glory Auction 151
O'Leary, Const. M. 263
O'Leary, Launce 92
One Hundred Francophone Assoc. 248
O'Neill, John 110

O'Neill & LeBlanc 62
O'Neill, Tom 62
Ontario 76, 77, 95, 179
Opera House 33, 94
Order British Empire 269
Order of Canada 233, 281
Ordre de Forestiéres Catholique 45
Ordre de Pleiad 248
Oromocto 182
O'Rourke, Ann 125
O'Rourke, J.J. 125
O'rourke, Mrs. J.J. 124
Osborne, Marg 61
Ottawa 17, 52, 111, 153, 225, 252
Outhouse, E.S. 293, 296
Outhouse Point 296
Overland Garage 31
Oxford Univ. 224, 238, 245

Pacific Junction 211, 220
Pacific Ocean 82
Painsec 97
Pakistan 308
Panama Canal 81
Panama Isthmus 81
Parker, Al. 164
Parkton 192, 260, 305
Palm Beach 281
Palmer's Pond 216
Parlee, Emma 120
Parlee, T. Babbitt 120, 121, 126, 127, 128, 182, 252
Parlee, William and wife 120
Parrsboro 83
Parsons, Genevieve 168
Parsons, Jess 162
Parsons, Lloyd 162
Parti Acadien 253
Patterson 93
Peake, Cecil 123, 124
Peake family 123
Peake, Florence 125
Peake, William 123, 125
Pearson, Rt. Hon. L.B. 233, 283, 284, 300

Peck, H.F.
Peking 224
Pellerin 93
Pennsylvania 28, 197, 278
Pennsylvania Germans 294
Péres de Ste. Croix 235
Peters 93
Peters, A.E. 93
Peters, George 19
Peters Lock Factory 22, 142
Petitcodiac River 106, 111, 115
Petitodiac Tidal Project 113
Pictou 59
Pincombe, Alexander 162
Pine Glen Road 293
Pine Hill Divinity School 299
Pittsburgh 28
P.L.O. 252
Point de Bute 167
Pointe du Chene 97, 156
Point St. Charles 107
Pontine Marshes 304
Ponzi 174
Pope Pius XI 117
Port Elgin 61, 298
Port Hope 239
Portland, Me. 157
Pottinger, David 22, 101, 102, 104
Post Road 106
Powell, Albert 211, 216 et seq.
Power Corp. 239
Power, Tyrone 124
Pre d'En Haut 288
Price 93
Price, Hanford 129
Price, Capt. H.N. 166
Price, Dr. L.N. 166
Priest's Lake 40
Price, Dr. O.B. 19, 61, 98, 99, 167, 283
Prince Edward Island 36, 81, 82, 167, 171
Princeton Univ. Press 224
Prix Goncourt 246
Procter, Maggie 137
Progressive Cons. Party 249, 261
Protestant Orphanage 215
Proust 65

Provident Fund 141
Public Library 63
Pugsley, Hon. W. 111, 124
Pujolas, William 32
Purdy, Mrs. C.T. 49
Purdy, Dr. C.T. 75
Purdy, Tom 154

Quebec 44, 47, 51, 76, 88, 89, 95, 107, 116 et seq.
Quebec Aces 35, 148, 186
Queen Mary the Catholic 294
Quiberon Bay, Battle of 99
Quinn, Frank 185

Radcliffe, Tom 38, 39
Radford, Tom 185
Radio CKCW 155
Radio CNRA 153, 154
Radio CRCA 154
Rainbow Melody Boys 154
Ramsay, Allan 228
Ramsay, Archie 228
Rand, Allan 105
Rand Formula 229
Rand, Mr. Justice I.C. 52, 105, 225, 226, et seq.
Rand, Nelson 229
Rand, Rev. Silas 229
Randall 93
Randall, Benjamin Sr. 61
Randall, Ben 61
Randall, Fred 61
Randall, George 61
Randall, John (Cons. J.K.) 61, 214, 219
Randall, Kent 61
Randall, Percy 61
Randall, Russell 61
Randall, William 61
Randall, Willard 61
R.C.A.F. 168, 171
R.C.M.P. 167, 168, 212, 213 et seq.

Reciprocity Election 230
Record, Charles B. 93
Record, E.B. 26
Record, E.A. 93
Record Foundry 22, 93, 105, 229, 274
Red Cross Clinic 84
Red Indians 187
Redmond, C.W. 180
Red Square 206
Read, Maizie 161
Reid, H.B. 178
Reid, John 223
Reid, Thomas 223
Reilly, Hon. E.A. 57, 58, 67, 70, 184, 230
Reformed Baptist Church 183
Renton, James 296
Republica, La 225
Restigouche 204, 208
Restigouche River 36
Restigouche & Western Rly. 208
Rexton 70
Rich, Harry 123
Richard 93
Richard, Hon. Clovis 203
Richard, Ernie 279
Richard, Dr. F.A. 42
Richards Government 297
Richard, Stanis 178
Richard, Mrs. Stanis 178
Richardson, Dynamite 98
Ricker, George 296
Ricker, Jacob 296
Rideout, Chief George 14, 23, 24, 25, 131
Rideout, Margaret 283, 300
Rideout, Sherwood 283
Ritchie Road 293
Rimouski 112
Ripley 93
River Hebert 194, 195
Riviere du Loup 97, 101
Riverview 10, 106, 260, 262, 265 et seq. 287, 292 et seq.
Riverview Heights 292
Robb, Bruce 193
Roberts, Dr. W. 231

Robertson, Mrs. Brenda 296
Robertson building 46
Robertson, Dr. D.E. 223
Robertson, George 166
Robichaud Government 184, 242
Robichaud, Hon. Hedard 237
Robichaud, Hon. Louis J. 239, 241
Robidoux family 44
Robidoux, Ferdinand 52
Robin Hood Flour 88
Robinson 93
Robinson, Hon. Clifford W. 18, 52, 70, 108, 110, 111, 115, 129, 134, 155, 184, 189, 191, 229, 230
Robinson, Frank and wife 34, 62, 63
Robinson, William 110
Rochon, Cpl. R. 255
Rodd, Marjorie 65
Rodd, W.R. 65
Rogers, J. 293
Rogers, William 60
Rogersville, N.B. 258
Rome 225, 304
Rooney, E.A. 303
Roosevelt, Pres. F.D. 229
Roosevelt, Teddy 84
Ross, Dr. George 228
Ross, J.M. 71, 122
Rotary Club 162
Roy 93
Roy, Alfred 202
Royal Air Force 167, 171
Royal Can. Army Med. Corps 65
Royal College of Organists 228
Royal Commission on Bilingualism 254
Royal College Physicians and Surgeons 282
Ruisseau des Renards 288
Russell, L.T. 127
Russia 208, 277
Russian 165, 309
Ryan, Claude 233, 237
Ryan, Farm 298
Ryan, Frank 32
Ryan, Fred 32
Ryan, J. 293

Ryan, James T. 73, 196
Ryan, Sanford 296, 298
Ryan, Tilley 296

Sacre Coeur College 244
Sackville 19, 93, 155, 169, 192, 254
Saint John 33, 35, 52, 54, 64, 76, 79, 84, 89, 106, 125, 140, 172, 183, 189, 193, 194
Saint John Globe 52
Salisbury 61, 106, 107
Salisbury Road 68, 306
Salvage Corps 64, 151
Salvation Army 215
Samphire Greens 295
Sangster, J.B. 63
Saskatchewan 154, 167, 204, 220
Saskatoon 154
Savage, Rev. Edward 42, 44, 51, 52, 54, 56, 67, 204
Savoie, Adelard 244, 246, 247, 290
Savoie, Dr. Alexandre 48
Savoie, Claude 254
Savoie, Roger 255, 256, 258
Sayer, F.R. 99
Salter, 105, 112
Scadding, Alfred 223
Scott Act 23
Scott, H. 34
Scott, Jessie 105
Scott's Waverley Novels 227
Scotland 83
Schelew, Nathan 277
Scoudouc 97, 179
Selick, Bessie 275
Selick, Freda 276
Selick, Isaac 275
Selick, Isaac & Sons 188
Selick, Ruth 274
Seneterre, Que. 169
Shediac 15, 16, 44, 48, 76, 82, 97, 117, 123, 125, 200, 208, 229, 304
Shediac Cape 87, 134, 152
Shediac Inn 87
Shediac Road 138, 141

327

Shemogue (Bristol) 76
Shepody Hills 37
Sherbrooke 206, 227, 228
Sherron, James 37, 138
Shields, T.T. 133
Shippegan 246
Sigogne, Abbé Jean-Mandé 47
Simpson-Sears 290
Sisters of Charity 20, 49
Smith (Victorias) 35
Smith, Sir Albert 15, 16, 70
Smith, A.P. 293
Smith, B.E. 71
Smith, Charles 194, 295
Smith, H. 60
Smith, Hon. Lewis 297
Smith, J.W.Y. 29, 70
Smith, Howard 127
Smith, Jigger 186
Smith, Lady 70
Smyth, Harry 33
Snow, Mrs. 113
Snowdon, Arthur 168
Sobey chain 175
Social Credit 261
Societé Assomption 46, 151, 200
Societé Assomption Mutuelle 46
Societé Nationale des Acadiens 259
Somerset 300
Somme 92
Song My 252
Sophie, The 294
South Africa 28, 29
Southern N.B. League 185
Southampton School 112
Spanish 308
Speedway, Moncton 20, 152
Spencer, G.O. 71, 72
Spencer, Mrs. G.O. 154
Spigleman, M.S. 44, 95
Spiro, Rabbi Joshua 276, 277
Springhill 97
Square Lake 88
Stanfield, Hon. Robert 252, 261
Stadium 185
S.S. Stanholm 223
Stanstead College 227

Stanley Cup 35, 148, 185, 186
Star Weekly, The 36, 223
Starratt 93
St. Agathe Parish 37
Ste, Anne de la Pocatiere 47
St. Anselme 93, 288 et seq.
St. Bernard's 44, 47, 50 et seq. 82, 107, 125, 236
St. Bernard's cemetery 56
St. Catherines 107
St. Francis Xavier U. 67, 68
St. George 37
St. George Food Market 275
Saint John diocese 204
St. John River 56
St. Joseph's College and University 44, 47, 89, 118, 148, 169, 206, 233, 237, 238 et seq.
St. Leonard's 208
St. Louis College 245
St. Louis de France 51
St. Malo 107
St. Mary's, Newcastle 125
St. Patrick's Cathedral 123
St. Paul's 232
St. Sauveur 255
St. Vincent de Paul Soc. 193
Steadman 93
Steeves family 293
Steeves, David and wife 62, 63, 65, 67
Steeves, Early 138
Steeves, Dr. E.O. 64, 65, 78
Steeves, Harold 66
Steeves, Isaac 64
Steeves, J.F. 65
Steeves, Mrs. L.W. 166
Steeves, Stephen 66, 67
Steeves, Winston A. 58, 66, 67, 303
Steeves, W.M. 10
Steeves Mountain 65
Stein, Cy 263
Stein, Raymond 263
Steif dynasty 293
Steif, Heinrich 193, 294
Steif, Matthias 294
Storey, Frank 64, 178, 182, 183
Storey, George 183

Stoney Creek 28, 30, 31, 75, 111, 222
Stratton, G.O. 73
Styles 93
Sudbury 239
Sullivan 93
Sullivan, John 216
Sullivan, Michael B. 10
Sumners 69, 175, 186
Sumner, F.R. 111, 155
Sumner, Fredrick W. 13, 82, 108, 130
Sumner wharf 105
Sunday Star 221
Sunny Brae 93, 184, 260, 305
Supreme Court of Canada 225, 226, 227, 256, 271, 272
Supreme Court of N.B. 256, 269, 271
Sussex 106, 111, 297
Sussex Corner 106
Sweeney, Dennis 59
Sweeney, Hon. Frank 67, 129
Swetnam, James 152
Swift Co. 277
Sydney 27, 97, 101, 116, 223
Sydney Pier 277

Talbot 93
Tammany Twins 284
Taylor, A.J. 166
Taylor, B.A. 188
Taylor, Claude 107, 297
Taylor, Dr. G.O. 67
Taylor, M.C. 88
Taylor, Robert 261
Taschereau, Cardinal 44
Teed, Annabelle 84
Telegraph-Journal 258
Tennant, F.M. 74, 142
Terrebonne 255
Thetford Mines 282
The Problem 151
Thibadeau, Pierre 295
Thibodeau 93
Thibodeau, Bliss 290
"Thirty Years in Moncton" 51, 56
Thomas Aquinas, Sister 163

Thomas, Rev. B.E. 39
Thomas, Charles 261
Thomas, Rev. H.E. 23
Thornton, Sir Henry 107, 112, 113, 167
Tiferes Israel congreg. 275, 276, 277, 278
Tilley Government 203
Tilley, Hon. L.P.D. 202
Times, Daily 17, 38, 48, 52, 62, 65, 69, 74, 117 et seq., 120, 129, 156, 191, 195, 257
Times—Transcript Bldg. 113
Tingley 93
Tingley, Frank H. 92
Tingley, George 165, 290
Tingley, Luther 181, 182
Tip Top Tailors 123, 145
Titanic 91
Toombs Building 45
Tompkins, M.F. 154, 166
Toronto 35, 36, 62, 77, 79, 116, 133, 162, 172, 174, 179, 227
Toronto Maple Leafs 183, 188, 222
Toronto Star 188, 220, 284
Torrie, Alexander 73
Torrie & Winter 159
Tottenham 62
"Trail of Blood, Canadian Murder Odyssey" 221
Trans-Canada Airline 169, 170 et seq., 222
Trans-Canada Highway 303
Transcript 15 et seq., 36, 37, 39, 75, 97 et seq, 110, 117, 143, 151, 156, 173, 176, 179, 189 et seq. 200, 220, 237
Travellers Aid 214
Travolta, John 174
Trerice, Burton 164, 169, 171
Trimble, H.H. 117
Trinity School 239
Trites 93
Trites, family 293
Trites, George 35
Trites, Milton 211, 214, 215
Troop, Capt. C.R. 167
Trotter and Pacer, The 151

329

Trudeau, Rt. Hon. P.E. 53, 229, 261
Truro 35, 112
Tupper, Ray 294
Turks 308
Turtle Creek 192, 295
Turney, J.V. & Son. 139
Tuttle Bros. 213
Tweedie, Hattie 20, 49
Tweedle, Dr. 28

Ukrainian 308
United Church 84, 87, 231
United Financial Mg'm't. Ltd. 279
United States 80, 112, 136, 193, 252
Upper Canada College 239
U.S. Congress
United Way 299
Université de Moncton (University Moncton) 55, 89, 235 et seq.
University of N.B. 193, 244
University of Pennsylvania 282
University of Toronto 224, 225, 228
University of Western Ont. 36
Urquhart, George 303
Uspenski Cathedral 206

Vanier High School 254
Veniot, Hon. Peter 52, 57, 230, 231
Verdun 107
Verne, Jules 236
Vernon, B.C. 60
Vietnam 308
Vietnamese War 251
Victoria 35
Victoria Garage 70
Victoria Rink 33
Victorias (Hockey) 60, 148, 184, 186
Victoria School 227
Victory Loan Com. 148
Vimy Ridge 92
Vindicator, The 27
Virginia 227

Wade, Jimmy 171
Wade, Mason 252
Walker, J. 34
Walker, W.A. 77, 78
Wallace, Edson 295
Wallace family 294
Wallace, Fen 295
Wallace, Woodrow 295
Walling, H.F. 293
Walsh, Francis 223
Walsh, Frank 223
Walsh, Mrs. Frank 223
Walsh, Fred H. 295
Walsh, Jack 295
Walsh, James 59
Walsh, Waldo 295
Warman, H.H. 96
Warren Paving Co. 22
Warwick, Septimus 75
Washington 282
Watergate 252
Watson, James 294
Webster, Aubrey 186
Weeks, Wiley 168, 171
Welfare Appeals Board 297
"We Fought for the Little Man" 295
Weir's 105
Weldon, C.M. 266
Weldon, Col. D.B. 25, 36
Weldon, S.B. 293
Weldon, W. McKay & Son 299

Wells, Judge W.W. 70
Wentworth, Gov. John 46
Western Union 123
West Indies 105, 174, 223
Wesley St. School 50
Westmorland court 216
Westmorland Constituency 260
Westmorland Conservative Assoc. 84
Westmorland County 15, 48, 52, 116
Westmorland Historical Soc. 24, 86
Westmount 228
Westmount Apartments 105
Weston's 79
Wetmore, Elias 99
Weymouth, N.S. 44, 54

Wheaton 60, 93
Wheeler, Ambrose 180, 186, 188, 276
Wheeler, Gary 163, 264, 266, 269, 271, 273
Wheeler, Jason 157
White, Eddie 192
White, Garfield 88
White, Jim 156
White, Dr. F.J. 69
Wiggins, Rev. W.B. 61
Wilbur 93, 94
Wilbur, B. 293
Wilbur, Flewelling 137, 138
Wilcox, Mrs. Ora 120, 128
Willett, Sheriff 116
Williams, A.E. 69
Williams, Ovila 32, 55
Williamson, Ned 32
Willis, Miss 120
Wilmot Valley 297
Wilson 93
Wilson, Charley 185, 295
Wilson, Ruth C. 167
Wing, Rosie 137
Windsor, Ont. 229
Windsor Hotel 27, 94, 214
Winnipeg 95, 124, 125, 169, 185
Winter family 105, 188
Winter, Fred 73, 159
Winter, John 73
Winter's wharf 105
Wolstenholme, George 187
Wood, Albert 295
Wood, Herbert M. 155
Wood, R. James 10
Wood, T.W. 48
Woolco 73
World War One 58, 91, 106, 119, 145, 165, 182, 197
World War Two 59, 65, 68, 73, 89, 106, 223
Wortman 95
Wortman (Victorias) 35
Wren, Sir Christopher 272
Wright, Esther Clark 295
Wrynn, Mrs. Elizabeth 153
Wrynn, Maudie 153

Yale University 238
YMCA Greater Moncton 84, 89, 299
Yorkshire 197
Yorkshire family 298
Youngs 70
Yprés 92